D0590403
000000490404

Race to The End

Scott, Amundsen and the South Pole

Ross D. E. MacPhee

Published by the Natural History Museum, London

Originally published as *Race to the End: Amundsen, Scott, and the Attainment of the South Pole*
This edition published in 2011 by the Natural History Museum, Cromwell Road, London SW7 5BD

ISBN 978 0 565 09271 9

A catalogue record for this book is available from the British Library.

Interior design by Oxygen Design: Sherry Williams
Book cover image: *A Very Gallant Gentleman,*
John Charles Dollman, 1913.
From a lithograph of oil original.

Printed in China

Contents

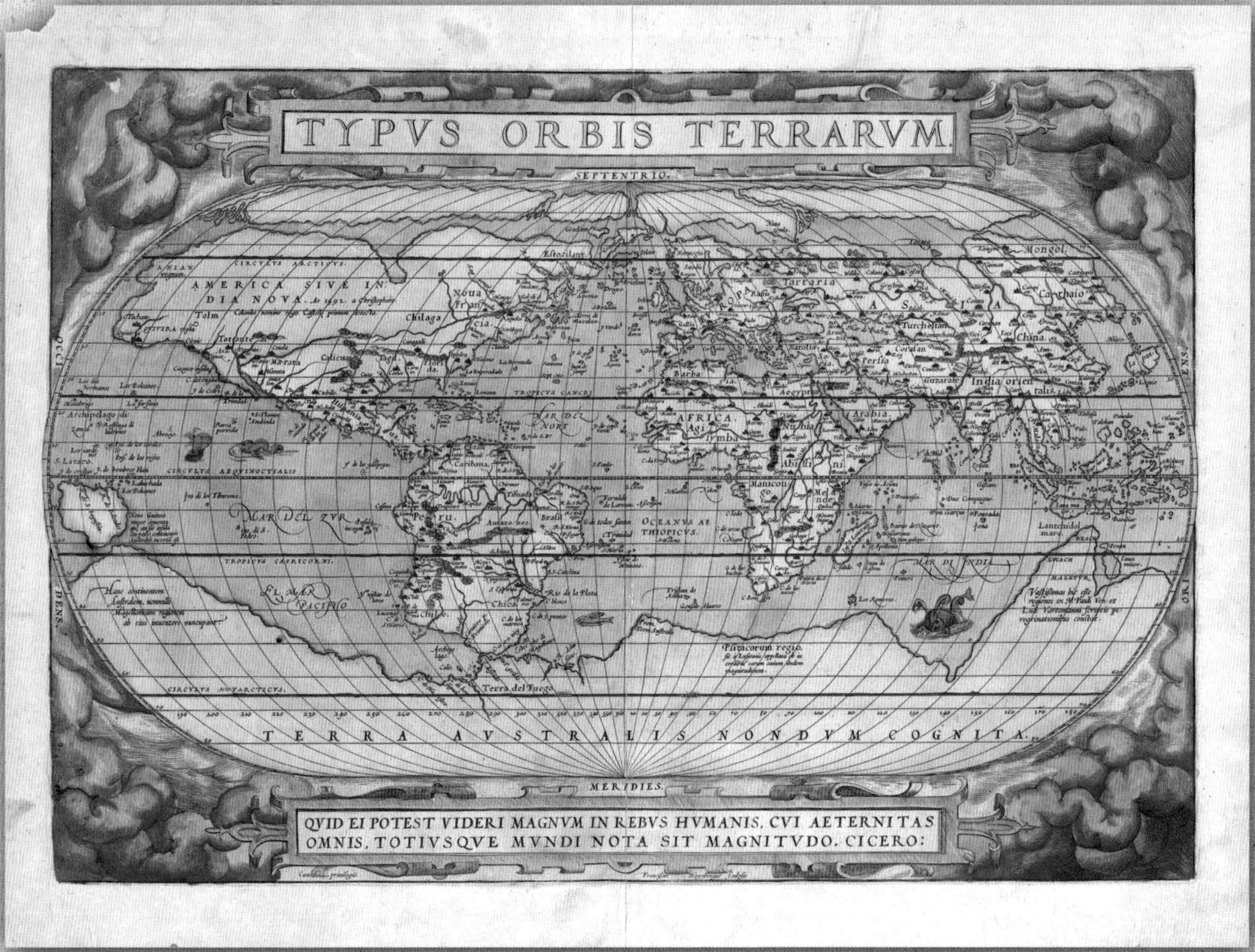

One of many diversely imaginative representations of *Terra Australis Nondum Cognita* ("Southern Land Not Yet Known") by geographers in the sixteenth and early seventeenth centuries. This version, by the Dutch cartographer Ortelius (Abraham Oertel), was published in Amsterdam in 1570. The solid coastline and regional divisions of the unknown continent imply some actual knowledge, but—ignoring the very doubtful possibility that part of Australia had been seen by early European seafarers by this time—all was sheer invention. As Mills (2003: 652) noted, Ortelius's southern continent occupied "every space where its presence was not yet disproved."

Preface

This book was written to accompany the American Museum of Natural History's new Antarctic exhibition, of which I have the honor to be curator. The show itself has a broad sweep, covering modern scientific endeavors as well as historical aspects of human involvement in Antarctica. The centerpiece, however, is a close study of the efforts of two men—Robert Falcon Scott on the British side, and Roald Amundsen on the Norwegian—to be first to stand at the South Pole. Whether they participated in an overt contest, or merely happened to overlap in time, target, and ambition, is to some degree a matter of definition and perspective. If it was not a race in fact, it was surely a race in form, whatever the contestants and their supporters might have wanted their contemporaries or later generations to think. The purpose of this volume is to present the race's circumstances for a modern audience: what ignited it, how the competing parties fared as they struggled toward their goal, and what was achieved of lasting value.

The documentation and imagery available for illuminating the works and days of these early Antarctic explorers is abundant, and revealing their stories in a compact fashion has been a prodigious task. For help in this regard I cannot sufficiently thank the two people I have continually interacted with at Sterling Innovation since this project began: Pamela Horn, editorial director, and Joelle Herr, senior editor, both of whom have been endlessly encouraging, even as the text increased to unanticipated proportions. Via Sterling Innovation, I also extend grateful thanks to Gil King, hard-working and conscientious researcher, and Susan Oyama, enthusiastic, dogged imagery consultant. These two have made the book so much more than I could have alone. This also applies to American Museum of Natural History (AMNH) senior photographer Craig Chesek, whose graceful color work is featured in many parts of this volume.

I am very grateful to the Scott Polar Research Institute (SPRI) and its director, Dr. Julian Dowdeswell, for unrestricted access to objects associated with the British Antarctic Expedition, especially the "last things" recovered from Scott's final encampment on the Ross Ice Shelf. Most of these objects have never been presented photographically, and are here given special prominence. Equal thanks go to the Frammuseet and Nasjonalbibliotek in Oslo for similar access to documents and artifacts associated with Amundsen, Nansen, and *Fram*. None of this would have happened, and certainly not in the way it has, without the cooperation of the librarians, archivists, and curators I have had the pleasure to meet in the course of writing this book. I would here like to especially commend Heather Lane, librarian and keeper of collections at SPRI, for her unequaled help, good cheer, and amazing ability to do at least three things at once. SPRI photo librarian Lucy Martin and archivist Naomi Boneham gave me immediate, gracious access to collections in their care and answered many questions. Geir O. Kløver, director of the Frammuseet, spent many hours showing us the contents of his museum with great enthusiasm; I also thank Geir for allowing quotation of his translations of relevant documents in Norwegian. Anne Meldgård, Guro Tangvald, Tove D. Johansen, and Jens Petter Kollhøj at the Nasjonalbiblioteket provided information and access to important documents and imagery associated with Amundsen. Tom Baione (AMNH Library) and Barbara Mathe (AMNH Special Collections) showed me materials and objects connected with Lincoln Ellsworth's bequest of Amundseniana to the museum and permitted photography of objects. Finally, my special thanks to representatives of the Scott, Wilson, and Oates families for permission to reproduce certain images and diary passages.

Arti Finn, former senior director of licensing and publishing at AMNH, and her colleagues Caitlin Roxby and Molly Leff, efficiently oversaw development of the museum's relationship with Sterling Innovation; everyone involved, I think, should be tremendously gratified by the results. Also deserving my warm thanks are my AMNH colleagues David Harvey, senior vice president of exhibitions, and Michael Novacek, senior vice president and provost.

For identifying errors and infelicities in the manuscript, and also for much else, I am grateful to several people who read part or all of the manuscript: Martin Callinan, Louis Jacobs, Heather Lane, Geir O. Kløver, JoAnn Gutin, Clare Flemming, and John D. Flemming.

I conclude this preface on a personal note. I am not an Antarctic historian, but a systematic biologist with Antarctic interests. Like many others who have worked or spent time in Antarctica, I have often delved into the stories of those who have gone before, if only to try to imagine their experiences in light of my own. Ten years ago, as co-curator of the AMNH's *Endurance* show, I had my first introduction to the scholarly side of Antarctic historical research. This new opportunity to spend fascinating hours reading works new and old on Scott and Amundsen has been a complete delight. I have relied heavily on published works for most details and interpretations. In this regard, and in no particular order, I would like to make special mention of Tor Bomann-Larsen's *Roald Amundsen*, Sara Wheeler's *Cherry*, Roland Huntford's *Scott and Amundsen*, Ranulph Fiennes's *Captain Scott*, David Thompson's *Scott's Men*, and David Crane's *Scott of the Antarctic*. Each of these works has a certain point of view that the reader needs to appreciate and respect, as well as question and compare. That is what good history should do: educate and entertain, certainly, but provoke at the same time. A list of other works consulted may be found at the end of the text, together with notes on quoted passages and source material. Issuance of this edition permitted me to correct a few minor errors of fact, for the detection of which I am indebted to Michael Rosove and Robert Stephenson.

Finally, I can only thank from my heart my dear wife, Clare Flemming, Brooke Dolan Archivist at the Academy of Natural Sciences in Philadelphia, who has read or heard every word of this work, much more than once. Her own profound knowledge of polar exploration has benefited me greatly, and saved me from many a grievous mistake in fact or interpretation. I dedicate this book to her.

A note on names and units. To preserve a sense of time and place, I have used geographical names that were current in the heroic age rather than their modern equivalents (which are however noted where suitable). Units of length, temperature, volume, and so forth are also cited as given in original texts, but ISO (metric) conversions are provided in rounded form immediately thereafter. My only departures are to omit unit conversions in quoted remarks, where they would disturb the flow, and to express all lengths in miles as statute miles (rounded, except where greater precision seemed needful). In the heroic age, geographical and nautical miles, which are virtually identical in any case, were preferred for distance logging because they could be easily computed from sextant and theodolite readings. That hardly applies to modern experience, and nothing of significance is lost by omitting them. Thus Shackleton's farthest point south on the *Nimrod* expedition is cited as three digits, 112 (statute) miles, rather than the more dramatic two, 97 (geographical) miles.

Accurately determining the historical relative worth of currencies is an undertaking fraught with uncertainties, none of which can be examined here. For simplicity, I used the calculators at www.measuringworth.com, especially the relatively conservative estimators "GDP deflator" and "Retail Price Index," for the relative worth of monetary units denominated in UK pounds "today" (in fact 2007, the last year for which estimates are available). For the relative worth of Norwegian kroner, I used as a proxy the equivalency 1 Swedish krona (SEK) in 1909 = 55 SEK in 2005, and 1 US$ = 7.5 SEK (see www.historicalstatistics.org). Although Norway was independent by 1909, it was still part of the Scandinavian monetary union at that time and krona and kroner were in a fixed relationship.

R. D. E. MacPhee

'Our sons will die like
English Gentlemen'
Wendy
"LIKE ENGLISH
GENTLEMEN"
TO PETER SCOTT
FROM THE AUTHOR OF
WHERE'S MASTER?

CHAPTER 1

The End Observed

On November 29, 1910, in the harbor of Port Chalmers, New Zealand, thirty-two-year-old Kathleen Bruce Scott stepped off the deck of *Terra Nova* onto a waiting launch and bade farewell to her husband of only two years, Robert Falcon Scott, the leader of the grandly named British Antarctic Expedition (1910). As she did so she did not pause to kiss Con—his family nickname—because she did not want "anyone to see him sad." With the other wives she watched the aged, overladen ship begin her journey southward, carrying the small group of men who intended, among other things, "to reach the South Pole and to secure for The British Empire the honour of this achievement."

And that was it; she never saw him again except through the warm haze of recollection: "With a queer elation and serenity I said good-bye to him as his ship left New Zealand for its long voyage to the South. I watched his face radiating tenderness as the space between us widened, until I held only my memory of that upturned face, but held it for a lifetime."

Con was scheduled to be away for two years, more or less; it all depended on opportunity and the ice. During this time Kathleen intended to keep herself busy in London, tending to the couple's infant son, Peter, and awaiting any news of the expedition. She had hoped to bring in some money through her sculpture, but commissioned work was slow in coming, and she sometimes had a difficult time making ends meet on Scott's navy pay. To make matters worse, rumors flew as time went on, especially in the early months of 1912: One erroneous cable reported, "Scott at South Pole—Brilliant victory." But Kathleen was not taken in by

FACING PAGE: A children's story, but one with a hook: Cover illustration of the anonymously written *"Like an English Gentleman": To Peter Scott* (London: Hodder & Stoughton, 1913). The author, writing of the southern journey in simple language, poses as a storyteller in the tradition, if not the person, of J. M. Barrie, author of *Peter Pan*. In the text the author frequently has recourse to Wendy's line, "We hope our sons will die like English gentlemen"—the reference needing no explanation.

The Scotts—Kathleen and Con—aboard *Terra Nova* in Lyttelton Harbor, just before the ship's departure for the south.

these unsubstantiated reports, insisting, as she wrote in her diary, "I was certain there was something wrong."

And something was wrong. Early in March 1912, the news came that a known rival—the Norwegian polar explorer Roald Amundsen—had reached the pole. Sailing in complete secrecy to Antarctica aboard *Fram*, the legendary ship of the Norwegian explorer Fridtjof Nansen, Amundsen had set out for the South Pole in late October 1911 at the end of the austral winter; he reached it less than two months later. Scott's expedition had been in the field at the same time as his, but Amundsen saw no sign of British presence at the pole when he was there. If they came at all, he concluded, they came later.

Cheered by well-wishers, *Terra Nova* prepares to depart from Port Chalmers, New Zealand, on November 29, 1910. The ship reached New Zealand from Melbourne, Australia, on October 28. Provisioning and coaling took place in Lyttelton over the next month, when dogs and ponies were also brought aboard. The ship then continued on to Port Chalmers, the jumping-off point for the Ross Sea.

Scott may have lost the gamble for immediate fame, but Kathleen was consoled by the thought that he had always intended his polar expedition to be a scientific quest. By furthering science, her friends assured her, Scott would ultimately win greater glory than Amundsen, whose entire accomplishment, it was said, amounted to no more than a long and rather uneventful ski trip. Still fiercely certain of their reunion, after traveling through the United States, Kathleen stepped aboard SS *Aorangi* in San Francisco in early February of 1913. She was sailing back to New Zealand, back to greet her husband and his bronzed and sturdy shipmates as they strode ashore, leaving Antarctic rigors behind as they fell very publicly into the arms of their loved ones.

Or so she might have daydreamed through listless days on the long journey across the Pacific. But a few hours south of Hawaii her reverie was ended, permanently, by a sharp knock on her cabin door and the message that *Aorangi's* captain wanted to speak to her urgently.

"I've got some news for you," the captain said. "But I don't see how I can tell you."

"The Expedition?" Kathleen asked.

"Yes."

"Well," she said. "Let's have it."

The captain showed her the message:

Captain Robert Falcon Scott in 1909, in a studio portrait taken during the time he was preparing the *Terra Nova* expedition.

> "Captain Scott and six [sic] others perished in blizzard after reaching South Pole January 18."

In a daze, she excused herself. She'd received fictitious reports before; was this another? For more than an hour she distracted herself with a previously scheduled Spanish lesson, and then she went on to lunch, where she discussed American politics with other passengers. She had asked the captain not to tell anyone else about Scott's death, but she could tell from the looks on their faces that the officers were aware of her husband's fate. Then, to keep her mind off the subject until she was sure she could compose herself, she retreated to the deck and read about the recent sinking of *Titanic*.

To the modern reader Kathleen's apparent sang-froid may seem contrived or even absurd, a denial of reality. Yet it was not out of character. Kathleen had always prided herself on her ability to control her circumstances, whether while vagabonding through Greece as an unaccompanied female, living a bohemian artist's existence in Edwardian London, or, regally certain of her attractiveness to men, being doted on by the likes of Auguste Rodin, Henry James, and H. G. Wells. She particularly loathed being ganged together with other women in after-dinner gossip sessions, where nothing of consequence was ever discussed, while the men retired to the billiard room to linger over cigars and earnest conversation. In short, she preferred men, and men's lives. Thus while news of Con's death surely came as a shock, she would never have allowed herself to collapse openly with grief: That was something *women* did.

Reports of Scott's death had reached London from New Zealand on February 11, several days before she heard the news. In a hastily organized but nonetheless magnificent memorial service for Scott and his companions in London's St. Paul's Cathedral on February 14, "The Dead March" from Handel's *Saul* was played; this moved mourners to tears, much as it had less than a year before when played for *Titanic*'s dead. Inside

Aftenposten

Nr. 123 | Morgennummer | Fredag 8de Marts 1912 | Morgennummer | 53. Aarg.

Norges Flag plantet paa Sydpolen!

Alt vel!

Roald Amundsen

Christiania.

Hobart, 7de Marts, Kl. 3.40 Em.

Polen naaet fjortende syttende December nitten elve. Alt vel.

Roald Amundsen.

Til Kristiania

Idag

flager By og Land!

Vi er alle

Roald Amundsens

Landsmænd.

Roald Amundsen,

tegnet af "Aftenpostens" Tegner.

LEFT: In early March 1912, papers all over the world blazed with the headline that Amundsen had attained the South Pole. This March 8, 1912 edition of *Aftenposten*, an Oslo paper, reads, "Norway's flag planted at the South Pole! All well!"

INSET: Captain Roald Amundsen in his polar kit. This was evidently one of his favorite photographs of himself; he used it in his lecture presentations and, tellingly, as the frontispiece for volume two of *The South Pole*.

£1,000

THE DAILY GRAPHIC, FEBRUARY 13, 1913.

THIS ISSUE OF THE "DAILY GRAPHIC" CARRIES A FREE INSURANCE OF £1,000 UNDERTAKEN BY THE OCEAN ACCIDENT & GUARANTEE CORPORATION, Ltd. (See p. 19.)

£1,000

No. 7234.—Vol. XCIII. LONDON: THURSDAY, FEBRUARY 13, 1913. REGISTERED AS A NEWSPAPER.

MRS. SCOTT LEARNS IN MID OCEAN OF HER HUSBAND'S FATE.

Not the least tragic circumstance connected with the Antarctic disaster, in which Captain R. F. Scott and four of his comrades lost their lives after achieving success and almost reaching safety, is Mrs. Scott's journey to New Zealand to meet her husband. Mrs. Scott was ignorant of the fate of the expedition until tidings were conveyed to her by wireless telegraphy when the Aorangi, the vessel in which she was voyaging across the Pacific, was a few hours' steaming from Honolulu and Hawaii. A merciful veil is drawn over Mrs. Scott's reception of the dreadful news, but she may be sure that all England shares her grief. In our map the position of the Aorangi when the wireless message reached her yesterday is shown, and the arrival of the Terra Nova at Lyttelton, New Zealand, is recorded. Inset are portraits of Mrs. Scott and her son and of Captain Scott.

745

A particularly poignant aspect of the Scott tragedy was that his wife, Kathleen, was on her way by ship to meet him in New Zealand when the news of his death broke, as was widely reported by tabloids like *The Daily Graphic* (February 13, 1913 edition).

the cathedral, King George V sat in an armchair under the dome facing the altar, dressed in the uniform of Admiral of the Fleet and flanked by military and government dignitaries. In an unusual gesture, cathedral authorities had decided that ordinary folk would be admitted, without having to acquire tickets, until the cathedral was full. Outside, thousands more gathered on nearby streets to pay their respects to the fallen heroes, exceeding the public outpouring of grief seen at the requiem for those lost on *Titanic*.

Still on her way to New Zealand, Kathleen knew nothing of the extraordinary reaction to Scott's death. In Britain, a special edition of the *Daily Mirror* set a record for copies sold, and one reporter lamented that he could not forget "one who is still ignorant of the frightful tragedy, that hapless woman still on the high seas, flushed with hope and expectation, eager to join her husband." Nor did she know that at the time of the service, "a million and a half children in the schools of London and other English cities were listening to a moving story of the deaths of Capt. Scott and his companions," where afterward, "many of them lined up in their school halls to sing Kipling's 'The Children's Song of Empire,'" which was "suited to the spirit of the occasion." They were then read Scott's "Message to the Public," found with his body at his last camp; one London reporter surmised that this day "will be strongly stamped on the malleable mind of childhood, and never forgotten through life, and from yesterday's service in the schools many thousands of men and women in years to come will be forever familiar with the splendid story of Scott and his heroic comrades."

Con's diaries, which had been recovered by an expedition search party in November 1912, were delivered to Kathleen once she reached New Zealand. As she read them, she learned that her husband had reached the vicinity of the South Pole in mid-January, only to find ski tracks and black flags—flags that Amundsen and his companions had planted on and around the estimated position of the pole a month earlier, to ensure that they had truly intersected it. After taking instrumental readings and a few sad pictures, Scott and his men turned around for the 900-mile (1,450 km) return journey from that "awful place." Plunging temperatures, debilitating blizzards, and snowblindness hampered their progress. Starving and poorly clothed, the five in Scott's party began to succumb to the elements; Scott may have been the last to go. "It's a glorious record wonderfully written stirring and inspiriting [sic] to the last degree," Kathleen wrote. "They would have got through if they hadn't stood by their sick and so I am very glad they did *not* get through."

Upon learning of his rival's fate, Amundsen, lecturing in the United States at the time, stated that he would "gladly forego any honour or money if thereby I could have saved Scott his terrible death." Amundsen's sympathetic words made no difference:

St. Paul's Cathedral, London, February 14, 1913. Memorial service for those who died in the conquest of the South Pole. King George V can be seen kneeling alone in the center of this painting in the *Illustrated London News.* It was highly unusual for a reigning monarch to personally attend the funeral or memorial service of a non-royal. Almost overnight, the story of Scott's pole party had become culturally transcendent: Even the king wanted to have—and to be seen to have—a personal connection with the honored dead.

They would not be enough to spare him from British scorn and derision for his usurpation of Scott's self-evident right to attempt to conquer the pole for the first time. The Norwegian never reconciled himself to the British reaction to his triumph; the librarian at the Royal Geographical Society later claimed that Amundsen was the unhappiest polar explorer he had ever met.

In Britain, Scott in death had been immediately elevated in the national mind from just another naval officer in charge of a disastrous polar expedition into an icon of courage and sacrifice, a latter-day Galahad with echoes of other romantic heroes from Beowulf to General Gordon. Thank goodness his death had been a clean one as these things go: no eating of one's fallen comrades, for example, or getting all whingey and maudlin in the last few pages of one's journal. During the past several decades, however, a different picture of Scott has supplanted the heroic one—one in which he is portrayed as being staggeringly ill-prepared, thus dooming his team to dreadful failure through unsound leadership and a series of poor decisions made along the way. The arc of his reputation, from hero to bumbler, has effectively dimmed the light on Scott's contributions, not only with regard to Antarctic exploration but also to Antarctic science. By contrast, recognition of Amundsen's seemingly effortless success has only grown.

One hundred years ago, the ambitions of these two competitors collided in an epic battle to claim the South Pole, the outcome of which was grand achievement mingled with bitter tragedy and selfless heroism, yielding one of the most powerful stories in the history of exploration.

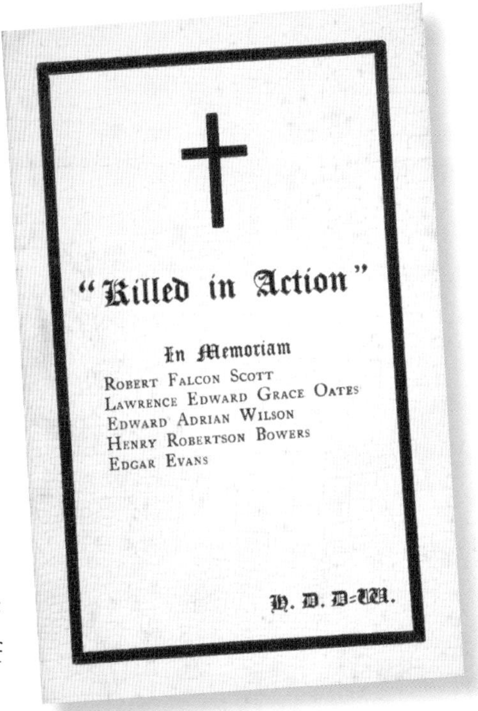
"Killed in Action"

In Memoriam

Robert Falcon Scott
Lawrence Edward Grace Oates
Edward Adrian Wilson
Henry Robertson Bowers
Edgar Evans

H. D. D-W.

Pamphlet accompanying a sermon preached in the Chapel of the Royal Naval College, Dartmouth, February 16, 1913. Because the polar dead had been, in effect, soldiers in a campaign to conquer the South Pole, in some quarters it was felt that they deserved the respect accorded those who had fallen for the nation's honor. They had been "killed in action," the Admiralty officially decided (Huntford 1979: 559).

At the turn of the twentieth century, Antarctica was the one place on the earth's surface of which it could still be legitimately said that it was almost completely undiscovered. At that time, only a century ago, even its basic outline was not known in detail. Because ships could only penetrate the sea ice in favorable areas, there were long segments of coastline that had never been seen or mapped. All that was clear was that the Antarctic region was fairly large, rather circular (if charted headlands were joined up by dashed lines), and mostly south of 60°S. Whether it comprised a continent, groups of islands, or some combination of terranes was an open question.

In antiquity it had been imagined that there must be a great, unknown southern continent, a *terra australis incognita*, to fill out and balance the bottom of the earth. Much later, mariners penetrating the Southern Ocean saw indirect indications of its existence: The occasional occurrence of huge tabular icebergs in high middle latitudes, sometimes adorned with grit and drift torn from land, implied that there had to be unrevealed realms, perhaps of great size, somewhere beyond the horizon. But this was inference, not observation; it was not until 1819 or so (the exact date is uncertain, and contested) that any part of what is now considered Antarctica (in this case, the South Shetland Islands) was actually visited by humans—possibly American sealers on the lookout for unexploited rookeries to supply their ghastly trade. The mainland—or at least ice connected to the mainland—may have been seen first by the Russian explorer F. G. Bellingshausen (1778–1852), in January 1820.

In this the sealers and the Russians succeeded where one of the greatest sailors of all time had failed. A half-century earlier, in 1772, a Royal Navy expedition under Captain James Cook (1728–79) was commissioned to find out what, if anything, lay beyond roughly 56°S, where knowledge of the terrestrial part of the planet mostly ended. With his two ships, *Resolution* and *Adventure*, Cook made the first documented crossing of the Antarctic Circle; but he found nothing for his trouble. After wintering in New Zealand, he headed

Three of the leading polar explorers of the day meet in January 1913. Sir Ernest Shackleton stands between Captain Roald Amundsen and Rear Admiral Robert Peary. Note the orientation of the globe between Shackleton's hands. Amundsen was on his American tour trumpeting his conquest of the pole. His agent, Lee Keedick, said that "Captain Amundsen's lecture in New York put more dollars in the kitty than any lecture given by any other explorer in this town" (cf. Bomann-Larsen 2006: 141).

south again the following year, this time venturing as far as 71°S before further progress was prevented by sea ice in the Bellingshausen Sea. And again he found nothing.

Ironically, both times Cook was very close to the Antarctic coast, within a day's sail, but ice conditions and poor visibility prevented his making what would have been the crowning achievement in an exploration career already adorned with numerous successes. If there was land there—and he suspected that there must be—then it had to be "a Country doomed by Nature never once to feel the warmth of the Suns [sic] rays, but to lie for ever buried under everlasting snow and ice."

Although parts of Antarctica and some subantarctic islands were occasionally spotted by ships from Britain, America, and several other countries in following

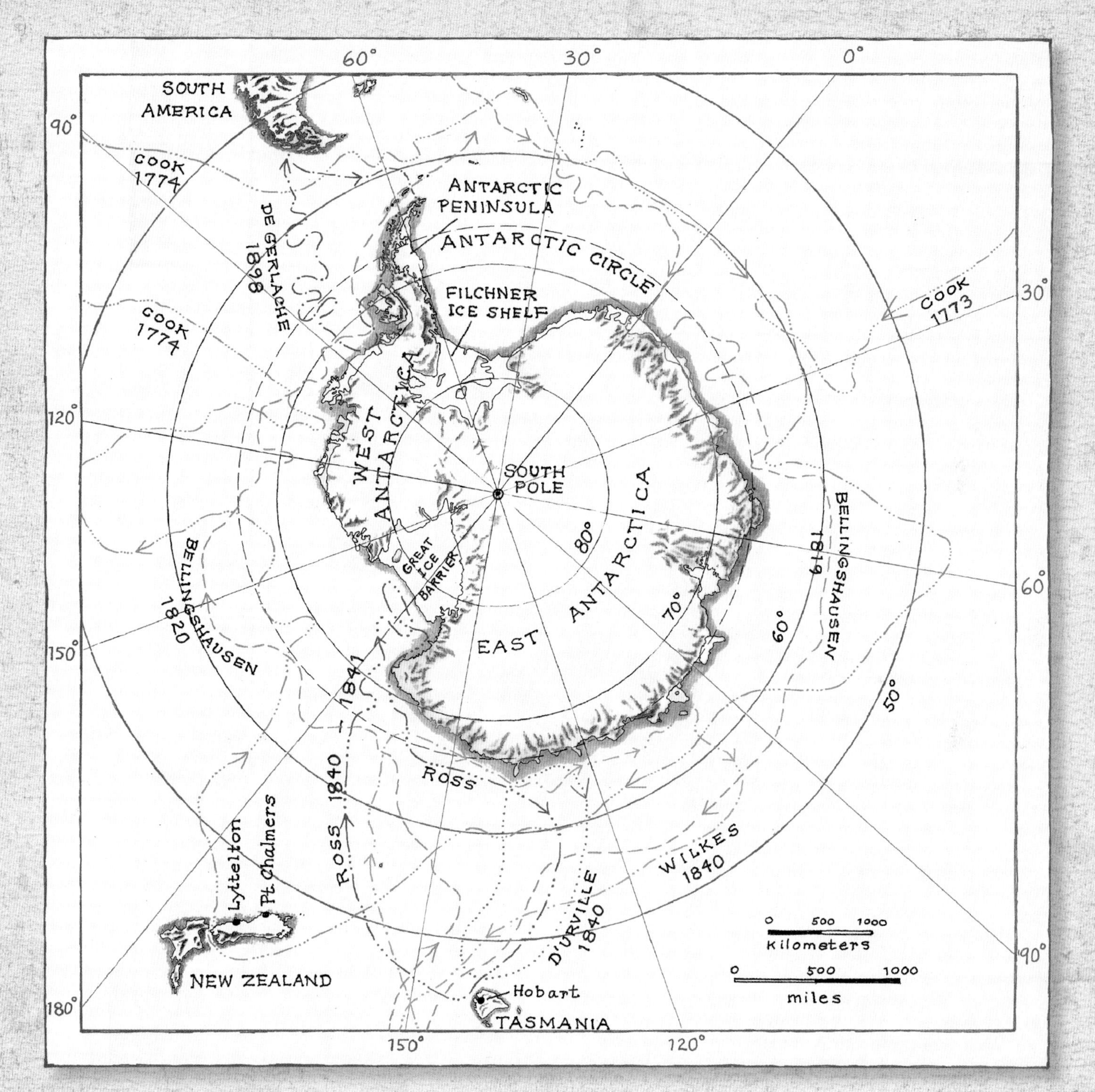

Before the heroes: early voyages of exploration to the Antarctic region (various sources).

decades, it was not until 1839 that the next major British campaign of discovery took to the field under the rather imposing name given it by the Royal Society, "Scientific Expedition to the Antarctic Regions," Lieutenant James Clark Ross (1800–1862) commanding. At forty, Ross was already a noted polar explorer, having located the position of the magnetic North Pole in May 1831 on his uncle John Ross's expedition to find the Northwest Passage. He now intended, eight years later, to do the same at the southern end of the world, and to find new lands if any existed. His ships were *Terror* and *Erebus*, built as "bombs" (in 1813 and 1826, respectively) for naval service and now in mothballs. Bombs looked like ordinary ships, but they were essentially seagoing platforms for firing mortar rounds; to this end their hulls were especially strengthened to absorb the mighty shocks produced during firing. *Terror* had proven its worth for polar work during an earlier expedition to locate the Northwest Passage in 1836–37. The Admiralty evidently decided it would be both smart and economical for Ross to use these now somewhat superannuated vessels on Antarctic service, for *Terror* had shown that bombs could navigate successfully in heavy ice—and in any case they would not be costly to refit. (One more polar excursion awaited them, their last: They were both lost during Sir John Franklin's disastrous third expedition to the Arctic in the late 1840s.)

In 1841, James Clark Ross discovered the Ross Sea and Ice Shelf; almost seventy-five years later, Scott and Amundsen would contend for the South Pole from this same region of Antarctica. Ross's snuff box (which had once belonged to his uncle, the Arctic explorer John Ross) holds open the Royal Society's compendium of instructions for his "Scientific Expedition to the Antarctic Regions" (1839–43). These included an emphatic statement regarding what to collect in any Antarctic lands that may be discovered: "*every thing* . . . is of the highest interest."

Sir Clements Markham, president of the Royal Geographical Society at the start of the heroic age and indefatigable supporter of both of Scott's Antarctic expeditions.

When Ross encountered, in Tasmania, reports that a French expedition under Jules-Sébastien-César Dumont d'Urville (1790–1842) and an American one under Charles Wilkes (1798–1877) had been working in Antarctica exactly where he planned to, he decided to avoid their areas of activity on the rather haughty argument that "England had *ever* led the way of discovery in the southern as well as the northern regions." It was a propitious decision. After four days in pack ice, Ross smashed through into broad, open waters never before seen by anyone, into the sea that now bears his name. Hoping that the South Magnetic Pole might lie in water, and would therefore be reachable by ship, in January 1841 he sailed toward a rocky headline where he discovered, and named after his vessels, the enormous active volcano Erebus and its extinct companion Terror. Seeing land before him to the west as he passed through McMurdo Sound and thence along the South Victoria Land coast, which he also named, he determined that the magnetic pole must lie inland and was therefore not achievable by ship. Turning eastward, to his surprise he found a continuous, high wall of ice that blocked further progress southward; this proved to be the vast expanse of the Great Icy (or Ice) Barrier, now the Ross Ice Shelf. He concluded, "we might with equal chance of success try to sail through the Cliffs of Dover, as penetrate such a mass."

During the next two years Ross made additional voyages toward Antarctica, wintering in Hobart and also the Falklands, but experienced formidable pack, bad weather, and near shipwreck; his exploring done, he sailed for England in March 1843. Some further voyages of discovery were made in the Southern Ocean during the latter half of the century—that of *Challenger* in 1872–77 being the most significant—but few of these went south of the Antarctic Circle, and the continental mainland was touched only once in this period, in 1895. This was a watershed year: The Sixth International Geographical Congress, meeting in London, declared that the exploration of Antarctica was "the greatest piece of geographical exploration still to be undertaken [and] scientific societies throughout the world should urge . . . that this work should be undertaken before the close of this century." This accorded well with the plans of the redoubtable Sir Clements Markham, president of the Royal Geographical Society, who had been pressing for years for renewed British exploration of the Antarctic, lest all the honors attending new discoveries should be taken by foreign hands. His plan was to claim The Bottom for Britain, and by 1899 he had bullied and pushed the reluctant Salisbury government into supporting an expedition. The role of leader eventually fell to an obscure Royal Navy lieutenant named Robert Falcon Scott. After a slow start, the so-called "heroic age" of polar exploration was about to enter an altogether different phase.

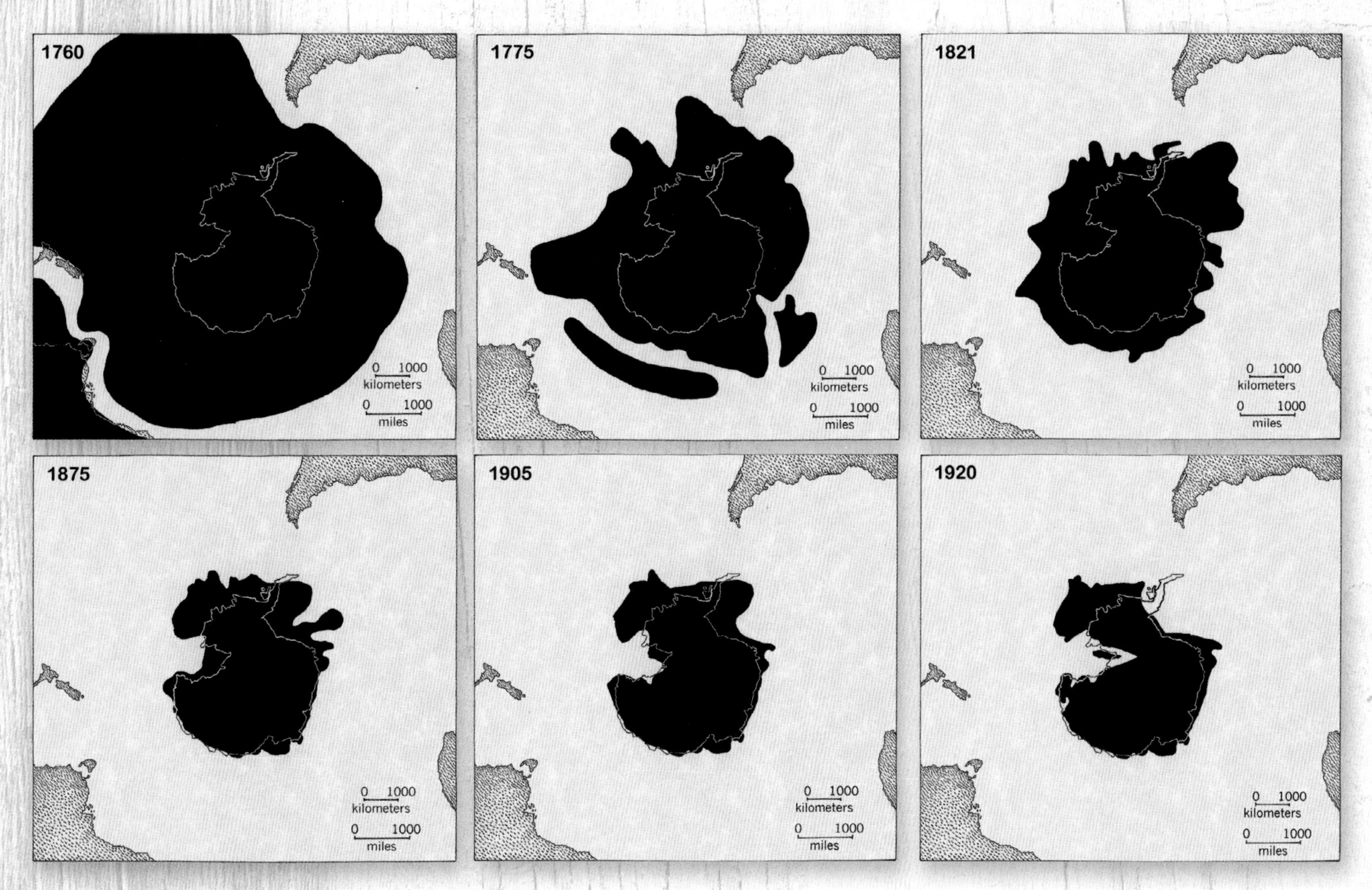

Increasing knowledge of the southern end of the world, 1760–1920 (chiefly based on Joerg 1930). Black areas in each map represent regions unexplored at the time. After the late 1920s, the geography of the still-unexplored parts of the continent was rapidly revealed by exploration from the air.

Financing the *Terra Nova* Expedition

Whereas Scott's *Discovery* expedition was, in the end, well financed, *Terra Nova* was much less so. In 1909 Scott went to the British government with an estimate of £40,000 (£3–3.8 million or $4.7–6.0 million today) for the cost of the expedition. He was turned down initially, but with the intervention of the Chancellor of the Exchequer (and future Prime Minister) David Lloyd George, the expedition was eventually granted half the projected amount (£20,000) toward expenses. The rest had to be raised from private sources: from donors large and small, even from schoolchildren, who would put their pennies and farthings together to help buy a pony or a sleeping bag. Scott was not a born money-raiser, and of course he felt it was demeaning to beg. But he soldiered on and the money trickled in, and by the spring of 1910 he had in hand £10,000 (£730–930,000 or $1.2–1.5 million today). And there were other ways to raise the necessary. Product endorsement was not a new tactic for polar explorers—American explorers such as Robert Peary were especially astute at this, flogging anything from tobacco to proper "Arctic dress" for money or in-kind donations. In the case of the British Antarctic Expedition, many companies came forward with goods and supplies, ranging from names still well known, such as Messrs. Heinz & Co., to Price's Patent Candle Co., Ltd., which provided candles that were "purposely made edible, though never eaten." Teddy Evans, who contributed an appendix for *Scott's Last Expedition* on "Outfit and Preparation," noted that Messrs. Simon Bros. supplied brandy, which "was particularly well put up in suitable bottles for sledging." It all helped, but the expedition was still short when *Terra Nova* sailed. Scott had to plead for cash from private and government sources as *Terra Nova* limped along from one imperial dominion to the next—South Africa, Australia, and finally New Zealand.

Polar expeditions were very expensive, and even with government subsidies, funding often fell woefully short. Beginning in the 1890s, explorers increasingly relied on finding sponsors and advertisers who would supply funds or materials in return for judicious product placement and personal testimonials. One medium of the day was the collectible card, inserted in cigarette boxes or other consumer items. The card issued by Shell (far left) capitalizes on the fact that this company provided lubricating oils for Scott's motor sledges. Another medium was the gummed stamp, which advertisers evidently hoped would be stuck by the consumer onto surfaces where people would see it. The one advertising Max Koch's jams was evidently issued before Amundsen postponed (until 1918) the northern leg of the Third *Fram* Expedition because of the outbreak of World War I.

CHAPTER 2

November—December 1910

Scott Sails South

Terra Nova was just two days at sea from New Zealand when the expedition nearly came to a bad end. "A day of great disaster," Scott would later remark concerning the mighty storm that almost caused his ship to founder. Too small for its load, the leaky, elderly whaler was at risk even before the storm brewed: With holds and decks packed to the brim, Scott worried that it might sink immediately upon leaving the dock at Port Chalmers. Laboring into the gale, the ship began to take on water in large quantity; the pumps, clogged after a few hours by a gummy paste of coal dust, dirt, and oil, eventually stopped working altogether. Bucket brigades, composed of officers, men, and scientists alike, struggled hour after hour in the dark. With water up to their chests at times, they sang shanties at the top of their voices to keep their spirits up, the bilge down, and the fear away, "the ship all the time rolling like a sodden, lifeless log." Later, a hole was cut by hand through an iron engine-room bulkhead to access the clogged suction inlets of the main pumps; it took twelve hours to make a hole large enough to wriggle through and clean them. There was no other way to do it, because the tons of water washing over the ship every few minutes would have caused her to founder almost immediately if the hatchways had been opened.

"It was a sight that one could never forget," Lieutenant Edward "Teddy" Evans, Scott's second in command, would recall. "Everybody saturated, some waist-deep on the floor of the engine room, oil and coal dust mixing with the water and making everyone filthy, some men clinging to the iron ladder-way and passing full buckets long after their muscles had ceased to work naturally, their grit and spirit keeping them

FACING PAGE: Snow goggles worn by R. F. Scott during the *Terra Nova* expedition. Scott experimented with lenses of different colors, but this pair lacks glass inserts altogether; instead the eye sockets have been reduced to narrow slits, Inuit style, with plaster tape.

Terra Nova as she appeared in Scott's day, by Sandy (Bruce) Clark, 1976. Acrylic and oil. After the British Antarctic Expedition, the ship was repurchased by former owners Bowring & Co and went back to whaling and sealing, especially in the waters around Newfoundland and Greenland. She sank in a storm near Simiutak Island, Greenland, in 1943; all hands were saved by the timely arrival of a U.S. Coast Guard vessel.

Terra Nova in a gale: After leaving New Zealand on her way to the Ross Sea, Scott's ship was buffeted by a great storm during the first days of December 1910. Water streamed into the leaky ship at a tremendous rate, and on the second day the pumps failed. "Thus were we driven to a method almost unique with a ship of 750 tons—that of bailing out with buckets!" (Taylor 1916: 41). This photo was taken by Herbert Ponting in March 1912, on his return from Antarctica, during weather conditions only slightly better than he experienced in the famous gale of '10.

going." If many were willing to make heroic efforts in dangerous conditions during that black night, it was Teddy Evans rather than Scott who knew how to keep them at their posts, hour after hour. Scott, ever ready to produce a sharp comment for his private journal, repeatedly noted over the next several months that in fact Evans was not second-in-command material; despite his excellent performance on board, on land he was "incapable" and "terrible slow to learn." These criticisms were expurgated from the version of his diary published in the posthumous *Scott's Last Expedition*. In Evans's case, it has been inferred that Scott was actually jealous of his second's greater ability to deal with the men. However, here as elsewhere it seems more likely that Scott was simply being Scott—continually forming snap opinions, often severe and based on limited evidence, but self-aware enough to alter them later if circumstances warranted.

On deck things were increasingly desperate. The ship's coal bunkers were too small to accommodate all of the coal required, so the excess—thirty tons of it—was stored in sacks on the main deck, along with such expeditionary wherewithal as lab supplies, sheep carcasses, motor sledges, dogs, and ponies, all lodged hugger-mugger wherever they might fit. During the storm many of the sacks became loose and skidded back and forth across the planking, hammering away at the ship's rails. Worse, overloading had affected the ship's buoyancy and handling. The only way to avoid catastrophe was to push some of the topside coal into the sea, even though there was no way of getting more. There was further mayhem on deck. Many of the thirty-three dogs, on short chains to keep them from fighting on the way south, were nearly strangled each time a breaching wave raced across decks. One dog, Osman, was washed overboard with such force that his chain broke, only to be miraculously tossed back onto the ship by another wave.

Lawrence "Titus" Oates, captain in the 6th Inniskilling Dragoons, with some of his charges on board *Terra Nova*. During the three-day gale that almost sank the ship in December 1910, he stayed with the ponies the whole time.

Ponies in cramped stalls in the forecastle juddered from wall to wall with each roll of the ship, legs flailing as they tried but failed to keep their footing, going down hard on their buckled limbs in pools of vomit and excrement. Indeed, if it were not for their handler, Captain Lawrence "Titus" Oates, literally forcing them onto their feet after they had fallen, it is unlikely that any would have avoided serious injuries during that long night.

To be sure, the ponies were a sorry lot to begin with. Upon seeing them for the first time, Oates described Scott's ponies as the "greatest lot of crocks I have ever seen." They had been purchased in Harbin in Manchuria by expedition member Cecil Meares, who originally had been commissioned to buy dogs in the Russian Far East but was charged by Scott to buy ponies as well. When Meares pointed out his total lack of experience with horses, Scott retorted that a good understanding of one domestic animal implied a workable understanding of all, and that Meares should get on with it. He had one other instruction: The ponies purchased should have white coats, since whites (or grays) had done better than horses of other colors on Shackleton's 1907–09 *Nimrod* expedition. There was no scientific basis for this conclusion, and it severely restricted Meares's choice of animals in the Harbin horse market because darker animals had to be passed over even if they seemed to be better choices. In New Zealand Oates examined the ponies carefully, pronounced the whole lot unfit, and told Scott so. Scott, reflexively reacting to an apparent challenge, told Oates that his opinion was both uncalled for and wrong. Oates stormed off.

Oates cared about horses; he cared less for convention and rank. He was one of the more unlikely participants in Scott's *Terra Nova* expedition. A career cavalryman, of few words and no relevant background in anything other than horseflesh, he had purchased a place on *Terra Nova*'s roster by means of a £1,000 donation (as much as £75–95,000 or $120–150,000 today.) He was also a war hero, having earned a name for himself as "No Surrender" Oates. Despite a shattering wound to his left thigh during an engagement in the Boer War, he refused to capitulate and remained in the field until rescued by his own side. He would later demonstrate the same unflinching strength of purpose—to the death—on the journey to the pole.

While in New Zealand, Kathleen and Con (on left in dark coat and cap), with others, inspect two of the ponies purchased in Manchuria. Oates, in a bowler, can just be seen behind Scott. The Owner, who knew nothing about horses, at first disagreed with Oates that they were of poor quality. He also disagreed with Oates concerning how much fodder the expedition needed to take—so Oates simply smuggled two more tons on board, which he paid for himself.

Officers and scientists crowded into the wardroom of the *Terra Nova* in December 1910. Scott sits at the head with Wilson two seats to his left. Farther up the table, the man in the jaunty bush hat is ski instructor Tryggve Gran. Second-in-command Teddy Evans is opposite Gran; his chin overlaps Scott's right shoulder. On the far right, the man sitting with hands cupped against his chin is Titus Oates; Apsley Cherry-Garrard, looking downward, stands directly behind him. The man with the goatee is geologist Griff Taylor, and the lad wearing the nightcap is physicist Silas Wright.

Apsley Cherry-Garrard—known to all as Cherry—was also among the least likely of the expedition's participants, but for different reasons. Wealthy, high strung, and extremely nearsighted, with little experience of life apart from getting a comfortable degree in modern history at Oxford and some travel right along the beaten track in the Orient, he wanted to do something that mattered. Like Oates, he paid £1,000 into the expedition's coffers, but was then rejected on medical grounds. He told Scott to keep the money anyway. This was the watershed: Scott, struck by Cherry's sense of *noblesse oblige*, arranged another medical exam—which Cherry also failed. But by this time it didn't matter; if Cherry were willing to assume the "additional risk" his poor eyesight engendered, Scott said, he would take him on as assistant zoologist. He also told Cherry to learn how to type, because no one else on the team did, and they would have need of a man with that secretarial skill. At many points during the next three years, Cherry would wonder whether providence had been kind or perverse on that day in April of 1909 when he was accepted as a full member of the team. Much later, he would publish *The Worst Journey in the World*, his stirring account of the *Terra Nova* expedition (and much more) that is widely considered one of the greatest true adventure books ever written.

But now, in the teeth of the violent storm they were experiencing, he was having the time of his life—even if he didn't think so at the time: "I have lively recollections of being aloft for two hours in the morning watch on Friday and being sick at intervals all the time. For sheer downright misery give me a hurricane, not too warm, the yard of a sailing ship, a wet sail and a bout of sea-sickness."

On December 3, seventy-two hours after the storm started, the winds and the sea began to calm, but the toll was heavy. Ten tons of coal were gone, as were 65 gallons (246 l) of petrol and 20 gallons (76 l) of lubricating oil. Two of the ponies were dead, two others badly incapacitated; one dog had drowned. The decks were covered with debris, equipment, and broken cases, and everything was soaked through and through.

But they had survived, and soon Scott was in good spirits at the expectation of sighting the "crystalline continent." "The scene was incomparable," he wrote a week later as they entered the southern pack, the fluctuating expanse of sea ice that annually surrounds Antarctica. "The northern sky was gloriously rosy and reflected the calm sea between the ice, which varied from burnished copper to salmon pink; bergs and packs to the north had a pale greenish hue with deep purple shadows, and the sky shaded to saffron and pale green. We gazed long at these beautiful effects."

Robert Falcon Scott was born on June 6, 1868, in Devonport, England, the third child of five of John Edward and his wife, Hannah. The Scotts owned a small brewery in Plymouth, which was the source of the family's prosperity. Naval and military traditions in the family were strong, however, and after studying at the Stubbington House School in Hampshire, at age thirteen Con began his naval career as a cadet aboard the training ship HMS *Britannia*.

At fifteen he became a midshipman and began a steady progression up the career ladder of the Royal Navy. Scott was able and ambitious, and after service aboard various ships, he rose in rank to lieutenant in 1889. In 1894, he was serving on HMS *Vulcan* when he learned that his father had bankrupted the family by selling the brewery and blowing the proceeds on poor investments. To make ends meet, the elder Scott, at age sixty-three and in failing health, was forced to take a job managing a brewery in nearby Bath. "My father was idle," Robert Scott would write at the end of his life, "and it brought much trouble."

Three years later, John Edward Scott died of heart disease. Familial responsibilities were suddenly thrust upon the twenty-nine-year-old naval officer, who quickly realized that he was in dire need of a promotion to bring in additional income to support his mother and unmarried sisters. It was in June of 1899 that Scott, in London on leave, had a chance encounter with Sir Clements Markham, now actively organizing what would become the *Discovery* expedition. Scott had met Markham years before, at age eighteen, in the West Indies during a cutter race, which Scott won. "I was much struck by his intelligence, information, and the charm of his character," Markham noted. The two coincidentally ran into each other in Spain several years later, where again Markham was reminded how impressed he was with the young officer. Markham had, in March 1899, just announced that he was in search of a leader and officers for an Antarctic expedition, and when he encountered Scott yet again in London that June, he encouraged him to consider applying. At thirty-one years of age, a torpedo specialist in the Royal Navy with no previous acknowledged interest in exploration, Scott saw this opportunity as just what he needed. Polar expeditions, he had heard, were a quick way up the ladder of advancement.

A few days later, Scott went to Markham's house and volunteered to lead the Antarctic expedition. He became Markham's first choice, but the Royal Society was hoping to appoint a scientist in charge of the expedition's program. There was much wrangling over this and other appointments. Markham, a master of getting his own way in bureaucratic infighting, set about scuttling the candidacies of other officers preferred by various members of the joint committee supervising the organization of the expedition, but it took time. In the end, approval of Scott's nomination was held up for nearly a year. Finally, on May 24, 1900, Scott was confirmed by the committee; he was promoted to commander and put in charge of the expedition's purpose-built vessel, *Discovery*, then being constructed in Dundee. He now had slightly more than a year to complete the prodigious number of tasks that needed to be undertaken before he and his men could set sail for the south.

Markham's somewhat curious choice of Scott has been subjected to much scrutiny in recent years, with opinions running a lengthy gamut of possibility, from Markham's eccentric methods of character assessment to his psychosexual bent. In any case, although the direct evidence is slim, it appears that Markham had several candidates

Officers and scientists assembled on *Discovery*'s rear deck before departure for the south in 1901. Scott is near the middle, fifth from right. The three on the left are (l to r) Edward Wilson, Ernest Shackleton, and Albert Armitage.

Hut Point. McMurdo Sound April 7.11, by E. A. Wilson, watercolor. The *Discovery* hut was a much smaller affair than the one built at Cape Evans for the *Terra Nova* shore party. Nevertheless, it was a convenient way station for travelers on the "Southern Road," and its existence probably saved lives on more than one occasion.

in mind over the course of the lengthy process of garnering support for the Antarctic expedition, but over time all of them had fallen into disfavor for one reason or another. On that afternoon in June, it might have been someone else's lucky day, but Scott got to Markham's door first. He was of the right age, he was technically accomplished, and he was Royal Navy. That he had no pertinent experience in anything having to do with polar travel was a minor concern; like some pre-modern MBA, Scott, the product of a Navy education, had in Markham's estimation all the theoretical background needed to plunge into his new job and succeed brilliantly.

Scott quickly set about trying to run the expedition along naval lines, although with a lighter touch than he would have preferred since the expedition was to be a civilian, rather than a military, enterprise. From the Royal Navy came three other officers and several noncoms and seamen; additional men were drawn from the Merchant Marine. A number of civilian scientists and workers completed the ship's complement.

Thanks to the intervention of one of the expedition's major backers, the industrialist Llewellyn Longstaff, Scott was politely but pointedly requested to take on a twenty-seven-year-old Anglo-Irish third officer from the Merchant Marine, Ernest Shackleton. Scott agreed; such is fate. Shackleton's hearty, robust manner doubtless annoyed Scott, but they got on well enough, and he thought it would be safe enough to put him charge of "seawater analysis," "entertainments," and like duties until his abilities proved themselves. Shackleton would later make his own name—on the 1907–09 *Nimrod* expedition, where he and his companions came close to reaching the South Pole, and even more famously on the 1914–16 *Endurance* expedition, when his ship became trapped in the ice and was crushed, stranding his men. Shackleton formed a bold but unlikely rescue plan, and assured himself of heroic status when he was able to bring his men home without loss of a single life.

Also aboard *Discovery* was the twenty-nine-year-old physician Edward Wilson, who would serve as junior surgeon, zoologist, and expedition artist. Despite sharp differences in affect and outlook, Scott and Wilson became fast friends. Some years later, when Scott began organizing the *Terra Nova* expedition, Wilson was offered and quickly accepted the post of chief scientist, despite the fact that he was only months away from getting married. Although trained as a medical doctor, after a serious pulmonary infection (possibly tuberculosis) he essentially gave up practice and spent increasing amounts of time absorbed in natural history projects, such as investigating epizootic diseases of wildfowl. He was a talented painter; his lively sketches and fragile watercolors adorn the pages of several of the books written in later years by expedition members and others. In an era innocent of psychological counseling, "Uncle Bill" (as he was nicknamed on the *Terra Nova* expedition) was mediator and confidant for many of the men. Deeply religious and ascetic in habits, he was the one man Scott could open up to and not feel diminished. A confessor, in short; perhaps "Father Bill" would have been a better epithet. Scott would describe Wilson in his diary as "the finest character I've ever met," and he would be one of the four men Scott selected for the final pole party. When the two were later found frozen in their sleeping bags, it was observed that Scott's left arm was protectively extended across Wilson's chest.

Dr. Edward "Uncle Bill" Wilson, in a 1910 portrait.

Southern Attractor

Ernest Shackleton estimated that, on January 9, 1909, he and his *Nimrod* companions attained a position approximately 112 miles (180 km) north of the abstraction known as the South Pole, the farthest anyone had ever ventured toward it. One might ask, after this near-achievement, what portion or part of The End remained to be discovered in any meaningful regard. The answer is simple: Even though Shackleton was close, as these things are counted he wasn't *there*, any more than a sprinter who collapses just before parting the ribbon can be said to have crossed the finish line.

The modern reader might counter with the observation that, even if Shackleton's team had been able to go a few miles more, or somehow look over the horizon, what would there have been for them to see except more of the same unrelievedly white void? Was there in fact a *there* there, different from what was already all around them? Of course they knew there probably wasn't; so did others in the exploration game; and, presumably, at some level the whole world did too. But to those who cared, this didn't matter in the least: After *Nimrod*, there was still a scrap of geographical knowledge hanging just out of reach, which could only be obtained by physically standing at 90°S. Not only did the chase continue in the years after 1909, it also became more overtly competitive, with plans for German, French, and Japanese polar expeditions, among others, being lofted into the air to see whether they might catch support on the way down. For a brief moment, there was even the possibility of an American oar in the waters of the Southern Ocean, pulled by the aged arm of Robert Peary (or, more likely, by one of his Inuit "helpers").

If this remaining scrap still counted for much at the end of the first decade of the twentieth century, it was not because its acquisition offered the possibility of important discovery or revealing new science, whatever expedition organizers might have claimed at the time. The appeal was far more basic and primitive, that of the final conquest, to be first at one of the last untrodden places on earth. As Tor Bomann-Larsen succinctly framed it, one hundred twelve miles represented only "another two days' march, maybe three, in a headwind. One hundred and eighty kilometers, to become part of history, to be immortalized."

"WITH CAPTAIN SCOTT
TO
THE SOUTH POLE."
(First Series.)

A CINEMATOGRAPHIC RECORD of the work of the British Antarctic Expedition, from the departure from New Zealand to February of the present year.

A Further Series of Pictures will be ready very shortly, and a third and final set will appear soon after the return of the Expedition. Captain Scott will start on his **DASH to the SOUTH POLE** next month, and it is hoped that the news of his success will reach England in the spring or early summer of next year.

The Pictures are by Mr. Herbert G. Ponting, F.R.G.S., and are exhibited by arrangement with **THE GAUMONT CO., Ld.**, holders of the exclusive rights.

Synopsis of the Films.

Scene 1.—Captain Scott on the bridge of the *Terra Nova.*

Scene 2.—The Departure from New Zealand.

Scene 3.—Mr. Herbert Ponting, F.R.G.S., the cinematographer, at work on board.

Scene 4.—Lieutenant Rennick, R.N., cutting Dr. E. A. Wilson's hair. Dr. Wilson is the chief of the scientific staff on the *Terra Nova.*

Scene 5.—On December 9th, 1910, a huge iceberg which had broken away from the Great Ice Barrier 500 miles distant, was sighted.

In addition to his still-life photography, Ponting returned to Britain in early 1912 with thousands of feet of movie film. Gaumont Co., which owned the rights to the film, produced two episodes of *With Captain Scott, RN, to the South Pole* that year—before it was known that the men in the pole party had died. Just as today, advertising was important; the poster (facing page) illustrates an actual scene from the second series, while the flyer (left) attempts to build interest. Ponting purchased Gaumont's rights two years later, then spent the next two decades perfecting a film that he eventually named *90° South: With Scott to the Antarctic*. The film was a critical success but not a commercial one; it has recently been re-released on DVD.

WITH
CAPTN SCOTT R.N. TO THE SOUTH POLE
FILMED BY HERBERT G. PONTING F.R.G.S
SECOND SERIES
AUTHENTIC PICTURES EXHIBITED BY ARRANGEMENT WITH THE GAUMONT FILM HIRE SERVICE LONDON HOLDERS OF EXCLUSIVE CINEMATOGRAPH RIGHTS
CAPTAIN SCOTT R.N.
Gaumont
FEEDING AT 30° BELOW ZERO

CHAPTER 3

June–September 1910

Amundsen's "Small Excursion South"

Amundsen acquired *Fram* with Nansen's blessing on the understanding it was to be involved in an expedition to the Arctic. But the ship had been out of commission for some years and needed a refit; much preparation went into readying her for her new work, including installation of a diesel engine and a shakedown cruise in the North Sea that doubled as an oceanographic voyage. *Fram* finally left Oslo harbor on June 7, 1910, on the first leg of what was supposed to be a voyage to the North Pacific via Cape Horn. However, his men noted several things about this new adventure of Amundsen's that just didn't add up. The men had signed on under the impression that they were headed for a multiyear investigation of the northern end of the world, which would involve both exploration and science. Amundsen had received funds

FACING PAGE: Amundsen's binoculars, with three of his major accomplishments scratched onto its brass facings: first transit of the Northwest Passage, second transit of the Northeast Passage, and first attainment of the South Pole. The inscription displayed in the inset reads "*Sydpolen* [South Pole] *14-12-1911*" (that is, December 14, 1911, the date on which Amundsen originally thought he had reached the South Pole, but off by one day because he did not account for crossing the international dateline). While at the pole, Amundsen noted, "Everything we had with us had now to be marked with the words 'South Pole' and the date, to serve afterwards as souvenirs. Wisting proved to be a first-class engraver" (Amundsen 1912, 2: 124).

Fram under sail.

for this purpose, as well as the support of Fridtjof Nansen, possibly the most revered person in the kingdom next to the sovereign. Yet in addition to the expected mass of provisions and equipment for polar work, the men had stowed some unusual, or at least unexpected, cargo before leaving Norway. One example was an "observation house"—of what use would such a structure be on the jumbled, ever-moving sea ice of the Arctic? Another was the ninety-nine Greenland dogs on board—what was that about, when such animals could easily be purchased in Alaska or Siberia, where *Fram* would have to make landfall anyway? To queries and quizzical looks, Amundsen gave whatever reasons he thought would satisfy the inquirer, without seeming to be hiding anything. Fortunately, suspicions never amounted to much more than idle curiosity, but, even so, something was clearly afoot.

Once the winds were favorable, the small ship was finally able to reach the open waters of the Atlantic, heading for the mid-Atlantic island of Madeira. Amundsen retreated below deck to his cabin and set about the task that he had been dreading. He needed to write to Nansen, because he was about to confess that he had betrayed Nansen's trust.

Roald Amundsen in a studio portrait from 1909. At this stage in his life he had a liking for the kind of moustache popularly associated with Kaiser Wilhelm II of Germany. His attitude toward Germany, and with it his moustache couture, changed during the course of World War I.

> *Fram* 22 August 1910
> Dear Professor Fridtjof Nansen,
>
> It has not been easy to write you these lines, but there is no way to avoid it, and therefore I will just have to tell you straight.
>
> When the news from the [Frederick A.] Cook, and later from the [Robert E.] Peary, expeditions to the North Pole came to my knowledge last autumn [of 1909], I instantly understood that this was the death sentence for my own plans. I immediately concluded that after this I could not be expected to secure the financial support I required for the expedition. The Norwegian Parliament's decisions of March and April 1910, to decline my request for 25,000 [kroner] proved me right [equivalent to $185,000 or £115,000 today].
>
> It never crossed my mind to abandon my plans. The question became how I could raise the necessary funds. Something had to be done to increase the public's interest. Only one challenge remains in the Polar Regions that can be guaranteed to awaken the public's interest, and that is to reach the South Pole. I knew that if I could do this, the funds for my planned expedition would be assured.

Professor, it is not easy for me to tell you that my decision to take part in the competition to reach the South Pole was made in September 1909. There have been many times I have almost confided this secret to you, but then turned away, afraid that you would stop me. I have often wished that Scott could have known my decision, so that it did not look like I tried to get ahead of him without his knowledge. But I have been afraid that any public announcement would stop me. I will, however, do everything I can to meet him and announce my decision, and subsequently he can act as he decides.

As this decision was made in September last year, I think I can say that we are well prepared . . . . From Madeira, we will set course southward for South Victoria Land [now Victoria Land]. My idea is to take nine men ashore with me and then let the *Fram* continue doing oceanographic research . . .

It is not yet possible to decide where we will go ashore, but it is my intention not to get in the way of the English. They do of course have the first right to choose. We have to settle for what they do not want. At some point in February or March 1912, the *Fram* will return to pick us up. We will first go to Lyttelton in New Zealand to cable the news, and from there to San Francisco to continue the voyage north . . . . And when you make your verdict Professor, do not be too hard. I have followed the only road which stood open for me, and then it has to end as it will.

I am currently sending the King the same message, but nobody else. A couple of days after you receive this message, my brother [Leon Amundsen] will make a public announcement about the new addition to the expedition's plan.

Once more I beg you. Do not judge me too harshly. I am no hypocrite, but rather was forced by distress to make this decision. And so, I ask you to forgive me for what I have done. May my future work make amends for it.

Respectfully yours,
Roald Amundsen

There is much that is obscure and unspoken in this heavily nuanced letter, clearly meant for posterity's eyes as well as Nansen's. The reference to resuming "my planned expedition" *after* reaching the South Pole was a sop to Nansen, who was meant to understand from this that the excursion to the south was a necessary money-raising addition to the promised northern voyage, now delayed but not forgotten.

Amundsen had been openly discussing his proposed north polar expedition since returning from the 1903–06 transit of the Northwest Passage aboard the tiny *Gjøa*. The crowning touch of the new project was to be the exploration of the northern part of the polar basin—where the North Pole was situated, which the first *Fram* expedition under Nansen in 1893–96 had not been able to reach. Amundsen emphasized the novel scientific work that would be undertaken, such as making depth soundings, measuring seawater salinity and temperature, charting currents, studying terrestrial magnetism, and so forth, but the gleam in his eye was always for the North Pole, waiting, still unachieved. Suddenly, the prospect of reaching it for the first time fell out of Amundsen's grasp into the hands of not one but two bickering claimants, the Americans Cook and Peary. Amundsen had not planned for this; what to do?

Roald Amundsen came from comfortable circumstances, but he was not then and never would be a wealthy man. From an early age, all he really cared about was either being on an expedition or planning another. This required that he find and keep backers, such as newspapers willing to pay generously for exclusive reports, which in turn required that he continually accomplish new and wonderful things. His *Gjøa* expedition had garnered some respectable attention by scientific bodies, but the resulting popular book and his lectures did not find a large audience abroad. Refining the position of the North Magnetic Pole and contriving a way through the labyrinthine Northwest Passage were accomplishments, but not stirring ones. To stay in the exploration game, he had to do something that would assure him extraordinary publicity. His quandary was that he had made plans for work in the north, secured a boat, and received some money to do so. To say now, suddenly, that all this was off and he was heading instead to Antarctica to find the South Pole might have been greeted with stares and blank looks at the very least.

Then as now it was typical that would-be explorers would announce their intentions well before the fact, as much to advertise their plans to the media and possible backers as to warn off anyone else presuming to do something similar, or forewarn them of a struggle for the prize. To so radically change direction, as Amundsen intended to do,

Dr. Fridtjof Nansen in 1909, in his study at Polhøgda, his villa outside of Oslo.

would invite questions not only about his commitment but also his competence. With backing weak and evaporating, Amundsen saw himself left behind in his house near Christiania (now Oslo) with only his dreams—and ultimately creditors pounding at his door, for he was almost always short of money. Thus, at least in his own mind, he was "forced by distress to make this decision."

But why did he go on to tell Nansen that he was "afraid that you would stop me"? It is quite uncertain whether Nansen would have been privately as judgmental of Amundsen as this letter implies he would be. Indeed, Nansen's reported reaction upon hearing of Amundsen's change of plans was a left-handed endorsement: "The idiot!" he is said to have shouted, "Why couldn't he have told me. He could have had all my plans and calculations." There is more to this. The reference to plans concerns Nansen's own somewhat inchoate intention to give the South Pole a try, an intention he finally abandoned in 1907 when Amundsen asked him for the loan of *Fram*. Maybe, as biographer Tor Bomann-Larsen has claimed, Amundsen could not risk telling Nansen about his change of objectives sooner, because the professor might have insisted on leading the expedition, thus becoming not Amundsen's benefactor but instead "his most dangerous rival in the battle for the South Pole." Maybe; but Nansen's South Pole ambitions seem to have been carried over as a sort of emotional charge from younger days, when he was at the height of his powers physically and could, he was sure, accomplish anything. No one likes to abandon such aspirations; they allow you to think that you are still a contender. Even so, Nansen never publicly, nor privately as far as is known, said that Amundsen had stolen the South Pole from him as well.

How concerned was Amundsen about adverse reaction in Great Britain and elsewhere? Britain had already colored a good portion of the map of the world in red, and until now the most publicly celebrated of the Antarctic expeditions had all been British. That neither Britain nor any other nation that had touched the shores of Antarctica had instituted any form of effective occupation, which might provide grounds for putative ownership, was beside the point: Most of the European powers of the time had acquired their empires in an opportunistic, willy-nilly kind of way that had little to do with international conventions or observation of treaties. One wag said that the British Empire was acquired in a fit of absence of mind. Yet the British could claim that they certainly had some rights to a big part of The Bottom,

Uranienborg, Amundsen's home from 1908, looking out onto Bundefjord.

if anyone did. Beginning with James Clark Ross's voyages in *Erebus* and *Terror*, all of the major expeditions in and around the shores of the Ross Sea had been British at least in name, including most of those that had made any kind of serious landfall (*Southern Cross*, *Discovery*, *Nimrod*, and latterly *Terra Nova*). If anyone had the right to call this region theirs, the British did. In all justice, how could some Johnny Foreigner now presume to come along and start out for the pole from their very front porch, with an expedition of their own already in the field and making for the same goal?

Yet it does not seem likely that John Bull attitudes would have deterred Amundsen overmuch, or explain his secrecy. Germany, Japan, Australia, and France all had Antarctic expeditions in the field around this time, and some intended to undertake extensive land explorations. In stating that the British had "the first right to choose" a starting-place for their try for the pole, Amundsen was giving the expected lip service to custom. What he really thought is revealed by the next sentence, "We have to settle for what they do not want"—in other words, McMurdo Sound is yours; outside of that, I'll land where I please. And, indeed, why not? Amundsen had been to Antarctica *and* overwintered there, before Scott had even assumed command of his first Antarctic expedition. Whose claim of priority was stronger?

Perhaps Amundsen's feelings for the Norwegian monarchy, which he ardently supported, provide at least an indirect route to his thoughts at this time. Maud, the wife of Haakon VII, the highly regarded king of Norway, was a granddaughter of Queen Victoria; Britain had been in quiet favor of the dissolution of Norway's former union with Sweden in 1905, and this young and comparatively poor country knew it was in need of large, well-intentioned friends. Indeed, Nansen himself, who had been instrumental in the dissolution and had served as independent Norway's first ambassador to the United Kingdom in 1906–08, would have counseled that Amundsen's intrusion into nominally British territory might be seen as an insult to the monarchies of both countries, further damaging the explorer's reputation. After it was known that he had successfully reached Antarctica and was on the ice, Amundsen's financial backers attempted to secure a government grant to cover the expedition's expenses, but in the ensuing uproar politicians favorable to Amundsen were afraid to show their support. Whatever Amundsen's calculations, he realized from the start that success was the only thing that would justify his subterfuge and quiet his detractors.

Amundsen continued to struggle, writing letters and press announcements that were to be delivered later by his brother Leon, once the news of his true destination was made public. That was hard enough, but he had another matter to deal with, one that would require great tact. As far as his crew was concerned, they planned to reach

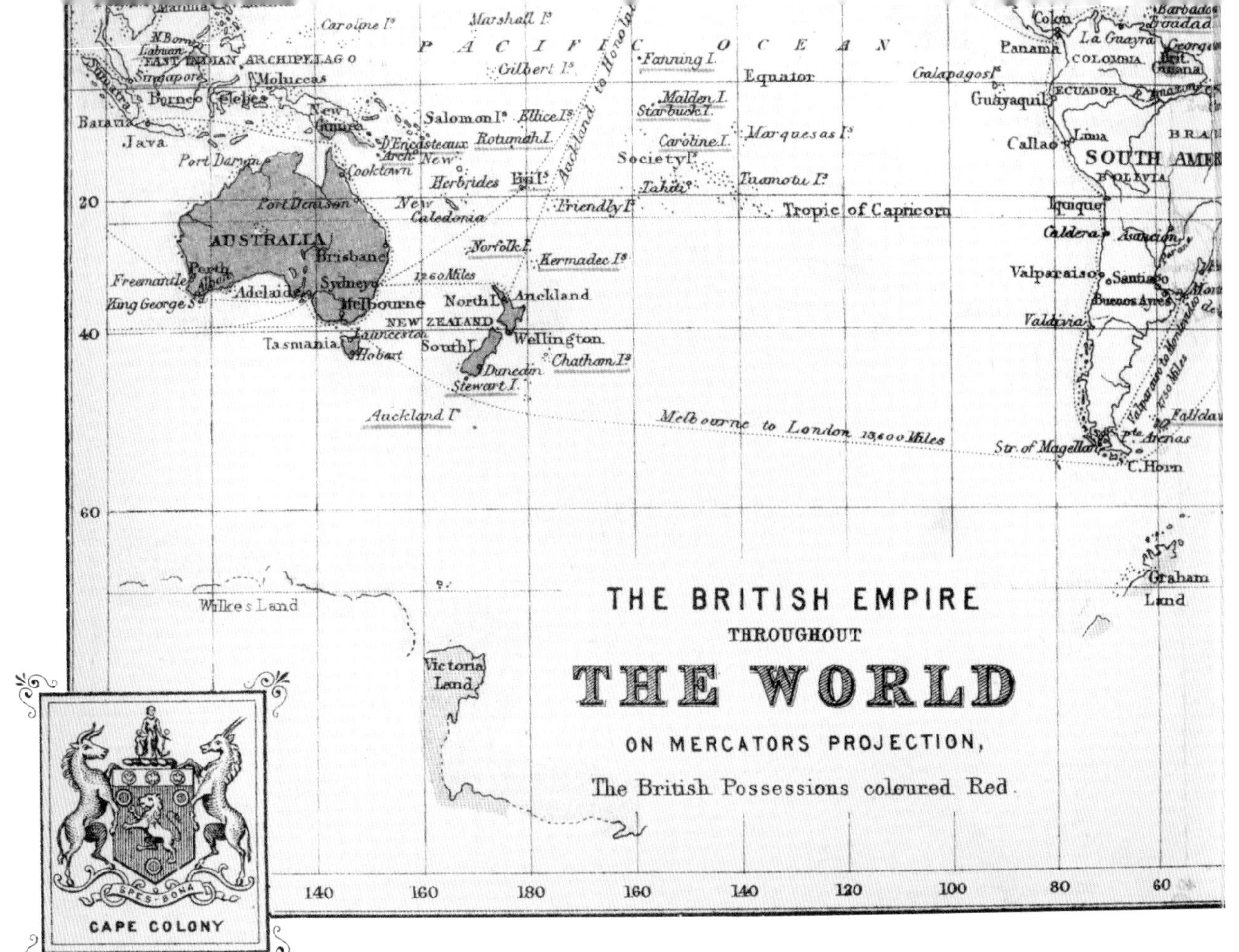

An empire, gained in a fit of absentmindedness: On this 1884 map, Graham Land (now known to be part of the Antarctic Peninsula) and South Victoria Land are colored pink, as though they were candidate parts of the British Empire, apparently because James Clark Ross had sailed by them more than forty years previously.

the Arctic via the Bering Strait, which in 1910 still required a trip around Cape Horn because the Panama Canal was not yet completed. The stopover in Madeira was normal for ships making the run thence to South America. However, in Amundsen's new plan, after Madeira they would sail straight for their objective, the Great Ice Barrier, without making another landfall unless absolutely necessary.

So it was to be on this small Portuguese island that Amundsen intended to let his crew know that they would not head toward the Arctic after all. During the past two months aboard *Fram* he had had ample time to get to know his men. He imagined they would be startled at first, but he was confident that they would be enthusiastic about the remarkable challenges that lay ahead. Lieutenant Thorvald Nilsen, the ship's commander, had been informed earlier, as were *Fram*'s other officers when the ship departed from Norway. Amundsen worried about the reaction of Sverre Hassel, an experienced dog driver and a man of strong personality who was one of the men Amundsen had in mind for the shore party. If he felt he'd been misled, Hassel might be able to persuade the crew to abandon the expedition. So Amundsen took Hassel into his confidence, and, cozened by the trust placed in him, Hassel agreed to keep the secret from the rest of the ship's company.

Two weeks later, on September 6, *Fram* arrived at Funchal, Madeira's main port, where the ship was restocked and minor repairs were made over the next few days. When Amundsen ordered the anchor raised on September 9, shortly after coming aboard at 4:30 P.M., the crew was taken aback. They were not scheduled to depart for several hours. There was grumbling as they were summoned on deck, where Nilsen was waiting with a large map, which he unfurled before the disbelieving crew. It was a map of Antarctica; Amundsen strode up beside it. According to Lieutenant Fredrik Gjertsen, one of *Fram*'s officers, Amundsen simply went straight to the point: "There are many things on board which you have regarded with mistrustful or astonished eyes, for example the observation house and all the dogs, but I won't say anything about that. What I will say is this; it is my intention to sail Southwards, land a party on the Southern continent and try to reach the South Pole."

Fram dockside in Christiania in May or early June 1910, getting ready for departure. The four persons in front are (l to r) Leon and Roald Amundsen, Lieutenant Fredrik Gjertsen, and Captain Thorvald Nilsen.

The men were poleaxed, not quite sure what to make of what they were hearing; Amundsen went on to explain why he had misled them regarding their destination, and, somewhat puckishly, why this new direction for the expedition did not amount to a major change in the plan at all. They had to sail around Cape Horn anyway, where they'd be three quarters of the way to the South Pole: If they were nearly there in any case, why not go the distance and grab the prize? Carefully, Amundsen was building his case. He described the expedition as not "his" but "ours," and spoke of common goals and achievements. Then, he delivered the knockout blow, informing the crew that they would now be racing England. "Hurrah," shouted Olav Bjaaland. "That means we'll get there first!" These words had just the electrical effect on the others that Amundsen desperately wanted. Bjaaland was one of the finest skiers in the world; to him, the expedition was now a grand sporting match, a cross-country ski race against Britain. And, "as everybody knew, the Norwegians were better skiers than the English." Bearding the Lion indeed.

Amundsen continued to explain, in more detail, the task before them and the reasons for keeping his plans secret. He later recalled,

> At first, as might be expected, they showed the most unmistakable signs of surprise; but this expression swiftly changed, and before I had finished they were all bright with smiles. I was now sure of the answer I should get when I finally asked each man whether he was willing to go on, and as the names were called, every single man had his 'Yes' ready. Although, as I have said, I had expected it to turn out as it did, it is difficult to express the joy I felt at seeing how promptly my comrades placed themselves at my service on this momentous occasion. It appeared, however, that I was not the only one who was pleased. There was so much life and good spirits on board that evening that one would have thought the work was successfully accomplished instead of being hardly begun.

Before *Fram* left Madeira, there was one more item of business that Amundsen had to address: He felt compelled to let Scott know of his change of plans. By telegram would do, with the text of it to be transmitted by Leon Amundsen, who had sailed to Funchal separately to meet *Fram* at a prearranged rendezvous. Leon's job was to take back to Christiania whatever last words his brother and his men wanted to send to the settled world before literally disappearing from it: letters, press announcements, instructions to supporters, and now one unexpected telegram. In view of the intended recipient, Amundsen thought it would be best to be brief and to the point.

Four who went with Amundsen to the South Pole (clockwise from top right): Olav Bjaaland, Helmer Hanssen, Sverre Hassel, and Oscar Wisting. Amundsen (1912, 1: 50) noted that he had chosen men "who were specially fitted for outdoor work in the cold," who could run dogs, ski, and make with their own hands whatever was needed for expeditionary travel or comfort.

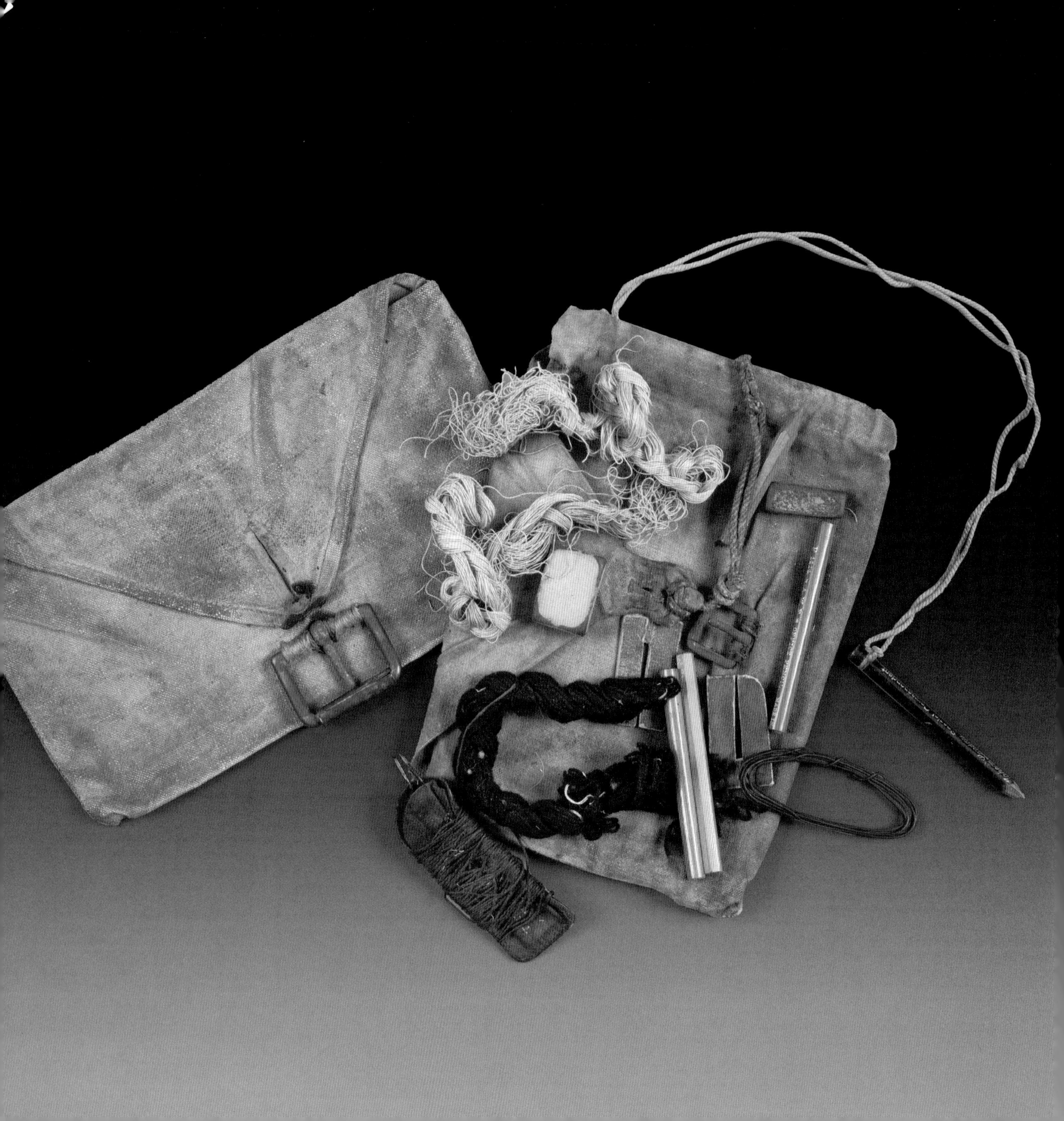

CHAPTER 4

October—December 1910

Challenge Served

The gale that nearly sank *Terra Nova* was behind Scott and his men, and the ship pressed on into the Ross Sea. Navigating around icebergs was easy by comparison to forcing a way through the pack, which the ship entered on December 9. *Terra Nova* had been built in Dundee in 1884; she was barque-rigged and carried coal-fired steam engines capable of 89 revolutions a minute to deliver 140 horsepower—which under unusually good conditions and with the assistance of sail yielded a top speed of 9 knots. (She mostly did much less, somewhere between slow and dead slow, as Oates pungently observed.) The ship was strengthened for working in polar waters, but it was no ice-breaker in the modern sense—it had neither the mass nor, especially, the engine-power to ram its way through meter-thick floes. Instead, it had to find its way by following slips of open water between floes—called leads—when possible. When not, the only choice was to wait for winds and sea currents to move the pack around and open new leads, or search for thinner or weakened floes that looked like they might be split by a strong blow with the ship's prow. If the ice was fairly thick, hitting it in this headlong manner was little different from hitting a rocky shoal: The whole ship would convulse and groan as it struck, then rise up, more or less sickeningly, on the floe's lip. If the ice then gave way and split, the prow would

FACING PAGE: Wilson's canvas wallet, which held his southern journey diary, and his "timinoggy" bag with its contents displayed, both found at the last camp. Timinoggy, with various spellings and meanings, is ultimately a nautical term for a rope used to prevent the fouling of a ship's running rigging, thus metaphorically (as here) a potentially useful collection of odds and ends. Wilson kept his full of scrap string, thread, pencils, and the like.

Terra Nova took three weeks to pass through the pack ice in the Ross Sea. Herbert Ponting, the expedition's somewhat eccentric but meticulous official photographer, did what he had to in order to get spectacular shots. He constructed this unsteady-looking scaffold (inset) in order to film the ship as she cut through the pack.

nestle down into its newly created slot and scrape forward toward the next obstruction. If not, there was nothing to do but back off and try again or look for another way. Lieutenant Henry "Birdie" Bowers, fresh from chasing gun-runners in the Persian Gulf and pirates on the Irrawaddy River in Burma (now Myanmar) with the Royal Indian Marine, was seemingly impervious to Antarctic cold. He had a knack for knowing what kind of ice would crack and split under battering, and often took the helm during floe-breaking maneuvers. His diligence in dealing the most violent shocks to the ship would often send Scott scurrying to the deck in alarm.

It was slow work—very slow by comparison with *Discovery*'s swift passage through the pack in 1901, which had taken less than a week. The delays irked Scott, who wondered after three weeks of slight progress if they might be forced to winter in the pack. After finally passing out of the ice on December 30, Scott enthused that the "ship behaved splendidly—no other ship, even the *Discovery*, would ever have come through so well . . . . If only she had more economical engines she would be suitable in all respects." This observation was prompted by the fact that the ship had consumed "61 tons [of coal] in forcing our way through, an average of 6 miles to the ton. These are not pleasant figures to contemplate."

BRITISH ANTARCTIC EXPEDITION, 1910.

CABLE ADDRESSES:
KINSEY, CHRISTCHURCH.
ONWARDNESS, LONDON.

LONDON ADDRESS:
36 & 38, VICTORIA STREET, S.W.

CHRISTCHURCH, N.Z.

Nov 14. 1910

My dear Dr Nansen

My telegram to ask Amundsen's intentions may need some explanation. I have just received your answer "unknown"
On my arrival at Melbourne I received a telegram from Amundsen dated Christiania October 3rd – "Fram proceeding to Antarctic" On November 4th I received a telegram from England "Hear Fram going direct McMurdo" Since that one or two of my people have called my attention to newspaper notices which support that rumour. As you can imagine it is very difficult to get accurate information in this part of the world and having no ~~knowledge~~ information

Scott's letter to Nansen, dated November 14, 1910, asks for any additional information that might be available concerning Amundsen's apparently sudden alteration of his plans and, more particularly, his designs on McMurdo Sound. Elsewhere in the letter Scott stated that he assumed Nansen would agree with him in "deploring" Amundsen's behavior in hiding his intentions. It is hard to imagine that Scott expected to receive an answer to this letter before leaving New Zealand for Antarctica only two weeks later.

There were other things not pleasant to contemplate: Two and a half months earlier, on October 12, when *Terra Nova* docked in Melbourne, Scott had received a mystifying telegram with Amundsen's name on it as sender. What exactly did it mean, "*Fram* proceeding to Antarctic," if that was all that it said? (The exact text of the message was evidently not recorded at the time by anyone, including Scott, and the telegram itself is lost. Teddy Evans and Cherry-Garrard gave different versions of it in their diaries and later works. The text cited here is Scott's, from a letter to Nansen dated November 14, 1910.) After reading the telegram, Scott summoned Tryggve Gran, the young Norwegian ski expert appointed to the expedition on the recommendation of Fridtjof Nansen. Scott had hoped that Gran, as Amundsen's fellow countryman, could help him make sense of the message. But little could be gleaned from the deliberately curt wording, sent according to plan by Leon Amundsen after *Fram* was well away from Madeira.

Tryggve Gran, the twenty-one-year-old ski expert brought on the *Terra Nova* expedition to teach the men how to ski. Gran described his charges, after instruction, as "average" skiers, indicating that they did learn something.

For a man like Amundsen, whose exploration career was built on a continuing cascade of firsts, there could be only one goal in Antarctica. As Scott told Gran, "Amundsen is acting suspiciously . . . In Norway he avoided me in every conceivable manner . . . Let me say it right out. Amundsen was too honourable to tell me lies to my face. It's the pole he is after, all right." Scott had tried indeed to speak with Amundsen in Norway some three months before *Terra Nova*'s departure, to gauge his interest in making simultaneous magnetic readings when the parties were in place in opposite polar regions. Amundsen, patently avoiding Scott, never made himself available for this or any other discussion. Although Scott had no reputation for humor, sarcastic or otherwise, his assessment of Amundsen as being "too honourable" seems unlikely to have reflected his true feelings.

Titus Oates, who did possess a dry wit, was certainly not trying to be funny when alluding to the events of the day in a letter to his mother (his idiosyncratic spelling and grammar are preserved in this and subsequent quotes from his letters and diary):

> What do you think about Amundsen's expedition. If he gets to the Pole first we shall come home with our tails between our legs and make no mistake. I must say we have made far too much noise about ourselves all that photographing, cheering, steaming through the fleet etc. etc. is rot and if we fail it will only make us look more foolish. They say Amundsen has been underhand in the way he has gone about it but I personally don't see it is underhand to keep your mouth shut—I myself think these Norskies are a very tough lot they have 200 dogs and Yohandsen is with them and he is not exactly a child, also they are very good ski-runners while we can only walk, if Scott does anything silly such as underfeeding his ponies he will be beaten as sure as death.

Scott also wrote to Nansen, thinking that he should be able to shed some light on the matter. But Nansen telegraphed back a one-word answer—"Unknown"—to Scott's inquiry. Scott couldn't leave the matter there, and rephrased his question in a second letter. In it he assumed that Nansen would agree with him in "deploring" Amundsen's not telling anyone what he was up to. But Nansen had evidently made the choice not to inform Scott that he knew that Amundsen was headed for South Victoria Land, probably foreseeing that Scott would view this as an invasion of "his" sector. Ever the diplomat, Nansen was probably trying to keep the developing conflict between the two explorers from becoming a major issue.

As Cherry later recollected, "The last we had heard of [Amundsen] was that he had equipped Nansen's old ship, the *Fram*, for further exploration of the Arctic. This was only a feint. Once at sea, he had told his men that he was going south instead of north; and when he reached Madeira he sent this brief telegram, which meant, 'I shall be at the South Pole before you.' It also meant, though we did not appreciate it at the time, that we were up against a very big man."

While some explorers publicly debated whether or not Amundsen had the ethical right to challenge Scott at all, others were firm in their belief that the Norwegian was foolish to even try. Among them was Ernest Shackleton, who did not see "how Amundsen can hope to reach the South Pole unless he has a large number of ponies on board. He may have dogs, but they are not very reliable." Shackleton believed that ponies were a sensible alternative to dogs as draught animals because they could, at least in principle, haul heavier loads. This blindly overlooked every other consideration, such as the fact that horses require very specific feeds (and could not be fed to each other), are susceptible to extreme cold in ways that dogs bred to such conditions are not, and, in general, are among the least likely beasts of burden one could choose for Antarctic work, whatever their virtues in the far north.

Sir Clements Markham believed that *Fram* had "no more sailing qualities than a haystack . . . she is not adapted for very heavy seas, and may turn turtle . . . Scott will be on the ground and settled before Amundsen turns up, if he ever does."

But Scott was caught thoroughly off guard. Temperamentally unsuited to deal with the unexpected, and, at times, paralyzed by the possibility that his plans might not go as originally set, he chose to ignore the implications of Amundsen's challenge. Weeks later, when a reporter in New Zealand persisted in asking Scott to comment on Amundsen's intentions, Scott went silent, and then according to Gran finally bristled, "If, as rumour says, Amundsen wants to try for the South Pole from some part of the coast of the West Antarctic, I can only wish him good luck." That is, Scott wished him luck if he attempted the pole from some *other* part of Antarctica, not the broad region centered on the Ross Ice Shelf—that was his alone.

A race is only a race when there is a competition, acknowledged or otherwise. Amundsen was clear on this matter—he had no thought but to beat the British, and said so—but Scott's equivocal view of the matter became engulfed in the hagiographic mist that rapidly surrounded the tragic outcome of his expedition. The fact is that, whatever Scott may have said to influential backers about the vulgarity of racing for the pole, to the public he plainly and unequivocally stated that "the Pole was the main objective." Of course, it only became an actual race when Amundsen and his

LEFT: Herbert Ponting at work in his darkroom at Cape Evans in March 1911. RIGHT: The darkroom in 2003. Some of the fixed equipment, such as the acetylene gas line, is still in place after almost a century.

men showed up; but others had been sending out trial balloons well before the *Terra Nova* expedition left for the south, and no one could have been in any doubt that, if there was to be any kind of competition for the pole on the Antarctic ice, Britain intended to get there first.

Newspapers had begun to trumpet Amundsen's change of plans even before *Terra Nova* had docked in Melbourne. Challenge had been served, and the competition for the South Pole was now very much on.

The high seas they had previously experienced were hard on those unused to it, and Scott noticed that Herbert Ponting, the expedition's forty-one-year-old official photographer, was seasick much of the time. "Ponting cannot face meals but sticks to his work," Scott wrote. "I am told that he posed several groups before the cinematograph, though obliged repeatedly to retire to the ship's side." The day before, Scott was staggered to see Ponting still working, despite his constant nausea, "with the developing dish in one hand and an ordinary basin in the other!"

Ponting considered himself a "camera artist," and it was his beautifully rendered images of Japan and China that had captivated Scott and convinced him that Ponting was the man he wanted. On board *Terra Nova*, Ponting would spend a great deal of time setting up his images with his bulky 8 x 10 view camera, sometimes suspending himself from various shipboard contraptions to capture just the right angle and backgrounds. He also took along a movie camera and would become one of the first photographers to bring back moving images from Antarctica.

Ponting gradually acquired his sea legs, and he was able to entertain the crew with his banjo songs. As they approached land, the crew was in fine spirits, and overwhelmed by the beauty before them. "The sun also brought us wonderful cloud effects," Scott wrote, "marvelously delicate tints of sky, cloud, and ice, such effects one might travel far to see. In spite of our impatience we would not willingly have missed many of the beautiful scenes, which our sojourn in the pack afforded us. Ponting and Wilson have been busy catching these effects, but no art can reproduce such colours as the deep blue of the icebergs."

There were other diversions as well. They had left with sixty-five men and a menagerie of ponies, dogs, two cats, squirrels, and, improbably, a pregnant rabbit—a gift from well-wishers in New Zealand. The rabbit was the possession of Petty Officer Tom Crean, a hard-as-nails Irishman who later went on to sail with Shackleton. By Christmas, Crean's rabbit had given birth to seventeen little ones. Their individual fates are not recorded.

Roughhousing was part of bonding; Bowers and Wilson enjoy a playful shoving match on the deck of *Terra Nova* in late 1910.

They were a rowdy lot, these young men who were heading south. Their antics, detailed in some of the surviving diaries, seem comparatively childish and overexcited, like tearing off each other's shirts or playing silly practical jokes. Even Dr. Wilson and Lt. Evans—surprising only in view of the professional stature of one and the rank of the other—entered wholeheartedly into these activities. Nicknaming, an old Royal Navy tradition, was also part of the men finding (and

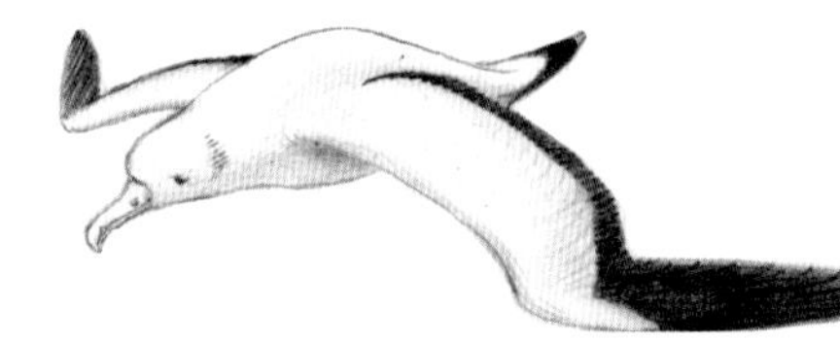

giving) places in the evolving hierarchy. Some of these were generic, such as "The Owner" for a ship's commanding officer (and thus applied to Scott). Others seem a bit cruel: For the little man with the large nose, "Birdie" was practically automatic; for the biologist Nelson, a man of fastidious habits, "Marie" stuck like one of Dr. Wilson's plasters. The point was that you were expected to wear your moniker as given, laughing it up to show you didn't mind and weren't going to be girly about a little ribbing. Sublimation at work, no doubt. If not exactly *Lord of the Flies*, the expedition was not a story out of *Boy's Own* either.

The men had been able to accomplish some scientific work already, using sounding lines to measure water temperatures at different depths and an apparatus called an electrometer to measure "penetrating radiation" (cosmic rays). They had also been observing whales, seals, penguins, seabirds, and other oceanic creatures. Of the scientists and researchers on board, some had professional standing but others (Cherry, for example) were hastily trained recruits or stand-ins for other appointees who had dropped out for one reason or another. This reduced the value of some of the scientific reports that eventually emerged from the expedition. But at this point Scott was not overly concerned about his staff's level of preparation: He believed in pluck and carrying on, after all. His view was that his men could accomplish whatever they needed to when they set their minds to it. Their goal was not only to claim the South Pole, but also to pursue science wherever, whenever, and however they could. Scott remarked that he had "never seen a party of men so anxious to be doing work or so cheerful in doing it . . . . The spirit of the enterprise is as bright as ever. Everyone strives to help everyone else, and not a word of complaint or anger has been heard on board. The inner life of our small community is very pleasant to think upon and very wonderful considering the extremely small space in which we are confined."

Christmas was spent in the pack, but by New Year's Eve prospects were finally improving. To combat feelings of loneliness and isolation, major holidays were aggressively celebrated both on board and, later, on the ice. Plum pudding, the usual opulent, sweet-but-savory finish to any heavy holiday meal, was provided in the wardroom on New Year's Day 1911. The men dug in, not only to experience the delicious mouth feel of the pudding, but also for the prospect of finding something purposely placed within, like a coin. Wilson found a button in his portion, which he must have liked because he took it with him all the way to The End.

On January 2, 1911, *Terra Nova* came in sight of Mount Erebus, the active volcano first seen by James Clark Ross. During the *Discovery* expedition a few years earlier, a post-office pole—a message depot for passing ships—had been set up on the island's

Polar toys for Midwinter "Christmas" on June 22, 1911. The label accompanying the little broom reads, in Cherry-Garrard's handwriting, "This brush is a toy taken down to the Antarctic and one of many gifts decorating the Christmas tree shown by Bowers on Midwinter Night 1911, just before we started on the Winter Journey. I was given this, Titus Oates a pop gun etc." Titus went around shooting everybody: "If you want to please me very much you will fall down when I shoot you" (Cherry-Garrard 1937: 232).

eastern end near Cape Crozier. As they drew near the cape they saw that the bright red cylinder was still standing, sparking welcome memories among old shipmates. Scott had hoped to land near the cape to set up winter quarters, and he launched a whale boat to examine the possibilities. The boat had a difficult time maneuvering, but eventually it drifted beneath lofty cliffs of ice, at which point the men joked that it wouldn't be much fun if one of those cliffs were to collapse while they were rowing beneath them. "So we were glad," Wilson wrote, "to find that we were rowing back to the ship and already 200 or 300 yards away from the place and in open water when there was a noise like crackling thunder and a huge plunge into the sea and a smother of rock dust like the smoke of an explosion, and we realized that the very thing had happened which we had just been talking about."

In the event, a landing proved impossible—the swells were everywhere enormous—and the ship set off for McMurdo Sound on the island's western side, where the *Discovery* expedition had been based. With his team at the ready and land off the bow, Scott was sure their efforts would deliver up some great success: "Fortune

Man-hauling pony fodder to the stable, with one of the motor sledges in the distance, January 1911. Once *Terra Nova* was firmly anchored to the fast ice off Cape Evans, offloading was completed in little more than a week. Ponies, dogs, motors, and men all worked to get tons of provisions, food, and equipment across the 1.5 miles (2 km) from ship to hut site. "The station is beginning to assume the appearance of an orderly camp," Scott enthused (Jones 2006: 79).

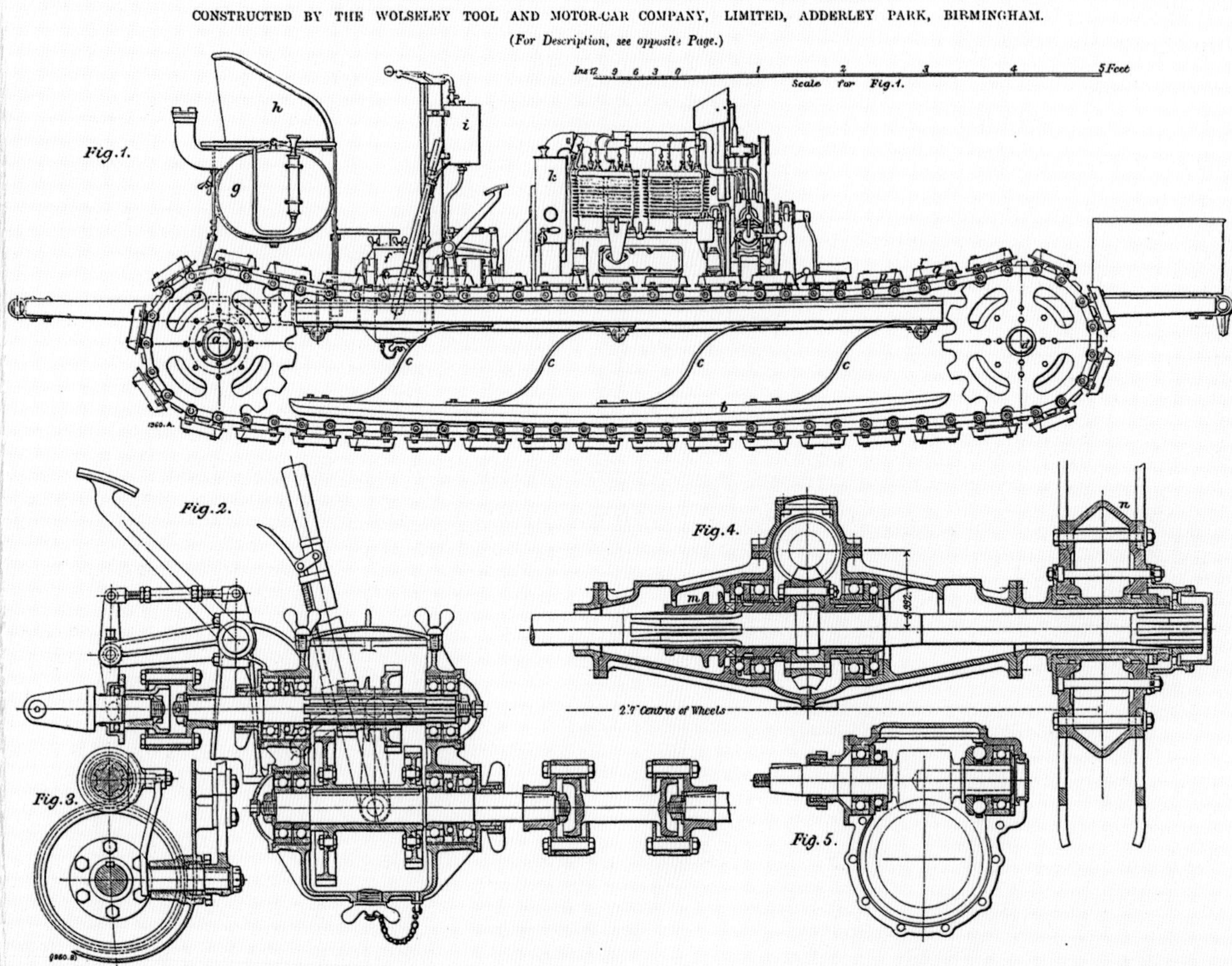

Technical drawing of the type of motor sledge used by Scott, depicted in the journal *Engineering* (December 23, 1910). Although field tests in Norway "proved thoroughly satisfactory," in Antarctic conditions the sledges performed poorly. Interestingly, the Birmingham manufacturer, Wolseley Tool and Motor-Car Co., also produced a slightly modified version of this motor sledge for the 1911–12 *Deutschland* Antarctic expedition under Wilhelm Filchner. Filchner decided to leave the sledge behind in Buenos Aires, but it would never have been used in any event because the expedition failed to make landfall in Antarctica.

would be in a hard mood indeed if it allowed such a combination of knowledge, experience, ability and enthusiasm to achieve nothing."

Cape Evans, a strip of rocky beach on the western side of Ross Island about 15 miles (24 km) north of Hut Point, was the site that Scott eventually settled on as the place to set up the base camp for the *Terra Nova* expedition. Known informally as the "Skuary" during *Discovery* days, the cape was renamed after Teddy Evans. *Terra Nova* was moored onto the fast ice about a mile and a half (2 km) from shore. Unloading and repacking was now the order of the day, as it was already the first week in January and the days before winter weather came on were slipping by. Two of the large motor sledges were unpacked and moved onto shore without trouble, and they were up and running later that afternoon. Using a large block and tackle, Oates struggled to get his ponies out of the ship and onto shore; eventually "the whole seventeen were safely picketed on the floe," rolling and kicking with joy. On the *Nimrod* expedition, four of Shackleton's ponies had died soon after reaching land when they ate salty sand on the beach, so Oates knew to rope his ponies in on a snow slope and keep them away from the shore.

Drivers Bernard Day and William Lashly (facing camera) tinkering with one of the breakdown-prone motor sledges. At the start of the southern journey in early November 1911, Day managed to coax his sledge only a few miles beyond Safety Camp before a cylinder cracked, disabling the machine. The other motor sledge, driven by Lashly, made it just beyond Corner Camp, only 50 miles (80 km) from Cape Evans. "So the dream of great help from the machines is at an end!" wrote Scott in some despair (Jones 2006: 315). However, he had never counted on the motors to get him very far, and the motor sledge party immediately became a man-hauling support party.

Scott had the dog teams taking light loads back and forth from the ship to the mustering site for stores; in his diary, he noted the initial meeting between his dogs and the most recognizable of Antarctica's birdlife:

> The great trouble with [the dogs] has been due to the fatuous conduct of the penguins. Groups of these have been constantly leaping on to our floe. From the moment of landing on their feet their whole attitude expressed devouring curiosity and a pig-headed disregard for their own safety. They waddle forward, poking their heads to and fro in their usual absurd way, in spite of a string of howling dogs straining to get at them. 'Hulloa!' they seem to say, 'here's a

> game—what do all you ridiculous things want?' And they come a few steps nearer. The dogs make a rush as far as their harness or leashes allow. The penguins are not daunted in the least, but their riffs go up and they squawk with semblance of anger, for all the world as though they were rebutting a rude stranger—their attitude might be imagined to convey, 'Oh, that's the sort of animal you are; well, you've come to the wrong place—we aren't going to be bluffed and bounced by you,' and then the final fatal steps forward are taken and they come within reach. There is a spring, a squawk, a horrid red patch on the snow, and the incident is closed.

Lumber and prefabricated sections for the base hut were moved onto the building site, and construction parties were organized to assemble the 50 x 25 ft (15.2 x 7.6 m) structure, with associated outbuildings and stables, as quickly as possible. But it was well into the summer season, and the fast ice around the ship was quickly deteriorating, making it increasingly dangerous to cross. Scott wanted the third and final motor sledge unloaded and taken to shore before the ice rotted completely. Too late: As the crew began to move the sledge toward the beach, the ice gave way and it plunged deep into the bay with no hope of recovery.

Although Scott's views on the utility of tractor transport would nowadays be considered prescient, Oates saw the motor sledges as a terrible waste of money: "3 motors at £1,000 each, 19 ponies at £5 each, 32 dogs at 30/- each. If Scott fails to get to the Pole he jolly well deserves it." In fairness, Oates didn't quite get the point. Introducing motors into Antarctic exploration, as Shackleton had done by bringing an Arrol-Johnston motorcar on *Nimrod*, was an attention-grabber, and implied that the expedition leader was on the cutting edge of science and technology, as well as donation management. In Scott's case, Baron Howard de Walden, a wealthy motorboat enthusiast, supported development of the design of the motor sledges. If more rigorous field trials had been undertaken prior to departure from Britain, the need for various improvements to the sledges would have doubtless become apparent, but Scott did not have—or did not make—the time for this.

Aside from the mishap with the third motor sledge, Scott was able to completely unload the ship and erect his hut in eight days. He was happy with his new home. "The hut is becoming the most comfortable dwelling-place imaginable," Scott wrote. "We have made unto ourselves a truly seductive home, within the walls of which peace, quiet and comfort reign supreme."

The ponies had been on board so long that Scott wasn't sure if they'd be able to stand up to the work expected of them, especially on slippery ice. Scott was accordingly amazed at the strength and endurance they displayed as soon as they were on land. He had Oates to thank for that. The dogs were a little more worrisome. They were getting better, Scott noted, "but they only take very light loads still and get back from each journey pretty dead beat. In their present state they don't inspire confidence, but the hot weather is much against them."

Scott was also pleasantly surprised by Gran's introduction of new skiing techniques. On the *Discovery* expedition, the men had used the old single-pole method for propulsion and balance, especially when pulling loads; now each man had two short poles for this purpose, a great improvement. "Everyone declares that the ski sticks greatly help pulling; it is surprising that we never thought of using them before." Although none of the men became outstanding skiers, those who went south with Scott certainly became accomplished enough under Gran's tutelage to make the use of skis an asset rather than a liability.

Further improvements were forthcoming during the long months ahead. Petty Officer Edgar "Taff" Evans, destined to play a tragic role during the pole journey, is often portrayed as a drinker with an exploring problem. Be that as it may, he was one of Scott's favorites, not least because of his skill in making or repairing virtually anything he set his mind to. He had, Scott commented shortly before they reached the pole, a "remarkable headpiece," and was obviously a natural tinkerer. One of the problems the men were having with skiing was the primitive design of ski boots, which restricted the ability of the foot to move around inside the boot, thus increasing the chance of frostbite. Evans designed and made rigid outer shoes of sealskin and wood, into which a flexible inner boot could be inserted, solving the problem.

On January 18, 1911, the new hut was ready to be inhabited. Scott divided it as though they were still aboard ship: The sixteen officers and scientists were given two-thirds for their quarters and labs, while the nine seamen and support personnel who made up the remainder of the shore party occupied the rest. Officers and men ate separately, although the food served was the same. It would have seemed odd to all concerned if anyone had protested this arrangement. Observance of class and social divisions 'tween decks was still automatic and unquestioned in the Royal Navy, and so it would be in Scott's Antarctic.

Fram

CHAPTER 5

October 1910–January 1911

Last of the Vikings

As *Fram* sailed from Madeira, the crew's spirits lifted considerably. To them Amundsen was—as he was to his own mother—the "last of the Vikings," and, just as their ancestors had done centuries ago, they were now setting forth on a rip-roaring adventure. They were simply going to take the South Pole away from Scott by getting there first. For his part, Amundsen was aware that he must not only beat the British expedition, but also ensure that he was the first to capture headlines by getting news of his triumph back to the civilized world before Scott did. Amundsen thoroughly planned for this as well: He had seen how wrangling over priority had helped to bring down his friend Frederick Cook, who had claimed to have reached the North Pole on April 21, 1908. This was almost precisely twelve months before Robert Peary's counter-claim, but Cook's return from the Arctic had taken a whole year. Neither of them was near a cable station until early September 1909; when finally sent, their victory telegrams came over the wires only four days apart. Thence followed heated exchanges, allegations, and a controversy that still has not ended.

The Norwegians had departed Europe three weeks before Scott's team, but on an even slower vessel; nevertheless, by January 3, 1911 they were inside the Ross Sea pack, without having made a single landfall since Madeira, even for fresh water. In Antarctica, everything is about timing. In contrast to the delays Scott and *Terra*

FACING PAGE: Cup from Amundsen's *Fram* expedition, bearing the phrase "14-12" (December 14, the Norwegians' "pole day") scratched into the enamel beneath the ship's name. Other scratches in the same area also appear to have been intentional, perhaps indicating a tent or ridges in snow. The spoon is probably from the *Norge* expedition.

Le Petit Journal

ADMINISTRATION
61, RUE LAFAYETTE, 61
Les manuscrits ne sont pas rendus
On s'abonne sans frais dans tous les bureaux de poste

5 CENT. SUPPLEMENT ILLUSTRÉ 5 CENT.

20me Année — Numéro 983
DIMANCHE 19 SEPTEMBRE 1909

ABONNEMENTS

	SIX MOIS	UN AN
SEINE et SEINE-ET-OISE	2 fr.	3 fr. 50
DÉPARTEMENTS	2 fr.	4 fr. »
ÉTRANGER	2 50	5 fr. »

LA CONQUÊTE DU POLE NORD

Le docteur Cook et le commandant Peary s'en disputent la gloire

Robert Peary and Frederick Cook—seen here in friendly discussion—both claimed to have reached the North Pole. In the exploration game, where priority is everything, this naturally led to a dispute (which continues still, as partisans doggedly argue for their man). To avoid a similar vulgar spectacle, both Amundsen and Scott were determined to acquire unassailable observational and photographic evidence that 90°S had been attained.

Nova had experienced throughout December, *Fram* had a relatively smooth passage through the floes. "For the first twenty-four hours after we entered the ice it was so loose that we were able to hold our course and keep up our speed for practically the whole time," Amundsen wrote. "Our passage through the pack had been a four days' pleasure trip, and I have a suspicion that several among us looked back with secret regret to the cruise in smooth water through the ice-floes when the swell of the open Ross Sea gave the *Fram* another chance of showing her rolling capabilities."

Low latitudes were hard on dog and man alike as *Fram* slowly chugged through the tropics. Amundsen sits on the spare mast in light clothing, next to sailmaker Martin Ronne, who made the tent that would be used at Polheim on the sewing machine seen here.

Fram at the ice front in the Bay of Whales in January 1911, during the process of unloading stores.

Amundsen recorded "no terrors to oppose us" and, given the time of year, saw surprisingly few icebergs. On January 11, they sighted their first goal, the Great Ice Barrier. In longitude 165°W Amundsen directed *Fram* toward the Bay of Whales, a deep embayment in the ice which existed at that time. He knew from reports of earlier expeditions, including Shackleton's *Nimrod,* that the height of the Barrier was much lower at this spot than anywhere else that had been properly surveyed, outside of McMurdo Sound. Here, he and his men could get onto its surface, build a base in which to wait out the winter, and make a run for the pole in late 1911. Of course, there was danger involved. According to the same reports, the ice front did not seem to have changed much over the past few years. Yet it was, after all, only the leading edge of a vast, elevated mass of inexorably moving frozen water that could suddenly fracture at any time, with possibly disastrous consequences for anyone encamped near its margin. Amundsen made his calculated decision: They would take the risk and make their encampment on the barrier about 2.5 miles (4 km) from the edge of the sea.

In keeping with his penchant for naming his major expeditionary bases after his vessels, Amundsen (at Kristian Prestrud's suggestion) called the camp on the barrier "Framheim" (Home of *Fram*). In the end, Framheim was much more than the simple prefabricated hut that Amundsen first had his unsuspecting men assemble on the grass next to his house, Uranienborg, outside Oslo. Discovering that the surrounding snows were sufficiently compacted to allow excavation next to the hut, the men eventually hollowed out a warren of passageways, storerooms, workshops, and—they were Scandinavians, after all—a serviceable, one-man sauna. A number of aboveground tents for provisions and dogs completed arrangements.

Amundsen started unloading *Fram* about a week after Scott had begun the same task on Cape Evans, but he was not in any sense behind. By landing at the Bay of Whales, Amundsen was 69 miles (110 km) closer to the pole in straight-line distance than the British expedition would be at their intended camp on the west side of Ross Island. In all that he would now do, Amundsen followed plans carefully laid out months before. The Norwegians had spent their time aboard *Fram* organizing their supplies, fine-tuning their equipment, and trying to anticipate their rivals' moves. Amundsen intended to hit the ground running.

Born to a family of Norwegian shipowners on July 16, 1872, Roald Amundsen was four years younger than Scott. Despite his mother's hopes that he become a doctor,

Amundsen knew, by the age of fifteen, that he would one day be an explorer. To please her, he enrolled at the university in Christiania, but he neglected his work, taking more pleasure in skiing, long nature walks, and attending lectures by Arctic travelers than in his courses. One such lecture was given by Eivind Astrup, a Norwegian of Amundsen's age who had accompanied Peary on his 1891–92 Greenland expedition. Amundsen learned that Norwegian skis were far superior to North American snowshoes for travel over snow, that Inuit dogs were perfectly suited to polar exploration, and that by imitating native peoples' dress and modes of living, Europeans could survive and even prosper in some of the harshest environments on earth.

Restless ambition was taking a firm hold on young Amundsen, and he only became more restless when he learned that the Norwegian naval architect Colin Archer was building a revolutionary ship for Nansen's next expedition. This ship would have a rounded cross section and virtually no keel. As a result, the immense horizontal forces generated by moving pack ice would be deflected under the ship, thereby preventing its being crushed—a common fate of ships of more conventional, deep-draft design. The theory was that this would enable the ship to remain intact even when beset—and to drift along with the ice for long periods. Although this concept was roundly mocked by some ship builders, Nansen paid no attention and put his full faith in Archer who, he believed, had designed an "almost unsinkable lifeboat." Nansen's wife, Eva, christened the ship (*Fram* means "Forward" in Norwegian) and on Midsummer's Day of 1893, when Nansen sailed from Christiania amid a fleet of escorts, the twenty-one-year-old Roald was there on the shore, watching, and dreaming.

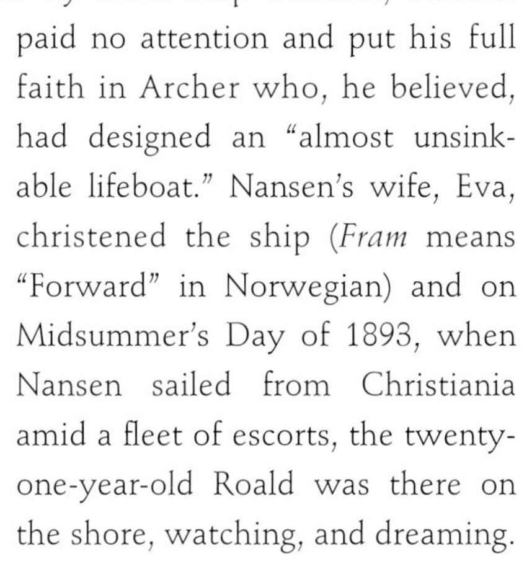

It came as no surprise to anyone who knew Amundsen that he failed his university exams that spring. His mind was elsewhere and medicine was not in his future. Still, he kept the bad news from his

Amundsen's movie camera, taken to Antarctica. Amundsen himself was too impatient to get good results with either still or motion-picture cameras, but others in the expedition, especially Bjaaland, were more proficient.

mother, and when she died later that summer, Amundsen no longer felt compelled to continue with a career that did not suit his interests. He left university, aiming now for a life at sea. Although he hoped to join an exploring expedition soon, he was not successful until Adrien de Gerlache, leader of the 1897–99 Belgian Antarctic Expedition, took him on as first mate aboard his ship *Belgica*. The expedition left Europe in August 1897, with the objective of exploring the western side of the Antarctic Peninsula as far south as conditions would permit. Amundsen's introduction to the dangers of Antarctic exploration began almost immediately. The ship hit a storm near the South Shetland Islands in mid-January 1898, and one of the sailors on board was washed away and drowned. According to Roland Huntford, Amundsen blamed himself, since he was the officer on watch at the time.

The hut at Framheim enclosed a single room used as a dining/sleeping area, with an adjacent galley. The pyramid tents (and snow tunnels hollowed out around the hut) contained the workshops and most of the equipment.

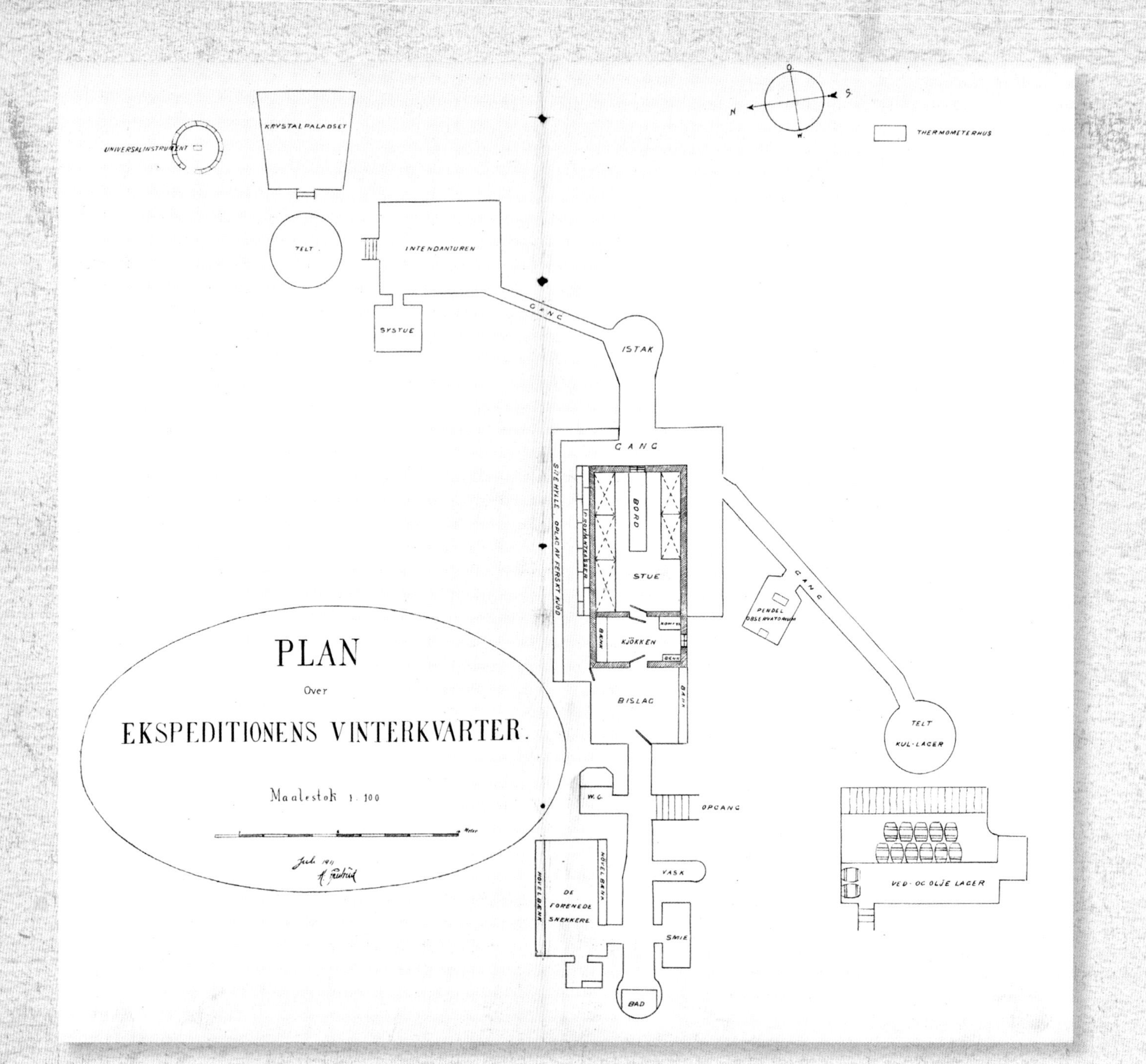

"Plan Over Expeditionens Vinterkvarter" or "Plan of the Winter Quarters of the Expedition", scale 1:100, July 1911, by Kristian Prestrud and published in *Sydpolen*, the Norwegian version of Amundsen's account of the South Pole expedition. The plan shows the footprint of the entire Framheim complex: the wooden building, pyramid tents, and the warren of tunnels, storerooms, and workshops dug into the snow over a period of months.

Despite the lateness of the season and the grumblings of the crew, de Gerlache pressed on and on, past the Antarctic Circle, past previously discovered lands, grinding ever deeper into the ice of the Bellingshausen Sea. By the beginning of March, *Belgica* was completely beset, forcing the ill-prepared crew to spend the winter frozen into the sea ice off Alexander I Island, well south of the Antarctic Circle. Nor did they escape the next summer; in all, the ship spent thirteen months entrapped in the ice. Amundsen's iron control over himself, as well as his instinctive insight into the odds they were facing, was evident from the start of their predicament: "I saw and understood fully the great danger [de Gerlache] exposed the expedition to, but I was not asked for my opinion, and discipline required me to keep silent."

In addition to a lack of adequate cold weather clothing, the effects of months of darkness, isolation, and fear gripped the crew. Two sailors became mentally unstable, and the threat of scurvy was ever present. Amundsen credited the expedition's surgeon and photographer, Frederick Cook, for saving them from this dreaded disease by organizing hunting excursions in order to feed fresh, underdone seal meat to the crew. At the time, this was not a widely accepted means of preventing scurvy. De Gerlache, who was himself beginning to suffer from the disease, did not approve of this diet and would not eat the meat until Cook forced it upon him as medicine. One *Belgica* crewmember did die of scurvy; he confessed earlier that he had such an aversion to seal and penguin that he "would rather die than eat either."

Yet despite these privations and discomforts, on June 20, 1898, with the sun having already disappeared for a month, the young Amundsen recorded in his diary words that revealed he just might have discovered his true calling in life:

> The sun finishes its wandering northwards tomorrow, and begins its return. I will naturally be glad to see it again but I have . . . not missed it for *one moment*. On the contrary, it is this that I have waited for so long. It was not a childish impulse that persuaded me to come. It was a mature thought. I regret nothing and hope I have the health and strength to continue the work I have begun.

Despite de Gerlache's mistakes in planning the *Belgica* expedition, which Amundsen never forgot and determined never to repeat, he learned important lessons about Antarctic survival and about himself.

Amundsen's 1903–06 *Gjøa* expedition deserves brief mention because in it we see the first public evidence of Amundsen on his own, as thoroughgoing planner and highly seasoned explorer. By this time it was well understood that the magnetic poles move, but not why or on what schedule. As a first step in the solution of these puzzles, continuous measurements were needed at these poles over an appreciable period. Amundsen stated he would go to the magnetic North Pole and undertake whatever measurements were needed, for years if necessary, to assemble the data required.

But of course there was more to Amundsen's plan. During the first half of the nineteenth century, ships looking for "the" Northwest Passage tested most of the possible routes around the islands making up the Arctic Archipelago. What they found was that none of them was realistically navigable because of ice, shoals, or both. Although Amundsen realized that probably no commercially feasible route existed, he also saw that he could gain stature as an explorer by the mere act of getting a single vessel through the length of the maze of ice-choked passages, something the Royal Navy had never been able to accomplish. It took three years from the first winter on King William Island in 1903 until *Gjøa* docked in Nome in the summer of 1906. He might well have been able to do it in less, but he was committed to collecting the promised observations, so he and his men stayed many months more than they needed to had geographical firsts been the only goal. Amundsen also showed an early ability to grab press attention, underlined by deeds of great endurance. To get out the word of his success, he skied from Herschel Island, where the vessel was iced in after passing through the Passage in 1905, to the closest telegraph station at Fort Egbert, 500 miles (800 km) away over the Brooks Range. Unfortunately, in this case he lost the possibility of selling an exclusive story due to the malfeasance of the local commandant, who passed on to Seattle papers Amundsen's telegram to Nansen that announced his victory. Nevertheless, by his feats he acquired considerable fame in Norway, as well as the plaudits of Nansen, who had been an early supporter, something he would put to use in future years. But perhaps the chief benefit of the *Gjøa* expedition for Amundsen was the lessons he learned from the Netsilik Inuit he encountered, particularly with regard to proper clothing and the handling of dogs. He had always sensed preparation was everything; now he knew he was ready for all that the polar regions had to show him.

One of the first things Amundsen did upon returning to Norway was to write a letter to Nansen, asking to meet with him so he could begin the next stage of his career in polar exploration, which would involve borrowing *Fram* to complete Nansen's original plan to reach the pole. As things turned out it just wouldn't be the North Pole that he went to first.

Roald Amundsen in 1906, after the *Gjøa* expedition successfully completed the Northwest Passage. Amundsen had now proven himself a competent leader and explorer and was ready for another challenge.

CHAPTER 6

January 1911

Making Ready

Scott's first foray south, the National Antarctic Expedition, had begun nine years earlier, in mid-1901. In a foretaste of problems on his second expedition, his ship *Discovery* leaked badly during the journey to New Zealand. But the expedition was treated royally in Lyttelton on New Zealand's South Island when it arrived in December, leaving Scott with pleasant memories. With repairs made and provisions stowed, he and his companions were ready for their entry into Antarctic waters. After some preliminary examination of the coast of South Victoria Land and the Barrier, in the third week of January *Discovery* entered McMurdo Sound and managed to anchor close to the peninsula (now Hut Point Peninsula) forming the southernmost extremity of Ross Island. There, for safety's sake, Scott allowed the ship to be frozen into the ice. Although a hut was erected on shore, for the most part the officers and crew continued to live and work aboard ship. Among Scott's instructions was a directive to explore his surroundings and bring back solid information about the nature and extent of any lands encountered. This obviously required that he and his men undertake long journeys over the ice, and to modern eyes the *Discovery* men were ill-prepared for their task: Not one among them was a skilled skier, nor were any of them adequately experienced in dog-sledging. But they could haul. Man-hauling had been the preferred—indeed the only—method of sledge travel utilized by most nineteenth-century Royal Navy expeditions engaged in exploring the Arctic Archipelago, despite the fact that the lighter

FACING PAGE: Herbert Ponting, official photographer of the *Terra Nova* expedition, described himself as a "camera artist." His compositional techniques were influenced by his previous exposure to artistic canons of Asia, especially Japan. Here Ponting's photograph of a grounded berg known as "The Matterhorn" is paired with "A Fisherman Standing on a Rocky Promontory at Kajikazawa in Kai Province" (inset), a woodblock print by the Edo Period artist Katsushika Hokusai (1740–1849). In the photograph, Mt. Erebus can be seen in the distance, a smoke plume rising from its summit.

Man-hauling for hours on end in deep snow like this was brutally hard work. Silas Wright, who traveled to the polar plateau with Scott, later reported, with a physicist's eye, on the things he had learned about expeditionary sledging. In one passage he emphasized how important it was that sledges—and sledging teams—be as equal as possible "when two or more man-hauling units are travelling together. No doubt the difficulties which may arise in such parties is largely a psychological one, but all who have sledged will bear witness to the reality of the effect . . . . [T]he friction of sledges varies greatly; if the party is pulling to the limit of its powers, the result upon the worst equipped unit may be quite serious. If equality of sledges cannot be attained, the personnel should be shifted among the units until the normal rates of travel are equal" (Wright 1924: 40). Scott tended to blame any sledging inequalities on poor packing or the men's lack of condition, and he did not shift team members around as often as he could have to ensure similar rates of travel.

sledges and dog teams used by northern native peoples were an obvious alternative (and one that had long since been embraced by Hudson's Bay employees, who had no need to prove their manhood by self-haulage).

The major trek of the *Discovery* campaign began at the end of October, 1902. Its original purpose was to determine whether the long line of mountains seen stretching away to the south along the South Victoria Land coast was a chain of closely spaced islands, or the actual edge of the southern continent. To accomplish their goal the men had to cross the unknown surface of the ice barrier—which, they hoped, might offer a veritable highway to the pole. They set out with a starting party of fifteen, which was gradually whittled down to Scott, Wilson, and Shackleton as the final

Shackleton, Scott, and Wilson on February 2, 1903, the day of their return to Hut Point from their Barrier trek. They had achieved a "furthest south" of 82°17'S.

team. They had a very difficult time in unfamiliar terrain, and were forced to turn around at the end of December, in latitude 82°S. They now faced a desperate slog back to the ship. By mid-January all the dogs were dead and the men were showing signs of exhaustion and imminent scurvy. Shackleton, the weakest of the three, could hardly pull and was coughing blood. Scott implied in his book that he and Wilson had to carry him on the sledge occasionally because he had "broken down," a claim that Shackleton disputed. But Albert Armitage, Scott's second-in-command, whose recollections were not always trustworthy, later related that Scott told Reginald Koettlitz, the expedition's surgeon, that if Shackleton "does not go back sick he will go back in disgrace." Shackleton was ordered back to England on the relief ship, *Morning*, which left for the north in early March, 1903.

There were other journeys later that year, including an exploratory trip to the unknown area to the west of McMurdo Sound (October 12–December 25, 1903), during which Scott climbed Ferrar Glacier to reach the polar plateau with Edgar Evans and William Lashly. (A half century later, Sir Edmund Hillary used almost the same route to attain the plateau, and eventually the pole, during the Commonwealth

The possibility of falling into a crevasse—and being unable to get out—must have preyed terribly on the minds of both the Norwegians and the British. This scene, entitled "Lieutenant Armitage's Fall Down a Crevasse," published by the *Illustrated London News* is loosely based on an incident that occurred during the *Discovery* expedition.

Trans-Antarctic Expedition.) Scott—whose bad luck at times seems boundless—almost died on the return journey by falling into a crevasse. Nevertheless, they made a major scientific discovery, one of the so-called "Dry Valleys" (a small group of valleys in western Victoria Land that have remained mostly ice-free for complex climatological reasons). But there was no new attempt on the South Pole in the remaining year of the *Discovery* expedition; that pinnacle of achievement was left unscaled for other years and other expeditions (and perhaps other men?). Scott's thoughts at the time are opaque; he was seemingly content to have accomplished what they did, and to be done with it.

Scott intended to leave McMurdo Sound early in 1904, but *Discovery* was still fast bound into the ice. Not one but two relief vessels appeared in January, *Morning* and another, replete with destiny for Scott: *Terra Nova.* The Admiralty had also sent orders to get *Discovery* out now, or abandon her. To a naval officer, having to abandon one's vessel is high among the worst things that can happen. A combination of dynamite, sea swell, and perhaps a dose of providence broke *Discovery* out just as winter was firmly closing in, and the expedition departed for home on February 16, 1904.

In September Scott returned to England, a tangible hero. The brutal Boer War that had so unsettled the nation was beginning to recede in the collective consciousness, and people were ready to hear about other kinds of deeds—ones that did not involve a lot of dead people. While the National Antarctic Expedition did not come close to reaching the South Pole, it set the stage for further explorations and was deemed a landmark success in the history of British Antarctic exploration. New research in geology, zoology, meteorology, and polar magnetism had been undertaken, with notable if somewhat mixed success. While the *Discovery* expedition was only one of several Antarctic expeditions conducted at the turn of the nineteenth century that had scientific inquiry as their chief motivation, it provided legacies that no other did, not least for forging a now-indelible linkage: "Scott" and "Antarctic."

Scott had a captain's job to return to in the Royal Navy, but first he requested time off to write the narrative of the *Discovery* expedition. Self-doubting as always, he was not sure he was up to the task, but the results put paid to any doubts on that score. The eventual book, *The Voyage of the* "Discovery," is the only lengthy work that Scott ever wrote, and it is magnificent. Within its pages Scott emerges as one of the most literate participants in the heroic age of Antarctic exploration. Although Scott's *Terra Nova* diaries were edited and published by other hands after his death, appearing in several editions under the original title *Scott's Last Expedition*, we shall never know what kind of book Scott would have written had he lived through the terrible events of early 1912. Thus the *Voyage* remains the one text, apart from his diaries, that can tell us how he wanted to be perceived by his contemporaries and by history. In a nutshell, what Scott wanted was respect, not so much for what he and his men actually accomplished, but for the fact that in all ways they tried as hard as they could: "If we had not achieved such great results as at one time we had hoped for we knew at least that we had striven and endured with all our might." He also heaped praise on his fellow participants, especially the naval ratings. His generous remarks concerning the hardiness and can-do spirits of the indomitable Edgar Evans and William Lashly earned each of them immediate promotions.

With his book published to strong reviews, Scott now had to look hard at his prospects. In 1906 he was given an excellent posting—flag captain of HMS *Victorious*, the flagship of Sir George Egerton, an old Arctic hand and supporter who was now a rear admiral. If there were no wars to hurry his advancement along, or blots on his service record to impede it, Scott estimated that he could expect to achieve a rank similar to Egerton's sometime around 1913. Somehow the prospect of many more years as a middle-rank, middle-aged salaryman in the Royal Navy failed to enthuse, because by 1907 he was in the throes of planning to do that which was left undone in 1903: He was going to return to the ice, and bag the pole.

It thus came as a bit of a shock to find out, as he did almost immediately, that another—one Ernest Shackleton, late of the *Discovery* expedition—was planning to do the same thing. Whatever it was that had really gone on between Scott and Shackleton in 1903, the two men had managed to submerge their feelings and endeavored to remain civil, for appearance's sake if nothing else. Now that they had become acknowledged competitors, their formerly collegial relations evaporated. Scott couldn't stop Shackleton, of course, but he could make things difficult. That is the only plausible interpretation that can be put on his peculiar insistence that Shackleton and his *Nimrod* expedition not set up their base anywhere near McMurdo Sound. Shackleton initially refused to submit to this egregious demand, but with Wilson arbitrating he eventually agreed to look into favorable spots along the margin of the Barrier, especially the Bay of Whales and King Edward VII Land, and stay away from the Sound. Shackleton's acquiescence is a little curious, since he had been on the *Discovery* expedition and knew that neither of these places was likely to be suitable. So, presumably, did Scott. But perhaps Shackleton, always a player, was going on instinct and thought that he would somewhere, somehow find a safe harbor far away from Scott's supposed property. In the event he could not, and, despite the agreement with Scott, he set up his hut on Cape Royds, just 20 miles (32 km) north of Hut Point

In June 1900 Scott received a promotion to commander, and it was at that rank that he led the *Discovery* expedition. At the expedition's conclusion in 1904 he was promoted once again, to the rank of captain, the uniform of which he is wearing in this 1905 portrait.

on Ross Island. This act would cause an irreparable breach with Wilson, who was a stickler for honorable behavior; as far as Scott was concerned, Shackleton's actions were typical of him, that is, devious, without blush of propriety.

Although he did not reach the pole, Shackleton came back to Britain a hero nonetheless. He also received a knighthood, which Scott hadn't; this surely rankled. But Scott's rival had indeed shot his bolt, and it had fallen short of the mark. In Scott's mind the way south was open once again. And there was now someone in his life who believed he could accomplish what others had not: "You shall go to the Pole. Oh dear me what's the use of having energy and enterprise if a little thing like that can't be done. It's got to be done so hurry up and don't leave a stone unturned," Kathleen had enthused early in their relationship. Two years later Mrs. Scott was on a tug in Port Chalmers, New Zealand, watching Con's ship recede toward the south.

Nimrod's southern party, on their return (l to r): Frank Wild, Ernest Shackleton, Eric Marshall, and Jameson Adams. Dwindling supplies and exhaustion forced the men to turn back after reaching 88°23'S. Shackleton and Wild reached the old *Discovery* hut on Hut Point on February 28, 1909, the day before *Nimrod* was supposed to depart for the north. To attract attention, the next day they burned some wood and sent heliograph signals; *Nimrod*, still in McMurdo Sound, saw their signals and returned to pick them up. All were saved: the Shackleton legend begins.

Five years after Amundsen had conquered the Northwest Passage, and seven years after Scott had returned to England aboard *Discovery*, both men found themselves looking out onto a limitless expanse of ice, imagining what it would take, what prices would be demanded and paid, just to stand for a hard-won moment at the South Pole.

With *Fram* and *Terra Nova* at anchor in their respective harbors, Amundsen and Scott set about finishing their base camps to wait out the oncoming winter. There was no other way of proceeding. Although the expeditions had arrived in Antarctica at the height of the austral summer, nothing like the long, 1,900-mile (3000 km) trip to the pole and back could be undertaken in the brief period of good weather remaining. They would have to wait for the following spring, by which time sunlight and manageable temperatures would have returned. December and January are, on

Orcas and Cameras

Unloading at Cape Evans continued around the clock under the midnight sun, with ponies and the two remaining motor sledges working well. Ponting was hard at it, taking photographs of the men at work. But the photographer didn't anticipate the adventure he was soon to be featured in, let alone as the central character. Near *Terra Nova*, six or seven orcas (killer whales) began swimming and diving around the ship, close to the floes where two dogs were tied. "I did not think of connecting the movement of the whales with this fact," Scott wrote, "and seeing them so close I shouted to Ponting, who was standing abreast of the ship." Ponting grabbed his camera and ran to the edge of the floe so that he could get a close-up photograph of the whales, which were "raising their snouts out of water" in the maneuver now known as spy-hopping.

Just as Ponting arrived, the whales disappeared for a moment, before the floe he was standing on shot up and fractured into jagged pieces. "One could hear the booming noise as the whales rose under the ice and struck it with their backs," Scott wrote. "Whale after whale rose under the ice, setting it rocking fiercely; luckily Ponting kept his feet and was able to fly to security."

The two dogs were badly spooked; miraculously, neither was plunged into the water. Scott surmised that the whales, which poked their "huge hideous heads" six to eight feet into the air to examine the results of their efforts, were equally astonished at the unsuccessful outcome. Scott noted their "tawny head markings, their small glistening eyes, and their terrible array of teeth, by far the largest and most terrifying in the world." The two men were struck by the whales' "deliberate cunning" in their coordinated hunting effort to topple both man and dog into the water. "In future," Scott concluded, "we shall treat that intelligence with every respect."

Among the entertainments at Cape Evans during the winter of 1911 were Ponting's banjo-playing (average), roughhousing and sports (whenever possible), lectures (variable in quality and interest), books, gramophone, and this Broadwood "pianola" or player piano, located in the wardroom section of the hut and played with a foot pedal. Here it is being put through its paces by Cecil Meares. The large metal object to the left is the Gurney's Patent Stove used for heating; above Meares' head on the piano top are a precariously situated microscope and a theodolite, used for surveying. The title visible at the end of the row of books is Ponting's *In Lotus Land: Japan*, which he positioned unashamedly in this scene.

average, the warmest months at the pole, with mean temperatures of –16°F (–27°C); thereafter, temperatures decline precipitously, with the July average hovering around –74°F (–58°C). In the long months ahead, both expeditions had to lay out the bones of their enterprises: Make the base camps functional and livable as soon as possible; keep their animals in good condition; organize supplies; and ready themselves for the crucial task of depot-laying. Food and fuel dumps, laid out at intervals, were the only way to make the run to the pole feasible, because the polar parties could not possibly carry all the necessities required for the round trip.

Scott pondered which men to choose for depot-laying; everyone assumed that it would be from this number that he would eventually select the few who would carry on to the South Pole. Scott was not one to let his choices be known until it was absolutely necessary, but he confided in Wilson, his old sounding-board. For depot-laying, Scott had decided that Wilson would be among those driving dogs; others would guide the ponies selected from the surviving animals, and Day and Lashly would coax the two remaining motor sledges as far as possible, with Lt. Evans in charge. The teams were gradually filled out under The Owner's watchful, critical eye.

By contrast, once *Fram* anchored, Amundsen's plan was carefully laid out so that each man was aware of his role, from start to finish. No one was kept in the dark. The Norwegians could not prepare enough for the task ahead: equipment, clothing, dog handling, efficient usage of skis—in short, everything was diligently gone over, time and again. "I may say that this is the greatest factor—the way in which the expedition is equipped—the way in which every difficulty is foreseen, and precautions taken for meeting or avoiding it," Amundsen wrote. "Victory awaits him who has everything in order—luck, people call it. Defeat is certain for him who has neglected to take the necessary precautions in time; this is called bad luck."

Cherry noted a peaceful contentment at the Cape Evans camp. "Scott seems very cheery about things," he wrote. And as the *Terra Nova*'s crew settled in, he couldn't help but wonder where *Fram* was. "They are supposed to have 140 dogs and 10 dog drivers on board: Meares says that if they were here now he believes they could go straight to the Pole . . . ."

In fact, *Fram* was not far away at all. One of *Fram*'s sailors had been expecting an eventual confrontation should the crews ever meet, and he wrote, "Well, if they are planning something bad (we were constantly asking ourselves in what light the Englishmen would view our competition) the dogs will manage to make them turn back . . . I had better be armed for all eventualities."

FRAM

CHAPTER 7

January—April 1911

The Road to One Ton

Once *Terra Nova* was unloaded and the shore party established, the ship departed on January 26 for the eastern end of the ice barrier in order to drop off Lieutenant Victor Campbell and his five-man team. Their objective as an "independent command" was to land on or near King Edward VII Land (now Peninsula), first seen and named by the *Discovery* expedition, and to undertake inland exploration wherever possible. Coasting along the Barrier, the ship encountered difficult conditions and heavy ice. In the early morning of February 3, still looking for a suitable place to land, the crew directed their vessel toward the Bay of Whales—where to their dismay they saw *Fram* riding quietly at anchor in the sea ice.

"Curses loud and deep were heard everywhere," one officer aboard *Terra Nova* noted. Campbell, who had been an avid skier in Norway and spoke the language, approached *Fram* and hailed the watchman, who was equally dumbfounded at the sight of the British ship. The Norwegians were not quite sure what to expect, but Campbell was friendly and, feeling less threatened, they invited their rivals to go up and see Framheim. They suggested a suitable spot nearby for the British to make camp if they wanted and even offered to help unload *Terra Nova*—an offer Campbell politely declined.

Then, in a dramatic entrance early the following morning, Amundsen came thundering along on a sledge pulled by his dogs. "The Englishmen [were] absolutely

FACING PAGE: Encounter at the Bay of Whales, February 3, 1911. *Terra Nova* can be seen off *Fram*'s bow. The two crews warily exchanged greetings, tours, and meals.

Two who did not go to the South Pole (l to r): Hjalmar Johansen and Adolph Henrik Lindstrom. Johansen had traveled with Nansen and in many ways was as experienced a polar explorer as Amundsen. He was down on his luck and battling alcoholism when Nansen specifically requested that Amundsen take his old companion on. Amundsen did so, against his better judgment; he eventually removed Johansen from the pole party for insubordination. Jovial Lindstrom was a completely different personality: The expedition's cook, he kept spirits up with his excellent meals. He is seen here with one of his renowned concoctions: hotcakes, American style.

flabbergasted," wrote Lieutenant Fredrik Gjertsen, one of *Fram*'s officers. "No, they had never dreamt that dogs could run in that way before a sledge, and already they felt contempt for their dear ponies. Suddenly they were gripped by wild excitement, cheered, and waved their caps. Our drivers returned their greetings and cracked their whips."

Amundsen was clearly showing off his ability to handle dogs, but of course he knew nothing about the trouble Scott had been having with his own animals, dog and pony alike. The Norwegians invited the British party to breakfast in their hut, which they had finished and provisioned on January 28. Adolph Henrik Lindstrom, Amundsen's cook, served pancakes, which he had learned how to make in America; the visitors were bowled over. On invitation they went aboard *Fram* and were astonished further: On this immaculately clean and comfortable ship, every man had his own small cabin, in sharp contrast to the deckside squalor and cramped conditions aboard *Terra Nova*. And unlike coal-burning *Terra Nova*, *Fram* had a diesel engine, a rarity on a private vessel in 1911. The British, with good-humored self-deprecation, entertained their hosts with tales of the seamen's mess table on *Terra Nova*, located

Ponting entitled this photograph, taken December 18, 1911, "Approaching snow storm." The film emulsions of the day favored the blue end of the spectrum: To avoid overexposed skies, Ponting used filters, which often yielded the dramatic, Turneresque result seen here. The small, snow-covered tent in the foreground has had an unexpected life of its own, perhaps because Ponting used it as a background image in his film *90° South*, when describing the finding of Scott's last camp. This scene has sometimes been claimed to show the *actual* last camp at the time of its discovery in November 1912, but this is obviously incorrect.

directly beneath the pony stalls, which had provided them with a yellow liquid for flavoring their food that was not mustard. The Norwegians were invited to luncheon aboard *Terra Nova*, a prospect that Nilsen thought "did not look very inviting."

The two parties were getting along pleasantly enough, but each was making rapid mental calculations. Campbell concluded that, despite the invitation to anchor nearby and do as he wished, his opportunity to be the first to explore the eastern Barrier and King Edward VII Land was forfeit. For his part, Amundsen was furtively looking around *Terra Nova* for evidence of a wireless system. Although 1911 was early days for long-distance wireless telegraphy on private ships, for the most up-to-date craft boasting every modern convenience—such as *Titanic*, under construction at this very time—it was already a necessary novelty. Scott was known to be interested in wireless technology, and Amundsen may have thought that Scott, as a Royal Navy man, might have been given a transmitter. If so, the British expedition would be able to relay the news of a successful trek to the South Pole as soon as their exploration party returned to base; Amundsen, by contrast, would have to await *Fram* and then beat his way back to Australia or New Zealand to find a cable station. He would thus lose the battle for media attention, even if he beat

The shore party at Cape Evans, fall 1911. All members are seen here except for the cook, Clissold, who had suffered a concussion a few days before, and Ponting, who took the photograph. Standing (l to r) are Day, Cherry-Garrard, Nelson, Taylor, Lt. Evans, Oates, Atkinson, Scott, Wright, Keohane, Gran, Lashly, Hooper, Forde, Omelchenko, and Gerof; sitting are Bowers, Meares, Debenham, Wilson, Simpson, P. O. Evans, and Crean.

ABOVE: The environs of the hut at Cape Evans in January 1911 resembled a large open-air warehouse while boxes of supplies were opened and contents organized and redistributed into groups by the indomitable Bowers. One of Ponting's considerations in framing shots like this one was good product placement: Colman's was an expedition sponsor.

LEFT: The powerhouse that was Birdie Bowers, in his element at Cape Evans in January 1911. His unprepossessing looks initially put people off, but Bowers quickly proved that he was a genius at organizing, much to the delight of Scott, one of the doubters. Cherry-Garrard, who was close to Bowers, looked beyond the exterior: "[T]he shop window is very different from the shop" (Wheeler 2002: 254).

the British to the goal. But he needn't have worried: The spark-gap equipment then available for long-distance wireless transmission was bulky and required high voltages, something that the British vessel would have had no way of generating in any case.

Another of Amundsen's concerns was the motor sledges. He had no real sense of how useful they'd be to Scott, but like wireless, motor sledges were a technology that the Norwegian expedition did not have. Amundsen had put careful planning into his assault on the pole, and was extremely confident in his ability to beat Scott's dogs and ponies. But Englishmen with motor sledges? He did not know what the machines would be capable of, so he asked about them. Campbell, still stung by the fact that the Norwegians had (in his mind) preempted his exploration of King Edward VII Land, was no longer feeling quite so genial: "One of them," he replied in reference to the sledges, "is already on terra firma." Amundsen and his men fell silent.

Campbell was, of course, referring to the sledge that had regrettably sunk to the muddy floor of McMurdo Sound during offloading, but he was not about to elaborate. Why not let Amundsen and his men consider the implications of a petrol-powered sledge speeding off to the pole, even if it was a fantasy? Sniggering over their slender psychological victory, Campbell and his men turned *Terra Nova* onto a course back to McMurdo Sound; The Owner would want to hear their news as quickly as possible. Campbell left a long message detailing his encounter with Amundsen for Scott, who was then laying depots on the Barrier. *Terra Nova* could not linger, however, because winter was closing in and the ship had to start back for New Zealand or stand in danger of becoming beset. On the way out, Campbell's team (now as "the northern party") was deposited on the South Victoria Land coast, so that at least some of the kinds of scientific and exploratory investigations originally intended for King Edward VII Land could be conducted.

Back at Cape Evans, and only a week after finishing their hut, Scott's team was preparing to lay depots on the Barrier; the outward trek was scheduled to begin January 25, with much to do. Unlike Amundsen, who considered the year he'd spent planning this part of the operation as insufficient, Scott had hoped to devise a workable plan on the fly, racing against the breakup of the sea ice. He had no fewer than four provisioning and exploratory excursions slated to go out before the onset of winter. "But my head doesn't seem half as clear on the subject as it ought to be," he would write. Indeed, Scott, in his haste to make arrangements to get this vital work started, ended up relying on Birdie Bowers to take over single-handedly the job of

A pair of pony snowshoes (left) and a pony head collar (below), with the man-hauling sledge harness (above) used by Frank Debenham during the *Terra Nova* expedition.

supervising the unpacking and repacking all the provisions from the ship. Yet Scott hadn't thought much of Bowers when he first met the man, and confided to Teddy Evans, "Well, we're in for it now, and must make the best of a bad job." But Bowers more than rose to every occasion. The squat Scotsman was a tireless worker who approached every challenge with good spirits and the resourceful, organized mind of a born logistician. Scott would later note that Bowers was "the hardest traveller that ever undertook a Polar journey as well as one of the most undaunted."

Oates, however, was once again seething over a number of issues. As he confided in a letter to his mother at the start of the depot-laying journey, "[w]e shall I am sure be handicapped by the lack of experience which the party possesses." Contrary to Oates's view, Scott believed the ponies were going to be "real good" on the pole journey because, having seen them at work in and around Cape Evans—his total experience with them in action—he was relieved to find that they could move about "with such extraordinary steadiness, stepping out briskly and cheerfully." He had to revise his opinion shortly.

More unexpectedly, lack of both experience and common sense brought grief on the head of the surgeon, E. L. "Atch" Atkinson, who had failed to report a blistered heel that had him limping badly a mere two days into the trek. The wound festered, incapacitating him and forcing Scott to leave him behind at Safety Camp with Crean, much to Atkinson's disappointment and Scott's displeasure: "I cannot have much sympathy as he ought to have reported his trouble long before." Deleted from the edited account of this incident was Scott's hyperbolic inference that Atkinson "kept silent fearing to be left out of the party—He might have wrecked it." It was Atch who would lead the search party in November 1912 that found Scott's last camp.

On the outward journey the dogs did well enough, as did the men on skis, who managed to remain upright most of the time. But for the ponies it was an unrelieved nightmare. Their comparatively great weight, transmitted through slender hooves, meant that in deep or slushy snow they would plunge up to their knees and hocks at every step; they had to exert all their energy pulling their legs out of one set of postholes only to enter another. Scott seemed amazed to find that "they go through in lots of places where the men scarcely make an impression." Thus the ponies went along but slowly, and painfully. "A more unpromising lot of ponies to start a journey such as ours it would be almost impossible to conceive," Oates noted.

Scott had seen to it that sufficient numbers of horse snowshoes of Scandinavian design (called hestersko) had been brought to Antarctica. These were made of canes bent into a tight spiral, the whole bound together with wire. Woven cane-fiber pieces fastened to the shoe's upper surface acted as a flexible clamp, into which the pony's hoof was introduced and secured with leather lashings. One of the ponies, Weary Willie, underwent a "magical" improvement once the shoes were attached to his hooves. But Oates had only brought that one set, leaving the rest at Cape Evans because he didn't think much of them. This annoyed Scott, who wrote, "If we had more of these shoes we could certainly put them on seven out of eight of our ponies. . . . It is trying to feel that so great a help to our work has been left behind at the station." Scott switched to traveling at night, thinking that on harder surfaces the ponies would sink less.

Thirty miles (48 km) from Hut Point, Scott and his men were caught by a "storm" (better described as a strong wind with blowing snow, as classical storm fronts do not occur in Antarctica). "Raging chaos," Cherry wrote, lasted for three days and three nights as they waited in tents. "Fight your way a few steps away from the tent and it will be gone. Lose your sense of direction and there is nothing to guide you back."

One Ton Depot, the southernmost of the caches deposited by Scott and his men during depot-laying preparations in January–February 1911.

After the blizzard, advance was slow, and Scott sent the weakest ponies back home with their handlers on February 12. The aptly named Weary Willie, who was kept on, was nevertheless lagging behind, sinking deep into the snow, with the dog teams approaching. "Suddenly," Scott wrote, "we heard much barking in the distance, and later it was evident that something had gone wrong." He and Oates rushed back to find that the dogs, on seeing Weary Willie fall, had attacked the vulnerable pony. Gran, Meares, and Wilson were able to whip the dogs away from Willie, but not before he had been savagely bitten. Scott and the others man-hauled the pony's load the rest of the way that day, and Scott blamed himself "for not supervising these matters more effectively."

Oates soon had to admit that the dogs were better suited to polar conditions than ponies—certainly so in the case of the ones on this expedition. When the ponies began to fail, Oates recommended that they kill the weaker ones, starting with Weary Willie, and prepare the carcasses for dog meat, to be stored in caches for the run to the pole later in the year. Scott was adamant: Killing ponies at this stage was not something he had planned for, and he would not consider it. Oates simmered, and according to Gran, he began to argue with Scott.

"I have had more than enough of this cruelty to animals," Scott told Oates, "and I'm not going to defy my feelings for the sake of a few days' march."

"I'm afraid you'll regret it, Sir," Oates replied.

"Regret it or not, my dear Oates, I've made up my mind, like a Christian."

Scott's intention was to lay depots at regular intervals along the first part of the route to the South Pole, with enough food and fuel at each to carry the party to the next cache on full rations—as long as they made an average of 16 miles (26 km) a day. By February 17, twenty-four days out and 150 miles (240 km) from Hut Point, Scott had had enough of distressed animals, piercingly damp cold, and the increasingly unwelcome remarks of his companions. He ordered the last load of supplies to be dumped where they stood—2,200 pounds' (1,000 kg) worth, hence "One Ton Depot"—at a position that was 37 miles (60 km) north of its intended placement at the 80th parallel. This decision would have consequences later. But for now, the end of depot-laying meant that, for the sake of efficiency, Scott could divide the tiny clot of men, ponies, and dogs coursing slowly across the borderless horizons of the Barrier into two groups. He took Meares, Wilson, and Cherry with him on the dog sledges, and left Oates, Bowers, and Gran to return at whatever pace they could manage with the remaining ponies.

On the way back to Hut Point, Scott attempted to take a short cut by going across a badly crevassed area. Wilson described what happened next.

I was running my team abreast of Meares, but about 100 yards on his right, when I suddenly saw his whole team disappear, one dog after another, as they ran down a crevasse in the Barrier surface. Ten out of his 13 dogs disappeared as I watched. They looked exactly like rats running down a hole—only . . . I saw no hole. They simply went into the white surface and disappeared. I saw Scott, who was running alongside, quickly jump on the sledge, and I saw Meares jam the brake on as I fixed my sledge and left Cherry with my dogs and ran over to see what had really happened. I found that they had been running along a lidded crevasse, about 6 to 8 ft wide, for quite a distance, and the loaded sledge was still standing on it, while in front was a great blue chasm in which hung the team of dogs in a festoon. The leader, Osman, a very powerful fine dog, had remained on the surface and the 2 dogs next [to] the sledge were also still on the surface.

They managed with great difficulty and numbed hands to pull out eleven of the thirteen terrified dogs that had fallen into the crevasse. The last two were on a snow bridge 65 feet (20 m) below surface; Wilson thought that it was too dangerous to make an attempt to save them, but Scott declared that he'd do it himself. They lowered him down, and he rescued the dogs; thus all were saved, but some had suffered internal injuries from their ordeal. Meanwhile, back on the surface a fierce battle had broken out among the dogs. The scene was one of uproar and despair as the men tried to separate the tangle of animals and traces. One of the

Petty Officers Taff Evans and Tom Crean, photographed by Ponting on their return to Cape Evans with Scott and six others on April 16, 1911, after waiting at Hut Point for nearly a month for the sea ice to thicken. Ponting made a point of posing field party members as soon as they returned to base, before they had an opportunity to clean up and thus wash away the rigors of travel etched into their faces and bodies.

dogs "had been considerably mauled before this was done—also, incidentally, my heel!" Cherry wrote.

When they finally made it to Safety Camp the next day the men met up with the pony handlers, who informed them that two of the ponies had died of exhaustion. This event, one of many similar ones to follow, was a window into the expedition's harrowing future—a future in which it would be men rather than ponies hitched up and straining in their traces, quickly growing thin and losing condition on a poor diet that was pitiably inadequate for the energy needs of the beasts of burden they had become; and dying thereby. Scott also recognized that the dogs were hardly better off than the ponies. They were "thin as rakes; . . . ravenous and very tired." "Hunger and fear," Scott had noted earlier, "are the only realities in dog life; an empty stomach makes a fierce dog."

Scott was also worried about Atkinson and Crean, who had left Safety Camp without leaving a message regarding their intended whereabouts. He went on to Hut Point, which was also empty. In fact, Atkinson was on his way *back* from Hut Point via a different route looking for Scott: He had a letter for him from Campbell, describing the unexpected meeting with Amundsen in the Bay of Whales. Scott, still reeling from the events of the day before, read the letter and observed that "the day pales before the startling contents of the mail bag which Atkinson gave me." Until now Scott had mostly been able to brush off, or perhaps simply not think about, the telegram he had received in Melbourne months before that had put him on notice concerning Amundsen's intention to sail for Antarctica. Some of the men became furiously angry over Campbell's news that not only were the Norwegians squatting at their back door, but were obviously well prepared for their own push to the pole. Cherry wrote that he and his companions were "possessed with an insane sense that we must go straight to the Bay of Whales and have it out with Amundsen and his men in some undefined fashion or other there and then."

March and April were a period of great tribulation for Scott. In trying to bring the ponies over the sea ice at the beginning of March, three were lost in hideous circumstances (see facing page). Pulling into Hut Point on March 5 with only two ponies remaining of eight that they started with, Scott expected to be able to cross over the sea ice to Cape Evans in short order. Instead, he had to wait five weeks. The problem was the sea ice: It was still forming, and until it was sufficiently thickened it would be inadequate to support the weight of men, ponies and sledges for the 15-mile (24-km) trek to the main camp. He had to wait it out, his impatience increasing, until they were finally able to leave on April 13.

The Lost Ponies

On the evening of March 1, Bowers, Crean, and Cherry-Garrard, on their way to Cape Evans after the depot-laying journey, had just passed Safety Camp and were near the end of the Barrier. The four ponies they had in hand were seriously weakened after the depot runs, and the men were trying to get them over to Hut Point as soon as possible by crossing the sea ice. The ice was riven with dangerous cracks, however, so they made an interim camp at a spot that they believed was safe near the Barrier's edge, and put up protective walls of snow blocks around the ponies (an innovation suggested by Scott).

The men were asleep later that night when a strange noise awoke Bowers. He thought one of the ponies had gotten into the oats, so he woke the others. When they emerged from the tent they were horrified to discover that they were stranded on a moving floe. Worse, the floe they were on had just split apart right under their camp, and one of the ponies, Guts, had already disappeared. They scurried to save the three remaining animals, sledges, and supplies, and led them from floe to floe in an attempt to reach the comparative safety of the Barrier. This went on for hours. Sometimes, there would be no floes to hop to, and the men would have to wait until another floe came close enough to reach. And then it got worse. They were greeted by "the arrival of a host of the terrible 'killer' whales . . . cruising there with fiendish activity."

As Bowers wrote, "the Killers were too interested in us to be pleasant. They had a habit of bobbing up and down perpendicularly, so as to see over the edge of a floe, in looking for seals. The huge black and yellow heads with sickening pig eyes only a few yards from us at times, and always around us, are among the most disconcerting recollections I have of that day. The immense fins were bad enough, but when they started a perpendicular dodge they were positively beastly."

Crean had managed to jump ahead on the floes, making it to the Barrier to look for help. He returned later with Oates and Scott, who was upset that Bowers and Cherry-Garrard had not jumped to safety with Crean.

"What about the ponies and sledges?" Bowers asked.

"I don't care a damn about the ponies and sledges," Scott replied. "It's you I want, and I am going to see you safe here up on the Barrier before I do anything else."

Bowers thought they could save everything anyway, and began to haul sledges and supplies off the floe and onto the Barrier. Just as he was about to move the ponies, the ice shifted again and the three remaining animals drifted away. Killer whales began to race beside them, but there was nothing the men could do. As the ponies' floe bobbed into the distance, the men gave up their vigil and made camp, despairing over their loss.

The others turned in, but Bowers decided to take a walk along the Barrier, and about a mile from camp, he spotted the ponies. "They were moving west fast, but they saw me, and remained huddled together not the least disturbed, or doubting that we would bring them their breakfast nosebags as usual in the morning," Bowers wrote. "Poor trustful creatures! If I could have done it then, I would gladly have killed them rather than picture them starving on that floe out on the Ross Sea, or eaten by the exultant Killers that cruised around."

Hastily gathering the others, Bowers made one more attempt to save the ponies, and managed to get one, named Nobby, safely onto the Barrier. But more than a dozen orcas appeared, spooking the other ponies as they made their way across the floes, and they toppled in. Having no means to save them, Bowers and Oates felt they had no choice: they killed their animals with pick axes rather than let them be torn apart by the whales.

"These incidents were too terrible," Scott wrote at the end of his summary of the events on the sea ice. It was indeed a horrific ending to the depot-laying journey. Scott was now left with just ten ponies for the coming summer's long trek to Beardmore Glacier. On returning to Cape Evans in mid-April, Scott examined their charges: "Have exercised the ponies to-day and got my first good look at them. I scarcely like to express the mixed feelings with which I am able to regard this remnant."

E. A. Wilson, del. Bale & Danielsson, Ltd.

CHAPTER 8

February—March 1911

42,000 Biscuits

At the same time that Scott was laying his depots some 400 miles (640 km) to the west, Amundsen was ready to begin doing the same for his pole journey. Unlike Scott, who was traveling through territory that both he and Shackleton had previously crossed, no one had ventured into the lands stretching out interminably to the south of Framheim. Amundsen the meticulous planner now had to endure some persistent uncertainty: "We could not tell, even approximately, how long the journey would take, as everything ahead was unknown." But as things looked from his vantage point at Framheim, at least, there didn't seem to be any serious difficulties immediately ahead. From 60 feet (19 m) up on the Barrier, Amundsen could see only a flat, snowy surface extending to the horizon.

Her job done for the time being, *Fram* was to sail to Buenos Aires, undertake an oceanographic survey, and then return to the Barrier in early 1912. At the same time as preparations were being made for the ship to leave the Bay of Whales, Amundsen and his men began a combined reconnaissance and depot-laying journey. On February 10, Amundsen, together with Johansen, Hanssen, and Prestrud, set off with three sledges, each carrying an average of 770 pounds (350 kg) of supplies. From the surface of the Barrier the men were able to look behind and see *Fram* still at anchor, with her "flag at the mainmast,—a last farewell." Then they turned their faces southward, and whips cracked over the dogs' heads.

FACING PAGE: Study of head and interior of mouth of light-mantled sooty albatross, *Phoebetria palpebrata*, by E. A. Wilson. Although Wilson was accomplished in many areas of natural history, ornithology was his special interest. His bird portraits, collected together and edited by Roberts (1967), are exceptionally naturalistic and exhibit an exquisite understanding of morphology. This particular painting is reproduced from a report on seabirds collected by the *Terra Nova* expedition, written by two British ornithologists, Percy Lowe and Norman Kinnear (1930), many years after Wilson's death.

Although the Norwegians had prepared themselves for the possibility of bad traveling conditions, the going early on was smooth and uneventful. Amundsen was pleased with his choice of skis, and the dogs were pulling splendidly. They covered 15 miles (24 km) on the first day, and were soon traveling twice and even three times as fast as Scott and his men usually managed. "Cannot understand what the English mean when they say that dogs cannot be used here," Amundsen wrote in his diary. At one point, with the temperature a balmy +12°F (–11°C), Amundsen took off his reindeer-skin pants and skied in just his shirt and reindeer-skin undergarments.

Scott brooded over Amundsen's arrival in Antarctica. "One thing only fixes itself definitely in my mind," he wrote. "The proper, as well as the wiser, course for us is to proceed exactly as though this had not happened. To go forward and do our best for the honour of the country without fear or panic. There is no doubt that Amundsen's plan is a very serious menace to ours. He has a shorter distance to the Pole by 60 miles—I never thought he could have got so many dogs safely to the ice. His plan of running them seems excellent. But, above and beyond all, he can start his journey early in the season—an impossible condition with ponies."

Impossible because the hard lesson that Scott had learned from autumn depot-laying was that the ponies wouldn't survive the grim spring conditions on the Barrier—that is, they would not survive long enough to complete their task of getting him, his men, and their supplies to the base of the Beardmore Glacier. Ultimately, Scott did not leave for the pole until the first week of November, in the hope that warmer conditions would improve the chances of the ponies' lasting long enough to meet his objectives. By contrast, after a false start in early September, Amundsen and his men were finally able to push off on October 20.

In thus capitulating to reality, before either team was even in the field, Scott had to face the fact that he was no longer in a position to control one of the critical variables in the race, the timing of departure for the pole. To Tryggve Gran, what this meant was crushingly obvious: "*If we reach the Pole, then Amundsen will reach the Pole, and weeks earlier* [emphasis in original]. Our prospects are thus not exactly promising. The only thing that can save Scott is if an accident happens to Amundsen." Even if Scott had trusted the fitness and durability of his dogs, he didn't have enough of them for the job, and the motor sledges—whose sole purpose was to ease the awful slog across the Barrier—were but a distant, unhappy memory. In fact he had nothing he could rely on except his men, and the knowledge that they could pull; pull long after the last animal was dead, pull until the end, whatever that might be.

Vitamin C and "Meat"

In the heroic age, those who swore by animal tissues as an antiscorbutic usually referred only to "meat," even when organs (especially liver) were on the menu as well. According to Isobel Williams, it "is now known that it is the offal (liver and kidney) in animal food, rather than muscle, which contains ascorbic acid." However, contemporary sources specify that Inuit and other native peoples rarely, if ever, ate organ meat (especially livers of seal, bear, and dog, which are known to concentrate vitamin A; this vitamin is not water-soluble and has severe effects on humans in overdose). Then as now, a piece of skeletal muscle on a plate is rarely composed of true muscle tissue alone; there will be greater or lesser amounts of fat, dense connective tissues, vascular remnants, and entrapped red blood cells as well. Only trace amounts of vitamin C are required to offset, if not cure, the worst effects of scurvy; perhaps there is enough vitamin C hosted in most "meats" to do at least a partial job, as long as one eats a *lot* of it.

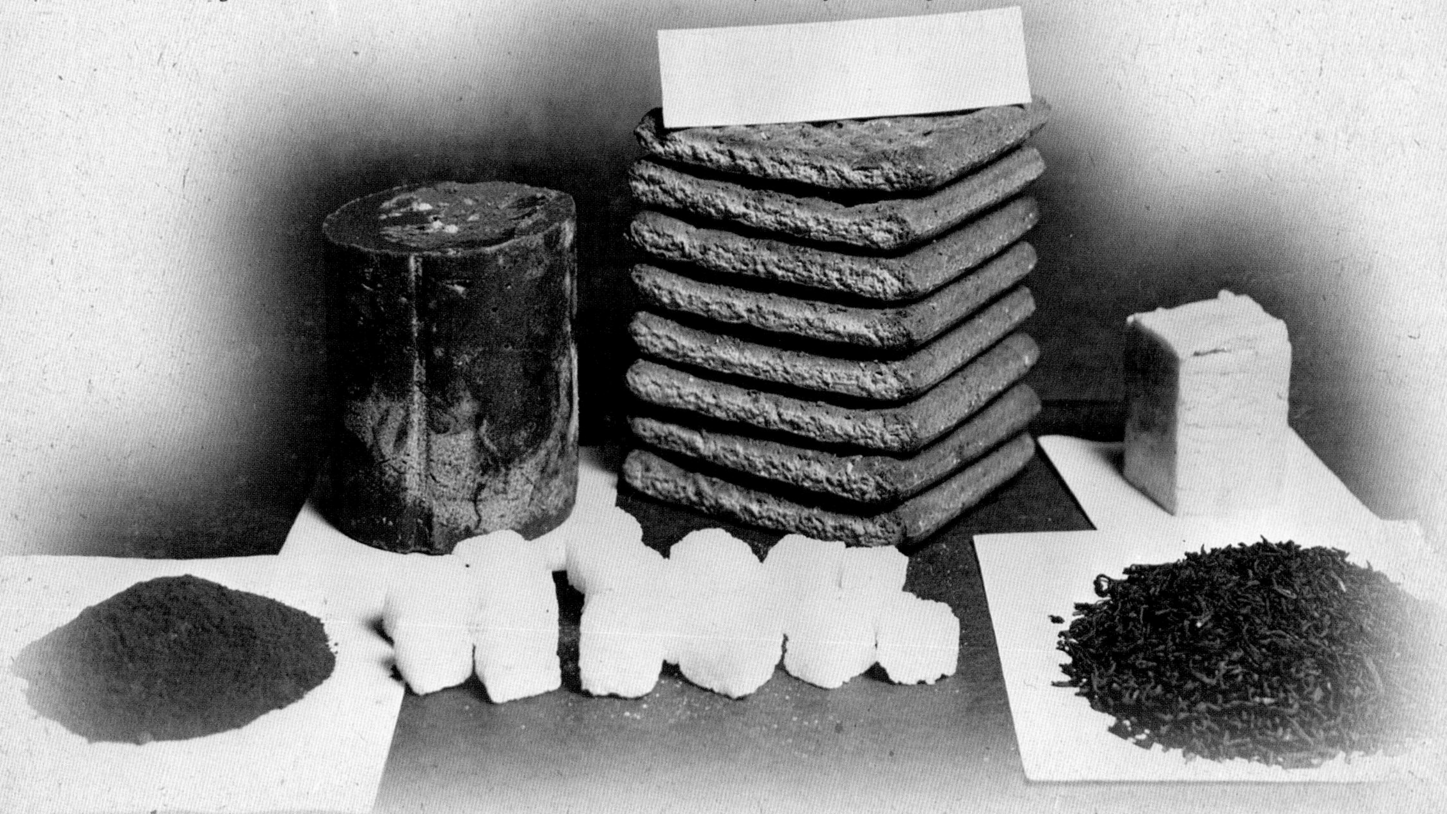

Scott's sledging ration for one man for one day: (front) cocoa powder, sugar cubes, and tea; (rear) pemmican, biscuits, and butter. Chocolate, cereals, and raisins were included on an ad hoc basis. The total value of one day's ordinary or "barrier" sledging ration was approximately 4,240 calories; the "summit" ration was slightly greater, at 4,590 calories. It has been estimated that man-hauling required 5,500 calories or more per man per day for sufficient nourishment. In addition to inadequate food, after months in the field the men probably also suffered from various vitamin and trace element deficiencies.

Olav Bjaaland planes down the runners of a sledge in one of the "workshops in the ice," Framheim, winter 1911. The sledges, manufactured in Norway by the firm that also supplied Scott, were overbuilt for Antarctic conditions. So were the sledge boxes; it was Jørgen Stubberud's job to plane them down until the sides were only a few millimeters thick. Through efforts like these, the Norwegian team reduced total sledge weight significantly without sacrificing strength.

Scott may have come to terms, temporarily at least, with the facts on the ground, but some of the men continued to fume. Bowers thought Gran was "so genuinely upset at the behavior of his countryman that one could not help feeling sorry for him and his awkward position." Indeed, Gran's view was that, "Amundsen's enterprise falls far short of what a gentleman would permit: There is nothing like it in polar history." Being a gentleman was probably not a useful prerequisite for becoming a polar explorer; if

Gran was truly shocked by Amundsen's behavior, he wasn't paying attention to recent polar history. Perhaps he chose not to recall the demeaning exchanges conducted the year before by Peary and Cook, as they argued publicly over who had been first to reach the other end of the planet.

Despite their early, easy marches, the Norwegians had some lessons to learn. As the British were also discovering, the boots they had been using for skiing were proving to be unsuited to Antarctic conditions, and Amundsen knew they would have to be rebuilt, using kamiks, the sealskin boots favored by the Inuit, for the uppers. And although they took care to clearly mark their depot trail with black flags, in Amundsen's estimation the flags were spaced too far apart. They ended up using the dogs' stockfish food (dried, unsalted cod) and broken crates to insure that the trail could be found in future.

Amundsen intended to lay a depot at each parallel, and on the first trip the Norwegians managed to place 1,200 pounds (545 kg) of provisions at 80°S. With their job completed in less than a week, they skied hard back to base camp in the hope that they might look on *Fram* one more time before she left for the winter. They covered 160 miles (241 km), 50 (80) of them on the last day, but missed seeing the ship by mere hours.

By this time Scott had already finished his depot-laying for the season, but Amundsen was preparing for a second run before winter conditions put a necessary halt to operations. This time, he'd take all the men except Lindstrom the cook, who would stay behind to care for the remaining dogs and the upkeep of the hut. Roly-poly Lindstrom might not have the body of a rugged polar explorer, but in his heart he was an adventurer nonetheless. "He has rendered Norwegian polar expeditions greater and more valuable services than any other," Amundsen wrote in his diary.

Before setting out again, Amundsen gave both man and dog a week's rest so that boots could be repaired and the sledges packed anew. Eight men, seven sledges, and forty-two dogs set off, following the markers they had laid on the previous journey. But this time the going was not so easy. The dogs were suffering from running over the sharp-edged sastrugi (wind-hardened ridges on the surface of the ice), which cut their paws, and they were becoming worn out and thin. Amundsen realized that he had been "over-taxing . . . these fine animals," a dangerous thing to do. Finishing their work with a depot of 1,250 pounds (567 kg) at 82°S, on March 10 the Norwegians headed home, thinking that the return trip with empty sledges would be a breeze. It wasn't. With temperatures hovering around –26°F (–32°C), after a 30-mile (48 km) day the dogs were unable to sleep and just huddled together through the night. The next morning, the poor animals had to be lifted to their feet. Amundsen, for his part, was suffering from a painful case of hemorrhoids—a common, agonizing complaint of polar travelers subsisting on constipating, high-protein diets.

One of the dogs, Thor, could no longer stand up, and because they were traveling without firearms on this trip, they had to put him down with an axe. Another hardworking dog, Lurven, pulled his sledge until he dropped dead. "All sentimental feeling had vanished long ago," Amundsen wrote. "Nobody thought of giving Lurven the burial he deserved. What was left of him, skin and bones, was cut up and divided among his companions." By the time they returned to Framheim on March 22, eight of the dogs had died, although in Amundsen's opinion this loss was compensated for by the fact that twenty-two puppies were now boisterously running around camp.

Amundsen ordered one last depot-laying party to go out and add supplies to existing caches, but because of his "rectal complaint" he stayed behind to work on the hut with Lindstrom. When the last group returned, a party was held to celebrate the end of the season's work. All of the required depots had been established: 7,500 pounds (3,400 kg), including three tons of seal meat, 40 gallons (165 l) of paraffin oil, and other necessary supplies were now lodged in three caches, ready for the start of the traveling season more than half a year away. For safety, at each depot signal flags were laid out along an east-west line to a distance of 5.75 miles (9.2 km), at a right angle to the intended north-south line of march. The flags were placed half a mile (1 km) apart, with the direction to the cache indicated. The Norwegians never missed a single supply dump during the journey to the pole or the return.

The men had learned other things as a result of their experiences on the ice. Back at Framheim, Bjaaland trimmed down the sledges with wood planes; at 150 pounds (68 kg) apiece they were far too heavily-built for the conditions encountered, and they would be much more maneuverable if lightened. Bjaaland managed to cut their weight by two-thirds without affecting their durability. Johansen packed the sledging boxes, using every possible space: "Of the 42,000 biscuits that were packed, each and every one was turned in the hand, before the right place for it was found." The contents of the food boxes were little varied—pemmican, milk powder, biscuits, and chocolate—but fresh frozen seal meat was available in abundance in the caches, and, of course, even fresher dog meat would also be on the menu.

Amundsen still worried about Scott's motor sledges, but he felt that, despite some setbacks, all his planning had been worth the immense effort to make his supply line secure. Both *Fram* and *Terra Nova* had left Antarctic waters, and the two expedition leaders had now only to wait out the long, dark winter months, dreaming of the South Pole, and who might get there first.

Like the British, the Norwegians laid depots of food and fuel at intervals, requiring that many hundreds of pounds of food and materiel be moved by dog sled. The main image depicts the depot at 80°S during construction: "It was made quite solid, and was 12 feet high" (Amundsen 1912, 1: 219). Amundsen was aware that fuel could "creep" out of stoppered containers at low temperatures, so he had Olav Bjaaland (seen here) make sure their soldered caps were secure. The inset shows the beginning of Amundsen's depot-laying journey in early February, 1911, with the men heading south from Framheim.

Celebrating the sixth anniversary of Norway's separation from Sweden, at Framheim, June 7, 1911. In this photograph by Lindstrom, the festive table is lined by (clockwise, l to r) Olav Bjaaland, Sverre Hassel, Oscar Wisting, Helmer Hanssen, Amundsen, Hjalmar Johansen, Kristian Prestrud, and Jørgen Stubberud.

Hjalmar Johansen at work in the "Crystal Palace"—one of the ice tunnels at Framheim—packing provisions, as compactly as possible, in sledging boxes: "They say that angels are specially gifted with patience, but theirs must be a trifle compared with Johansen's. There was absolutely not a fraction of an inch left in that case" (Amundsen 1912, 1: 323).

1910–1913
BY
APSLEY CHERRY-GARRARD
WITH MAPS AND ILLUSTRATIONS BY THE LATE DOCTOR
EDWARD A. WILSON AND OTHER MEMBERS OF THE EXPEDITION

CHAPTER 9

Winter 1911

Taking Stock

Antarctica is not only the continent with the highest average elevation, thanks to the ice, but it is also the windiest. Cold air, collecting over days or weeks in depressions and pockets on the plateau and its lateral spine of mountains, can suddenly start spilling down toward the distant sea. Mighty streams of air braid together, gathering speed as they go, as fast as 200 miles (320 km) per hour. By the time these katabatic winds reach the edges of Antarctica their energy has begun to dissipate, but they can still be extremely dangerous to those who are ill-prepared.

At Cape Evans in the early winter of 1911, Scott puzzled over extraordinary winds and accompanying whiteouts that prevented the men, for days at a time, from going outside for more than brief periods for the purpose of checking instruments and animals. Along with violent storms and waning hours of sunlight, dropping temperatures ushered in a long season of waiting. To pass the time, as well as to prevent the depression that living through long periods of polar darkness

FACING PAGE: Cherry-Garrard's snow goggles, fitted with colored-glass lenses, resting on the title page of his classic true-life adventure tale, *The Worst Journey in the World.* "The goggles supplied for the Expedition were of leather, quadrilateral in shape.... Two such pieces of leather, with glass between, formed each eyepiece.... [The goggles were poorly ventilated, so conditions were] particularly unfavourable for those individuals who normally wear glasses. With such persons it is most important that the coloured glasses should be ground with the correct curvature, so that two pairs of glasses need not be worn" (Lyons 1924: 32).

The South Polar Times was, in addition to being the expedition's in-house magazine, a works project designed to take the men's minds off their isolation while giving an outlet for their creative energies. The magazine was actually begun during the *Discovery* expedition; the idea worked well, and Scott revived it for his second expedition. In addition to typically anonymous stories, poems, and informational pieces, the magazine featured copious illustrations, mostly by Wilson, who drew this title page.

Apsley Cherry-Garrard, editor of *The South Polar Times*, winter 1911.

Silhouettes also appeared in the pages of *The South Polar Times*; this one by Wilson is of The Owner, Robert Falcon Scott. Debenham said Scott didn't like the depiction because his hair was "awry as it always is here" (Preston 1997: 151).

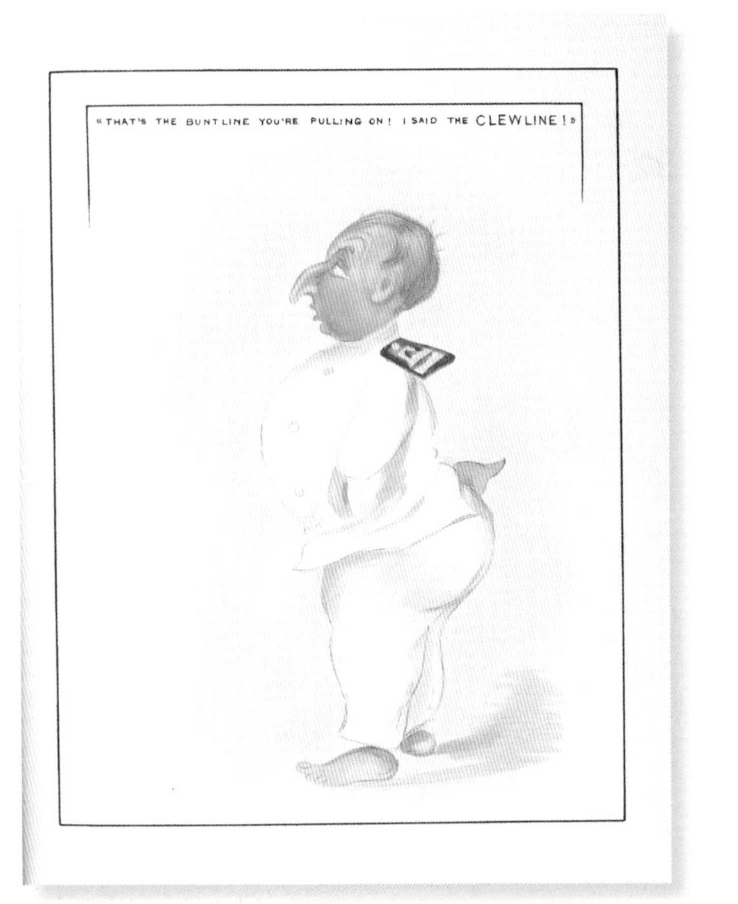

TOP LEFT: Birdie Bowers's physical attributes were a subject of notable, but not necessarily unkind, attention in *The South Polar Times*, as in this unsigned sketch by Wilson.

TOP RIGHT: Wilson could also laugh at himself: Here he caricatures his obsession with penguins.

may engender, the men played soccer and chess, took the dogs on runs, celebrated birthdays and national days, repaired their equipment, and even wrote and printed a sort of newspaper-cum-magazine, *The South Polar Times*. Cherry's newfound typing skills could now be put to use; he was appointed its editor. They also had lectures, on all kinds of subjects, which could involve much robust questioning and jousting for hours at a time. Some topics—and lecturers—were more popular than others. Ponting, who had brought along lantern slides of his photographic excursions in Japan, India, and Burma, was a definite favorite. Wilson gave a lecture on penguins, and, at other times, used his watercolor paintings and drawings to illustrate whatever topic he was discussing. Less popular was Dr. Atkinson's disquisition on the anatomy and physiology of parasitic worms, but the normally taciturn Oates held the house in his hands on August 11, as he warmed to possibly the only subject he cared deeply about, the management of horses.

Ponting was a popular lecturer during the winter season of 1911, partly because of his delivery style but also because his imagery reminded the denizens of Cape Evans that a larger, brighter, warmer world still existed.

Other scientists, like geomorphologist Thomas Griffith "Griff" Taylor and geologist Frank "Deb" Debenham, also spoke about their respective fields of study, often to intense questioning from The Owner, who had an undeniably sharp ear for detecting flaws in argumentation. Although not everyone participated, or appreciated Scott's sometimes heavy-handed interrogations, winter evenings in the Cape Evans hut were anything but dull.

On May 8, Scott rose to address the men on "The Future Plans of the Expedition." As Cherry duly reported for *The South Polar Times*, Scott's object was not "to lay down a definite plan for the future, but rather to discuss the details of the problem with a view to giving complete consideration of them before the plan is made." "Everyone was interested, naturally," Scott noted somewhat smugly in his journal. He began by unfurling a large map of Antarctica. He had marked key points along the way, and pointed out distances and times between stations. He also presented an evaluation of

Frank Debenham, Tryggve Gran, and Griffith Taylor in their "geological cubicle." Taylor wrote of their digs, "We have to live in this space for six months of darkness, and as we are limited horizontally to seventeen square feet each, it will not cause surprise to find that we have imitated the New York sky-scrapers" (Taylor 1916: 108).

how much food needed to be taken for men and animals. As a starting point for his calculations he used some of Shackleton's experiences in traveling over the ice three years before, drawn not from detailed discussions with his rival but instead directly from Shackleton's book, *The Heart of the Antarctic.* Although the two explorers had had some brief, frigid interactions between the time Shackleton returned from the south in 1909 and Scott's departure the next year, and although Scott had never publicly condemned Shackleton's use of "his" sector during the *Nimrod* expedition, they both knew the score: There could never be any cooperation, no sharing of information, between them. Roland Huntford, in his book *Scott and Amundsen: The Race to the South*

Edward "Atch" Atkinson, Royal Navy surgeon and enthusiastic parasitologist, is seen here at his lab bench in the Cape Evans hut.

Pole, argued that Scott's presentation amounted to no more than running through a crib sheet, as though he was so underprepared at this stage—"without any plan worthy of the name"—that that all he could do was summarize Shackleton's accomplishments.

Scott's lack of sources and his attitude toward Shackleton aside, viewing him as completely unprepared for the southern journey is not a plausible interpretation of the evidence of his actions at this time. He *had* prepared; the trouble is that all of the needed discussions about strategy on the ground, about the pros and cons of doing something this way as opposed to that, had taken place in his mind alone, with occasional requests for information from others. "I have asked everyone to give thought

Bench of Edward "Marie" Nelson, one of the expedition biologists, in 1911 (above) and in 2003 (right). Scott oscillated wildly in his assessments of the scientists on the expedition. Thus, in June 1911, which was midwinter, he observed (in comments that were expurgated from the published version of his diary) that "Nelson is very quick & clever, the makings of a man who might have gone far, but he is a skimmer, armed with superficial information on many subjects, profound knowledge concerning none, as a fact he will get nowhere in life" (Scott in Jones 2006: 464–65). Three months later, when Nelson could actually see what he was doing and could start collecting marine invertebrates again, Scott enthused that "Nelson . . . has made great strides and now I have every hope that his biological results will rank with those obtained by other workers" (Scott in Jones 2006: 467).

to the problem [of reaching the pole], to freely discuss it, and bring suggestions to my notice," he wrote in his diary after his lecture. If this is how he actually presented such requests to his men, as though it was their job to come to him rather than vice versa, it is unsurprising that they regarded him as rather remote. Debenham, for example, later recorded in his diary that "Amundsen's chances . . . are rather better than ours. To begin with they are 60 miles further South than we are and can make due south at once, whereas we have to dodge round islands." Debenham had concluded that for Scott to succeed, he would "need very careful organization . . . [I]f [Scott] will consult the senior men I think it can be done but if he keeps them in the dark as they were on this depot trip things are likely to go wrong." Many months later, on September 14, Scott presented his final lecture on his "Southern Plans." Once again, "everyone was enthusiastic," but "[a]lthough people have given a good deal of thought to various branches of the subject, there was not a suggestion offered for improvement." Indeed.

If Scott is to be faulted at this stage, the most obvious sign of his lack of sufficient appreciation of the situation is revealed by his intended departure and return dates. At this time Scott's plan was for departure on November 3, which, providing that the pole party made it to 90°S and returned on schedule at so many miles per day, would bring them back to the waiting ship 144 days later, by March 27. Setting so late a date bordered on recklessness: Shackleton was courting death in 1909 when he returned late in February, and Amundsen had long since decided that returning to Framheim any later than the end of January would be needlessly risky. And George Simpson, the British expedition's meteorologist, believed that Scott's plan left no room for error or bad weather, which "would not only bring failure but very likely disaster." In this regard Scott seems to have known what he didn't know—time and again in his journal he characterized the Antarctic climate and weather as "mysterious," "bewildering," "puzzling." But even though he acknowledged the possibility of outright catastrophe due to weather, he refused—there is no other word for it—to contemplate it as a problem for which he had to find a solution. If Antarctic weather was inherently capricious, well then, it was just something that he and the men would have to endure, as though they were so many brute beasts, lowing insentiently in the wilderness even as the tempest enveloped them. Scott intended to carry on "as if Amundsen did not exist"; he might equally have said "as if Shackleton's record was meaningless," because he was determined to prove that he could endure far harsher conditions than his countryman.

The motor sledges that Amundsen had feared all winter were, in Scott's estimation, not reliable enough to be counted on. And despite the fact that Scott was getting nearly 30 miles (48 km) a day from the dogs on his return from the February depot run, he considered their endurance over long distances to be suspect, and was "inclined to chuck them for the last part of the journey." The ponies, he explained, would lead the way to the Beardmore Glacier, but only that far and no farther. This pleased Bowers immensely: "I for one am delighted at the decision. After all, it will be a fine thing to do that plateau with man-haulage in these days of supposed decadence of the British race." In all, Scott and his men would spend an estimated eight weeks in the most extreme conditions, much of it at high altitude. "I don't know whether it is possible for men to last out that time," he told the men in closing. "I almost doubt it."

As the men settled into their winter routines, an unusual side journey was being readied: three men were about to travel from Cape Evans to Cape Crozier, in the middle of the austral winter, for the sole purpose of recovering emperor penguin eggs at an early stage of development to test a scientific theory that was already outmoded (see page 124).

At the Bay of Whales, as the last days of sunlight ended, the Norwegians prepared for four months of darkness. Amundsen was still refining his plans for his assault on the pole, which now included an intention to start much sooner than he thought Scott possibly could, with or without his damned motor sledges. There were no nightly lectures at Framheim, and about the only scientific measurements being taken by the Norwegians were meteorological in nature. Amundsen was very clear about his objectives:

> Our plan is one, one and again one alone—to reach the pole. For that goal, I have decided to throw everything else aside. We shall do what we can without colliding with this plan. . . .What concerns me is that we all live properly in all respects during the winter. Sleep and eat well, so that we have full strength and are in good spirits when spring arrives to fight towards the goal which we must attain at any cost.

Amundsen had even taken diet into consideration during the winter months, whereas Scott had not. Although Lindstrom's pancakes were delicious, Amundsen's experiences aboard *Belgica* taught him to take the ever-looming threat of scurvy very seriously. Amundsen knew nothing of vitamins—in 1911, no one did except for a few medical researchers whose results were not yet widely known—but he insisted that his men consume a diet of fresh or frozen seal, underdone, just as his old friend Dr. Cook

Wilson, Bowers, and Cherry-Garrard on their return to Cape Evans on August 1, 1911, after five weeks experiencing some of the harshest conditions on the planet in their effort to secure eggs of the emperor penguin at the Cape Crozier rookery.

had recommended years before. The livers of seals in particular contain significant quantities of what we now know as vitamin C (see page 103). Lindstrom's wholemeal breads and wheatgerm provided B complex, another essential vitamin. By contrast, Scott and his men were eating lots of refined foods—white bread and tinned meats—that did not contain these critical vitamins. When they did prepare seal meat, over-cooking destroyed much of the vitamin content. Later on, some of Scott's men would complain that they had been living indolently all winter, eating delicacies instead of training and preparing their bodies for the grueling work ahead.

The weather, Amundsen wrote, surprised him. He'd heard about the "continual violent winds" that British expeditions had experienced at McMurdo Sound. He would later note in *The South Pole* that "we were living on the Barrier in the most splendid weather—calms or light breezes" while "Scott at his station some four hundred miles to the west of us was troubled by frequent storms, which greatly hindered his work."

Oscar Wisting sews tent components in one of the workshops in the ice at Framheim. Unlike Scott's camp at Cape Evans, where the naval ratings did most of the handwork, in Amundsen's Framheim everyone had manual tasks to accomplish.

For his team Amundsen had deliberately chosen men who were good with their hands; he wanted workers, not an intellectual debating society or a "Universitas Antarctica," Scott's precious title for the winter lecture series at Cape Evans. When mistakes in planning occasionally revealed themselves—he had, for example, forgotten to bring snow shovels—Amundsen was able to improvise, requesting Olav Bjaaland, a skilled carpenter who made not only skis but violins, to make snow shovels out of iron plates. "Considerably better than one can buy," Amundsen boasted.

Amundsen had studied Shackleton's published account of the *Nimrod* expedition and he decided he would not try to do what the British seemed bent on doing—namely proving their toughness by struggling as much as possible against the elements. Amundsen did not view the race to the pole as a battle against nature, but rather as an opportunity to make nature work for him. He was prepared technically for the terrain he would face, in everything from skis to sledges to dogs to clothing, and he worked all winter long to adapt to whatever nature could throw at him. Ski boots were customized, cooking equipment was perfected and goggles were altered—all to optimize their gear for the polar trek.

Amundsen had his little quirks. Each morning over the winter, Amundsen held a contest to guess the temperature, requiring that the men go outside for several minutes right after they awoke from a night's sleep. Amundsen gave noteworthy prizes for the man whose guess was closest to the actual temperature, with the winner in the end receiving a telescope. Although probably more than a bit annoying, the contests had a purpose: They gave the men practice at judging temperatures in the event a thermometer broke, and got them used to quickly rising and getting outside to take in the morning air on a consistent basis.

They passed the winter at Framheim working and improving their equipment, and at night they read books, played cards, or partook of the Saturday night sauna ritual of rolling naked in the snow. The dogs roamed free and might even disappear for a few days, but only a few failed to return; Amundsen assumed they fell into crevasses. On August 24, the sun finally appeared above the Barrier for the first time since April. This was the day Amundsen had thought to begin the run for the South Pole. He was familiar with how quickly the Arctic warmed up at the beginning of spring; like Scott, he didn't comprehend that "spring" and "fall" do not exist in Antarctica as lengthy periods bounding summer and winter. But the thermometer told the tale: With temperatures approaching –72°F (–58°C), Amundsen knew the dogs would have a difficult time, and Johansen warned against starting out so soon. So day after day he postponed the start, and grew more restless with every lost moment. "The thought of the English gave him no peace," one of the crew later noted. "For if we were not first at the Pole, we might just as well stay home."

Another remarked, "I'd give something to know how far Scott is to-day."

"Oh, he's not out yet, bless you!" came the answer. "It's much too cold for his ponies."

Finally, on September 8, 1911, after several days of improving temperatures, Amundsen decided he could wait no more. A caravan of sledges and ninety excited, barking, rambunctious dogs burst forth from Framheim, intent on winning the last great polar prize.

Anxious to be on his way as soon as possible, on August 23, 1911, Amundsen ordered the fully loaded sledges to be hauled out of the ice tunnel in which they had been kept all winter: "[T]hey weighed 880 pounds apiece, and the way up to the surface was steep. A tackle was rigged, and by hauling and shoving they slowly came" through the previously excavated roof of the tunnel (Amundsen 1912, 1: 374).

The Worst Journey in the World: Why?

"For we are a nation of shopkeepers, and no shopkeeper will look at research which does not promise him a financial return within a year. And so you will sledge nearly alone, but those with whom you sledge will not be shopkeepers: that is worth a good deal. If you march your Winter Journeys you will have your reward, so long as all you want is a penguin's egg."

—

Apsley Cherry-Garrard, *The Worst Journey in the World*

In the heart of the Antarctic winter, Wilson, Cherry, and Bowers undertook a journey to Cape Crozier to collect eggs of the emperor penguin (*Aptenodytes forsteri*). Except for occasional moonshine, the three men man-hauled for 65 miles (105 km) from Cape Evans in complete darkness, in temperatures sometimes reaching −70°F (−57°C), with inadequate gear and no margin of safety. Yet they persevered, and became the first men to observe emperor penguins during breeding season. They returned to Cape Evans in early August, after five weeks on the ice. As they started stripping off their outerwear so that their condition could be seen, Ponting thought they looked like Russian prisoners of war he had once seen in Mukden.

Their expedition was thus very much a prequel to the southern journey to the pole later that year, with similar elements of unpreparedness and amateurism. The difference is, of course, that no one actually died during this particular worst journey in the world, which had the immediate effect of transforming it from a potentially tragic fiasco to the epitome of British courage and endurance. What could have possibly justified such an undertaking? The dreadful story of their journey has been told many times, but its actual scientific purpose is usually given only incidental treatment.

Let us begin with background. Scott has been faulted for allowing Wilson to have his way in conducting so dangerous a trek in the middle of the polar night, but what was he to do? Wilson had made it clear that one of his reasons for signing on to the *Terra Nova* expedition as chief scientist was so that he might collect emperor penguin embryos at the proper stage of development to reveal fundamental aspects of the phylogenetic, or evolutionary, history of birds, which Wilson correctly believed must converge in some manner on reptiles. (Contrary to the statements of some recent authors, however, he was not looking for evidence that birds were specifically derived from saurischian dinosaurs—that understanding was many decades away.) This is something that Wilson had had on his mind since *Discovery* days, when it evidently first occurred to him that penguins were not only the most primitive living birds, but also that the emperor penguin could be the most primitive of all. In short, Scott could hardly deny his right hand man the chance to make what might have been a major scientific discovery, one that might have won the expedition substantial credit.

One topic that caught Wilson's interest was the relationship between two kinds of integumentary structures, feathers and scales, one of course typical of

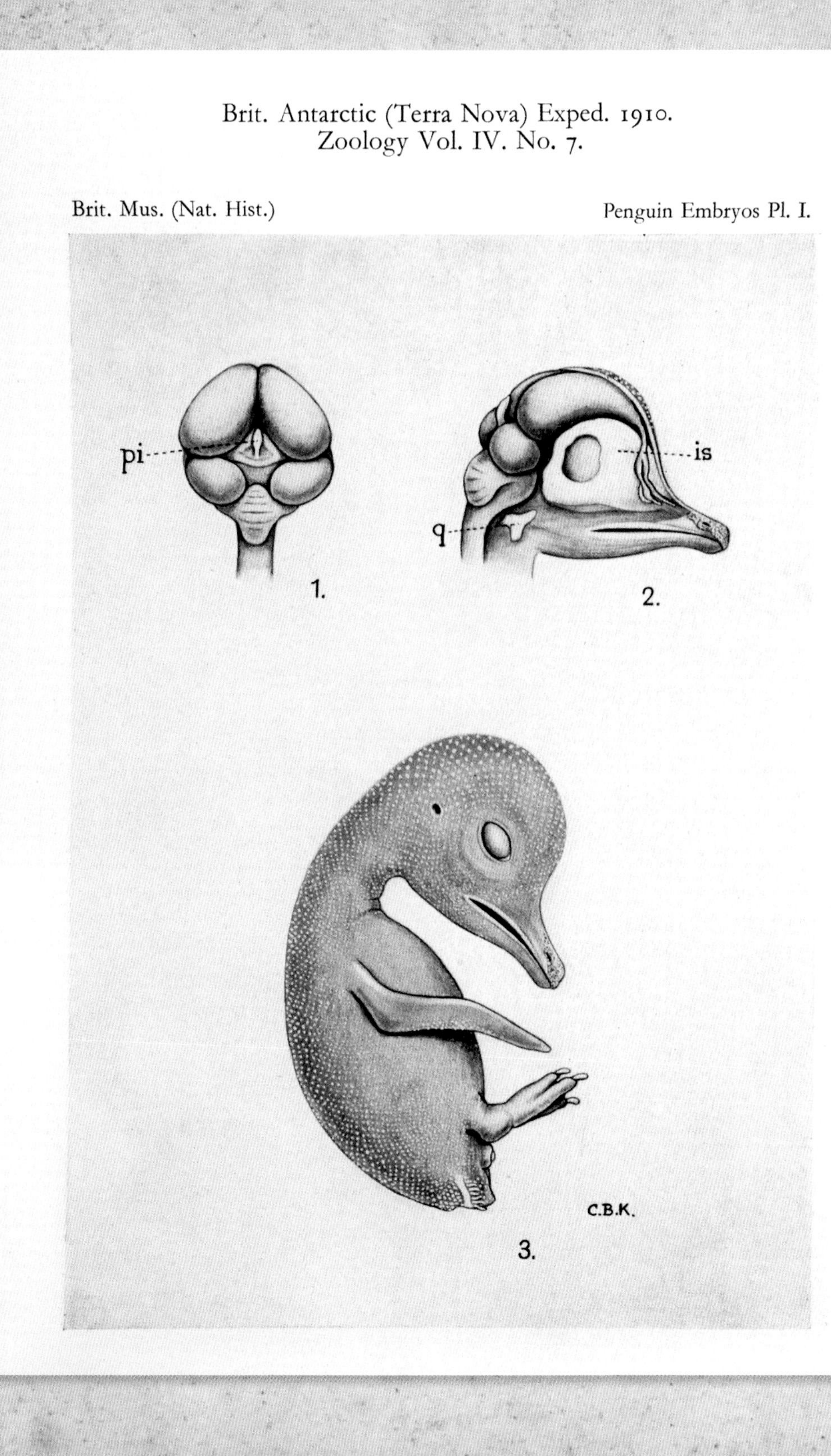

Embryo of an emperor penguin, from one of the eggs collected by Wilson, Bowers, and Cherry-Garrard during their winter journey in July 1911. "[U]nfortunately nothing decisive could be expected from the collection of the three Emperor embryos so close to one another in development as those that Dr. Wilson and his comrades obtained at such cost" (Parsons 1934: 261).

living birds and the other of living reptiles. He thought that a study of the development of feathers in emperor penguins might reveal evidence of the actual "transition" from conditions in their scaly forebears. For the study he had in mind he needed young stages—pre-hatchlings or embryos. His fascination with the alleged primitiveness of emperor penguin embryos is often presented in a condescending manner, as though his expedition to Cape Crozier was yet another example of the cocky dilettantism that pervaded Scott's expedition. But here it should be remembered that the genetic basis of heredity, first discovered by the obscure Austrian priest Gregor Mendel in the mid-1860s and published in an equally obscure local natural history journal in 1866, had absolutely no impact on the greater scientific world until his "laws" were rediscovered in 1900–01. Even then it was not clear what, if anything, genes had to do with evolution or, indeed, how evolution truly worked at all.

Somewhere along the line, Wilson must have come across the views of the prominent early Darwinist Ernst Haeckel (1834–1919), whose most famous aphorism was that "ontogeny is a shortened or recapitulated form of phylogeny"—that is, the individual, in the course of its development, shows evidence of the species' evolutionary history. This notion was still accepted well into the early twentieth century, even though the leading edge of evolutionary thought had by this time left it behind as void for ambiguity.

Haeckel's insights may have been superficial, but they were not ridiculous; like so much that reflects the interrelatedness of life on this planet, the fish, the bird, and the human do go through initially similar phases of gross structural development. It could hardly be otherwise, as the genomes of all vertebrates share much the same suite of genes concerned with early development. The unfolding of ontogeny in different biological lineages may be compared to the interwoven elements of a vast fugue, the voices (or species) of successive measures spiraling outward from common sources, repetitively, sonorously, exploring key after key. But because each biological species differs from every other in ways reflective of their separate evolutionary journeys since they last shared a common ancestor, mere comparison of arbitrary stages will not reveal the actual, adult ancestor (or its integument) in the way that Haeckel implied.

While Wilson's scientific hypothesis may not have been out of place, given the times, Scott's reaction to the Cape Crozier adventure was certainly so. It is objectively revealing that he seems to have taken almost no lessons away from the harrowing experiences of Wilson, Cherry, and Bowers. In his journal he merely expiated on how useful it was that Wilson had tested the seeming adequacy of a sledging diet, and how the incidents of travel to and from Cape Crozier, such as experiencing incredibly low temperatures while pulling 750 pounds (340 kg) on a sledging surface with the friction qualities of sandpaper, were tremendously uplifting and comprised "a tale for our generation, which I hope, may not be lost in the telling."

FACING PAGE: Most of the material published in *The South Polar Times* was lighthearted and often whimsical, even when the subject matter was far from it. Wilson's playful cartoons that ring this piece of doggerel, which concerns the winter journey to the emperor penguin rookery, is a good case in point. Each little picture refers to a specific, often extremely dangerous, incident that befell Wilson and his companions during their five-week trip: lost mittens, broken penguin eggs, missing cooker pieces, and, worst of all, the disappearance of their tent (which they however managed to recover the next day) during a gale. The image on the bottom shows the three men huddled in their sleeping bags behind the stone wall they built, watching their canvas roof being torn to shreds. Cherry-Garrard later wrote that Bowers bravely shouted over the din, "'We're all right'; [but] he only said so because we knew we were all wrong" (Cherry-Garrard 1937: 279).

The good old Blizzard of local fame,
Compared with which was considered tame
The best of the bracing South Winds cool
That blew all day, (and the next as a rule),
And cemented the Ice-blocks, hard and stout,
That were placed so carefully round about,
But failed to secure the Canvas strong
That formed a roof about ten feet long,
To cover the Rocks and Boulders "Erratic,"
Composing the Walls, - with lavas "Basic" -
That stood on the Ridge, that topped the Moraine,
And, somewhat collapsed, are all that remain
With some fragments of Bamboo Poles dejected,
Of the House of Stone that Cherry erected.

PATENT
STOCKHOLM
PRIMUS

CHAPTER 10

Spring 1911

The Race Begins

The temperature was hovering around –42°F (–41°C) when Amundsen and his men left Framheim; Lindstrom was left to look after things in their absence. Three puppies tagged along with the cavalcade; Amundsen, against his better judgment, allowed them to run alongside the sledges for miles. A return to Framheim could not be contemplated, so when they broke for lunch, he had them shot.

After driving for nearly 12 miles (19 km), they set up camp for what would be an uncomfortable night, as the dogs were fighting and the men had a difficult time falling asleep with the row outside the tents. By September 11, the temperature was dropping toward –70°F (–57°C) and the dogs were struggling. They lay huddled together and had to be lifted into their harnesses. The dogs' paws were frostbitten, and some of the men were having great difficulties with blistering, frostbitten heels. The fluid in their compasses had frozen, the weather became very thick with fog, and they couldn't accurately guess the position of the sun to guide them.

FACING PAGE: Primus stove, manufactured in Sweden by Hjorth. "Under all conditions a gallon of paraffin suffices for cooking three meals a day for a four-man unit for seven days, and with economy and under summer conditions a gallon can be made to last for 10 days." The stoves burned paraffin (kerosene), which was stored in 1-gallon (4 l) containers fitted with screw caps and leather washers: "After exposure to excessive cold, the leather washers harden and are less effective in preventing evaporation. . . . Returning parties found their supply at the depot short for this reason" (Lyons 1924: 31).

Amundsen's first depot, at 80°S, consisting of a pile of boxes marked by a flag. Because of excessively cold temperatures during the abortive September journey, this depot was as far as he got before deciding to turn back to Framheim.

Amundsen knew he had no alternative. "To risk men and animals out of sheer obstinacy and continue, just because we have started on our way—that would never occur to me," he wrote. "If we are to win this game, the pieces must be moved carefully—one false move, and everything can be lost." There was nothing for it but to return to Framheim. The supplies they carried were left at the 80°S depot on September 12. The superstitious Lindstrom chided them for starting their journey on a Friday—a day he felt would bring bad luck. "I told you so!" he scolded the men on their return.

But more than a mere turnabout had occurred out on the ice: Both Amundsen's planning and his leadership were called into question. When the decision to go back had been made, Amundsen uncharacteristically sped off with Hanssen and Wisting, leaving the other men to make their way as best they could. Some barely made it back to camp. Johansen, who had come in last with the inexperienced Prestrud, was livid that men had been left behind in this manner, without food or fuel. At breakfast the following day he confronted Amundsen in front of the others, stating that a leader should not become separated from his men. "I don't call it an expedition," Johansen said. "It's panic."

One might think had Amundsen had a choice to make. He could have acknowledged Johansen's remarks and apologized for his lapse in judgment, or he could have cut the man off at the knees for challenging him. Giving an apology under these circumstances was not in Amundsen's nature. Johansen, who had traveled with Nansen and was the most experienced of his ice men, had, just like an underperforming dog, rendered himself expendable. Amundsen's response to Johansen's insubordination was to take him off the pole party and put him on a team with Stubberud and Prestrud that would explore King Edward VII Land while the other five men went to the pole. But first, Amundsen had to wait for the men to recover from their frostbite.

Finally, with signs of spring conditions—essentially, slightly warmer temperatures—around them, Amundsen and his party departed Framheim with fifty-two dogs on October 18. (Amundsen thought it was October 19, but he was off by one day because he had not made an allowance for *Fram*'s crossing the international date line; he would also be off by a day when he recorded his arrival at the South Pole.) By October 24, fast sledging with dogs in top condition had enabled Amundsen to get a 150-mile (240 km) head start over Scott, who was still a week away from leaving on his own course to the South Pole.

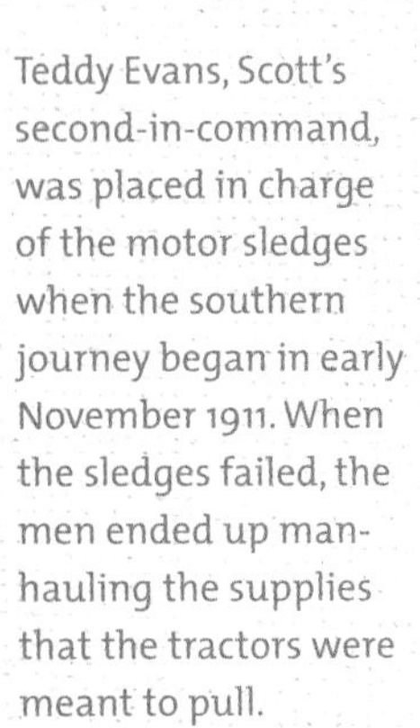

Teddy Evans, Scott's second-in-command, was placed in charge of the motor sledges when the southern journey began in early November 1911. When the sledges failed, the men ended up man-hauling the supplies that the tractors were meant to pull.

DRAWING ILLUSTRATING THE LOCALITY OF ROSS ISLAND.
No claim is made to geographical accuracy.

Bird's-eye view of Ross Island and McMurdo Sound during the heroic age of Antarctic discovery, looking south; from Herbert Ponting's book *The Great White South* (1923).

During these early days of spring, Scott had been testing the motor sledges under various conditions on the terrain around Hut Point. The engines were working well enough, but the cylinders were running hot on low-octane fuel, and required frequent lubrication. They were able to get the motor sledges going at a rate of 2 to 3 miles (3 to 5 km) an hour, which was a comfortable speed, but they had to stop every mile or so to allow the engines to cool. Also, blowing snow and dry wind wrought havoc with the carburetor, and the wooden tread rollers were splitting. "It is already evident that had the rollers been metal cased and the runners metal covered, they would now be as good as new," Scott wrote. "I cannot think why we had not the sense to have this

Bowers with Victor, the pony he led during the first part of the southern journey. Victor reached 83°S before the bullet came on December 2, 1911. "Sad to have to order Victor's end—poor Bowers feels it. [Victor] is in excellent condition and will provide five feeds for the dogs" (Scott in Jones 2006: 335).

done." Still, Scott believed that the "motor programme is not of vital importance to our plan and it is possible the machines will do little to help us, but already they have vindicated themselves."

On the evening of October 31, as the last of a blizzard was blowing through camp, Scott sat down at his desk. If the weather held, he and his men would leave for the South Pole in the morning. "So here end the entries in this diary with the first chapter of our History. The future is in the lap of the gods; I can think of nothing left undone to deserve success."

Acting Leading Stoker Edward MacKenzie's finnesko [boots made of reindeer skin, with hair side facing out], draped on a description of this kind of footwear: "Good finneskoe will last a year on snow surfaces with good treatment, but bad ones will last only a month or less" (Lyons 1924: 35).

Expert dog driver Cecil Meares with a favorite animal, the lead dog, Osman. This was the same dog that was washed overboard—and then returned by another wave—during *Terra Nova*'s stormy crossing from New Zealand.

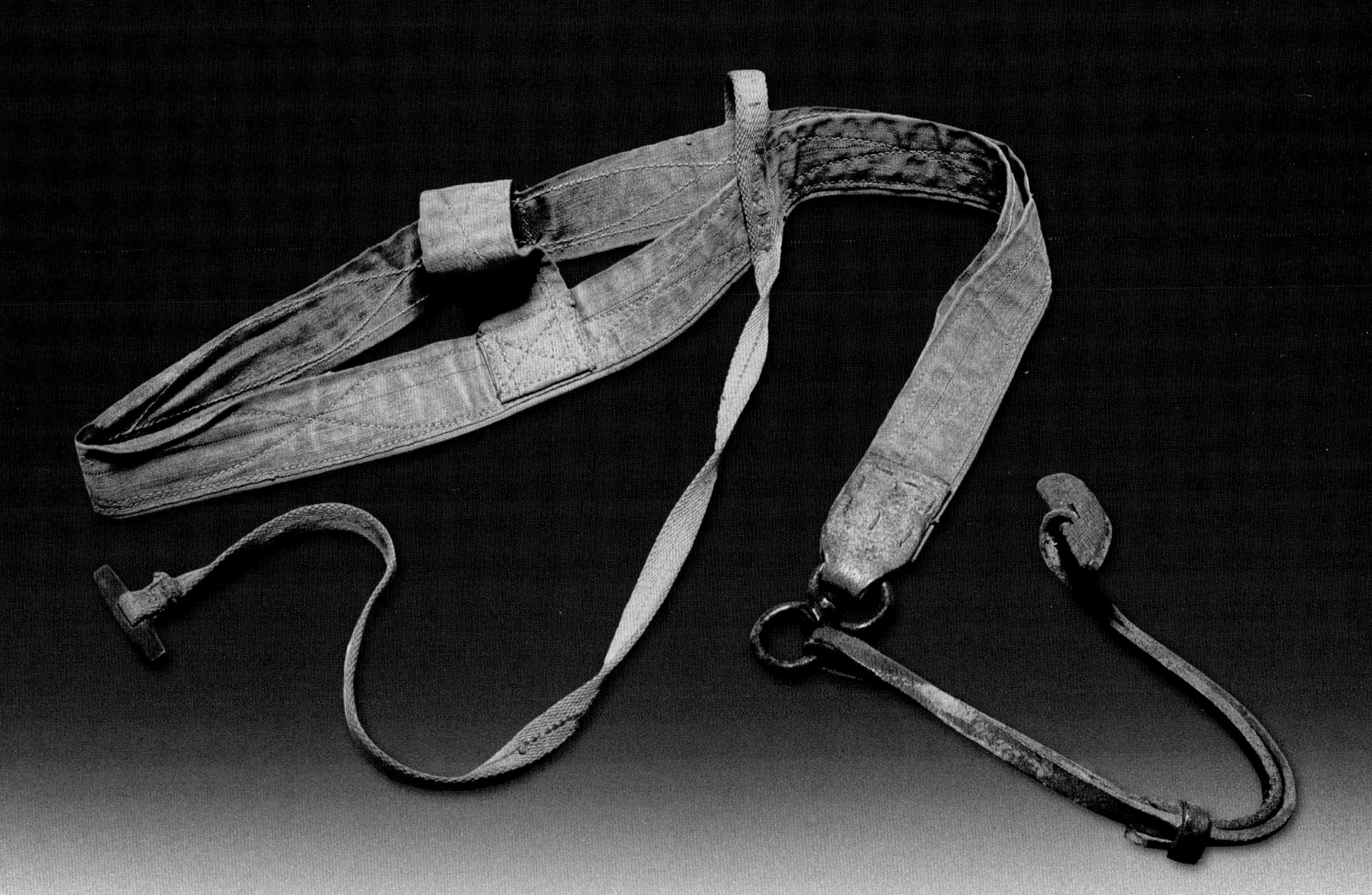

The harness of the dog Krisarovitsa. The canvas harness "consisted of a loop fitting over the dog's head, thus allowing him to pull from the shoulders.... The ends of the loop were finally sewn around the ring of a swivel, to which were attached two leathern thongs; these were fastened to a wooden toggle [to attach to the trace and thus the sledge]" (Lyons 1924: 39).

As Scott was making final preparations and thinking about what lay ahead, Kathleen Scott was also sensing something. "I had rather a horrid day to-day," she wrote. "I woke up having had a bad dream about you, and then Peter [now aged two] came very close to me and said emphatically, 'Daddy won't come back,' as though in answer to my silly thoughts."

If Amundsen was now having his own troubles with some of his men, Scott's troubles had never left him. Oates loathed Scott for several reasons, but chief among them was his arrogant ignorance concerning what the ponies needed if they were to do their job—or Oates his. In a letter to his mother written just before departure, Oates wrote, "I dislike Scott intensely and would chuck the thing if it were not that we are the British expedition and must beat the Norwegians. Scott has always been very civil to me and I have the reputation of getting on well with him. But the fact of the matter is that he is not straight, it is himself first, the rest nowhere, and when he has got what he can out of you, it is shift for yourself . . . "

On the morning of November 1, Scott and his men, along with ten ponies and a team of dogs, started south across the sea ice to Hut Point and thence onto the Barrier. Like Amundsen, who was already 200 miles (320 km) ahead, Scott had his own false start. He had left the Union Jack intended for the Pole, which was given to him by Queen Mother Alexandra, back at Cape Evans. Tryggve Gran set off on skis to get it.

On the very same day the last great unknown—the one that Amundsen had feared most—had resolved itself unceremoniously. The two motor sledges that had haunted the Norwegians' thoughts for many months had finally broken down, one just after crossing a short distance onto the Barrier and the other after traveling about 50 miles (80 km). "The dream of great help from the machines," Scott wrote, "is at an end!" This was not yet the Machine Age that the later twentieth century would become, and it was no surprise that the temperamental, breakdown-prone internal combustion engines had failed to perform. If Chief Stoker William Lashly and the others on the motor party were disappointed at now having to drag deadweight loads of 200 pounds (90 kg) per man, they did not show it.

A week or so into the journey, Scott increasingly had to face the limitations of the ponies, now that the motor sledges were out of the picture. They were unsuited for this frozen environment and required a great deal of care, as ice clung to their sweating bodies and they sunk deep into the snow, at times barely able to pull the sledges. Also, like the men, the ponies suffered from snowblindness and required eye protection. For no apparent reason they would sometimes avoid the harnesses and kick up a frightful fuss until Oates got them under control.

On November 7, a blizzard struck; because it was dangerous to lead the ponies in such conditions, Scott and his party remained stuck in their tents. Much to Scott's surprise, despite the weather Meares and the dogs reached the camp with no problem—proof to all that the dogs could pull in the harshest Antarctic conditions, and were the superior animal for this kind of expedition. From this moment on, Cherry noted, Scott began to doubt whether the ponies were up to the job ahead. Day after day, the dogs demonstrated their speed and strength in snow and bad weather, while the ponies slowly deteriorated. Some of the men who were now in man-hauling harnesses would soon begin to do the same.

THE TOLL OF THE ANTARCTIC: WHERE CAPTAIN SCOTT AND HIS COMRADES MET THEIR DOOM

The main features of Captain Scott's last journey are plainly indicated in this diagrammatic picture, as well as the route of his more fortunate rival, who reached the South Pole exactly 35 days before Captain Scott's party; while the inset map, drawn to scale, shows the furthest points reached by other pioneers in the siege of the Antarctic. It will be seen that, though the actual Pole has been attained, some nine-tenths of the great Southern Continent remain to be explored.

DRAWN BY G. F. MORRELL

Bird's-eye view of routes of Scott and Amundsen to South Pole, looking north, as pictured in *The Daily Graphic*, February 15, 1913.

"BOVRIL" PEMMICAN
sustaining food, consisting of Albumen and
Fibrine
Beef, and Animal Fat, etc. For use in cold
regions.
BOVRIL, LIMITED, LONDON, E.C.
A highly sustaining food,
Fibrine of Beef, and Animal Fat,
ESSENCE OF BEEF
PEA FLOUR
SOUP IN ONE
HIGH PRESSURE STEAM PREPARED

CHAPTER 11

November—December 1911

Barrier to Plateau

At the start of their journey south, the Norwegians paced themselves, sledging just five or six hours per day, saving their strength for later. Amundsen was meeting his daily goals, goals set not by hours on the trail each day, but by degrees and minutes of latitude gained, so that he and his men could visualize themselves inching across the empty map of the Barrier. His diary describes the reasons for his ebullient mood: "we had reason to be satisfied that we had come off so easily," and "thus far the trip had been a good one for the animals," and "[we] never had to move a foot; all we had to do was to let ourselves be towed." And still they were traveling twice as fast as Scott.

The Norwegians were driving their dogs expertly, resting them at hourly intervals to maximize their efficiency. Amundsen's attention to detail was now paying dividends. At their daily stops they were able to set up their tents, prepare meals, and unhitch and feed the dogs in less than an hour; it was a practiced routine, designed to avoid chaos in bad weather. Instead of having to untie, unload, open, and then close,

FACING PAGE: Packaged provisions used during expeditions of the heroic age (l to r): "Emergency ration" (*Discovery*), two bricks of pemmican (*Terra Nova*), beef "essence" (*Nimrod*), and pea flour (*Terra Nova*). The label of the emergency ration reads, "Not to be opened, except by order of an officer or in extremity. It is to be carried in the haversack and produced at inspections. The ration is calculated to maintain strength for 36 hours if eaten in small quantities at a time." The spoon, obviously broken and repaired, was used by members of the northern party during their enforced stay in the ice cave during the 1912 winter.

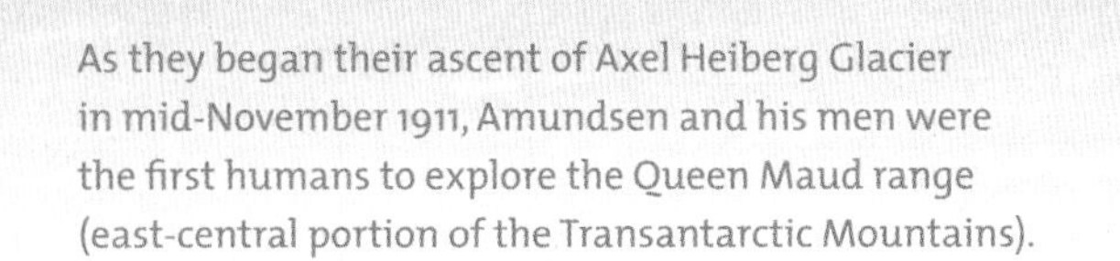

As they began their ascent of Axel Heiberg Glacier in mid-November 1911, Amundsen and his men were the first humans to explore the Queen Maud range (east-central portion of the Transantarctic Mountains).

reload, and retie sledge boxes containing ready bags, provisions, and other necessities at every stop, as Scott's men often had to do, Amundsen only had to remove a large, circular lid cut into the top of each of his permanently secured boxes and take out what was needed, saving much time and labor thereby. And thanks to their fall depot-laying trips, they had managed to cache, on a per man basis, ten times the food and fuel that the British had. Amundsen had built a safety net, allowing for a missed depot or a prolonged storm; by contrast, Scott was always skirting the edges of his possibilities: Any grave mishap or miscalculation would place him and his men in serious danger.

But even Amundsen could only manage his circumstances up to a point. On November 1, coasting into pea-soup fog that restricted visibility to a few sledge lengths, Amundsen pressed on despite being hampered by crevasse after crevasse. At one point, Hanssen, who had been leading the sledge train, fell into a crevasse; soon after his rescue, Hassel did the same. But, at least according to Amundsen's account, the Norwegians simply laughed off such interviews with disaster; once out of immediate danger they went back into position and carried on with their journey. And indeed, what else should they have done except laugh? In that harsh environment no amount of foresight or skill could control for every eventuality; you did your best, trusting in the strength and fortitude of your companions to get everyone through, facing each predicament with the armor of humor.

On November 17, the Norwegians reached the Transantarctic Mountains, which line the continental edge of East Antarctica. They left provisions in a depot, carrying enough for sixty days, and then began a laborious search for a way up and onto the plateau beyond. For Shackleton in 1909, the route to the plateau had been up the huge feature that he named the Beardmore Glacier, a frozen torrent of plateau ice 125 miles long (200 km) and 25 miles wide (40 km). Amundsen needed the same brand of luck to find his highway; after three days' search he saw what he was looking for, a great glacier 30 miles (48 km) long leading up to the plateau. He named it for Axel Heiberg, a venture capitalist who was one of his major sponsors. Amundsen discussed strategy with his men. They would use all the dogs for the climb, then slaughter twenty-four of them, leaving eighteen for crossing the plateau beyond the mountains. "The task we had undertaken was greater than we thought," Amundsen later wrote. "In the first place, the distance [to the top of the glacier] was three times as great as any of us had believed; and, in the second place, the snow was so loose and deep that it was hard work for the dogs after all their previous efforts." That night, they camped at nearly 6,000 feet (1,830 m) above sea level. The next day, to the sound of ice avalanches crashing in the distance, the Norwegians and their forty-two dogs fought their way up the middle of the glacier for 20 miles (31.5 km), reaching an altitude of 10,000 feet (3,050 m) on the snowy flanks of Mount Ole Engelstad. Looking back along their route, Amundsen was struck by the vista:

> The wildness of the landscape seen from this point is not to be described; chasm after chasm, crevasse after crevasse, and great blocks of ice scattered promiscuously about, gave one the impression that here Nature was too powerful for us. . . . It was not without a certain satisfaction that we stood there and contemplated the scene. The little dark speck down there—our tent—in the midst of this chaos, gave us a feeling of strength and power.

Amundsen's account understates what he and his team had accomplished. As Roland Huntford noted, "In four days they had found a way from the Barrier to the Polar Plateau. They had traveled forty-four miles and climbed 10,000 feet with a ton of supplies. In charted terrain it would have been a respectable performance, even by modern standards with mechanical aids. But they had been faced by unknown mountains. It was as if they had pioneered the first crossing of the Rockies or one of the Tibetan passes. Amundsen had brought off a *tour de force*." During the same four days, Scott had traveled fifty-two miles on level surfaces. "Come and say dogs cannot be used here," Amundsen wrote pointedly.

Amundsen also understated his increasingly poor management of relations with some of the men. At one point, after an argument with Bjaaland, he ordered the man to return to Framheim with Hassel as his companion. This could have placed the whole expedition in serious jeopardy, but Amundsen would not brook being challenged or contradicted. In later years and on other expeditions, this imperious streak would come through more and more: Cross him in any way and you would become superfluous, to be disposed of like any other form of offensive matter. This time Bjaaland apologized and the team moved on, but feelings were raw. "One might think the man has a screw loose," wrote Hassel. "He has many times in the last few days actually initiated quarrels, an extraordinary stand to take for a Governor and leader for whom peace and good camaraderie should be the main target."

Having achieved the edge, if not the actual top, of the Plateau, according to plan Amundsen ordered the dogs that would not continue on to the pole to be shot and butchered to feed those that would. This was a hard thing for these very hard men to do. They had grown fond of their animals and hated putting them down. But they

In addition to being a brilliant scientist and explorer, Fridtjof Nansen was also a technical innovator. His "Nansen cooker," which contained inner and outer compartments, was designed to melt snow for drinking water at the same time as food was being heated. Although it seems paradoxical, fresh, liquid water is one of the most important things an Antarctic traveler needs, but is among the hardest to acquire. A standard kit like the one illustrated here included four aluminum cups and spoons, all of which fit within the inner potlike container on the right. This example lacks the large lid used as a base to support the cooker on the primus stove, and the cups are reproductions. The accompanying strap was specially designed to attach the cooker to the sledge. "With these cookers it took from 30 to 45 minutes, according to the degree of cold, to provide a meal for four men" (Lyons 1924: 31).

Treatment of Animals

Much has been written about the treatment of animals on heroic-age expeditions. However one feels about the subject—and there is no question that such treatment was often barbaric by modern standards—historical accuracy requires that we remember that, in 1911, dogs and horses were among the several kinds of animated machinery that humans still relied on to perform a wide range of tasks. In Britain, breeding animals for man's work, using them up thereby, and finally discarding them when worn out, would not have been regarded as brutal treatment unless, of course, it was *conducted* brutally according to views accepted at the time. Bowers, contemplating the shooting of the pony Jehu on November 24, 1911, justified it this way: "A year's care and good feeding, three weeks' work with good treatment . . . and then a painless end. If anybody can call that cruel I cannot either understand it or agree with them." Amundsen's views on using up his dogs were no different; indeed, he was puzzled that Englishmen like Scott always had to convert what was, to him, simply a question of efficiency into a moral dilemma.

Wild animals, if worth the trouble to shoot and prepare, were regularly taken by both groups. Seals were considered especially valuable, because they provided blubber for fuel and meat that could be eaten by both men and dogs. If prepared and cooked properly the fishy taste of the meat can be greatly lessened, and fresh seal meat has at least some effect against scurvy. Few of the men on the British team seem to have relished penguin as long as there was anything else to eat. Petrels, skuas, gulls, and albatrosses were usually ignored, and, unlike some Arctic expeditions, few of the men were interested in shooting animals merely for the "sport" it afforded.

"The ponies' covers which were put on at camping time were of stout green-canvas with cover cloth. . . . On camping a wall of blocks of snow was built on the windward side of the ponies for shelter. . . . The average weight pulled by the ponies varied from about 490 lbs. for the weakest to over 600 lbs. for the strongest" (Lyons 1924: 66).

did what was required; this camp became the *Slakteri*, "The Butchery," for its blood-stained snows. "There was depression and sadness in the air," and the men were glad to leave this now-haunted place on the slopes of Mt. Don Pedro Christophersen. They were still more than 300 miles (480 km) away from the South Pole.

Meanwhile, Scott and his teams of men and animals were scraping along, up to nine hours a day, making slight progress in bad weather. "[A]t every step S.'s luck becomes more evident," Scott wrote in frustration as he reviewed Shackleton's greater rate of progress during the *Nimrod* expedition. The contrast between Scott's party and Amundsen's smartly moving team was both sharp and poignant. The ponies averaged 11.5 to 13 miles (19 to 21 km) per day; Amundsen with his dogs often did twice that, sometimes more. Because of the different rates at which the ponies, dogs, and man-haulers advanced during the course of a day, Scott had to start the groups at intervals so that they'd arrive at the intended camps at roughly the same time. The slowest ponies constituted the "Baltic Fleet," a sardonic reference to the Russian Imperial Fleet's taking seven months to travel from St. Petersburg to the Far East during the Russo-Japanese War (1904–05). The dogs required much less maintenance than the ponies; they simply curled up with each other to stay warm, but the shivering ponies needed blankets and snow baulks to protect them from cold and wind. The blizzards and gale-force winds that struck both teams kept the British in their tents for days at a time, but Amundsen, with his dogs and fur clothing, was usually able to keep moving.

During the last days of November, with morale slipping, Scott decided that some of the ponies—reduced now to shuddering scarecrows—could go no farther and ordered them shot. On November 29, the men were briefly buoyed when they passed Scott's 1902 furthest south, 82°11'S. A week later, with the party only a few more miles more toward its destination, a blizzard descended that kept the men tent-bound for four days. The remaining ponies, sinking to their bellies in the new, wet snow, eyes wild with terror and exhaustion, could move no more than 5 or 6 yards (4.5 or 5.5 m) before collapsing. There was nothing for it: On December 9, the last five were shot, skinned, and their meat cached at a depot—aptly named Shambles Camp. Wilson had had enough: "Thank God the horses are now all done with and we begin the heavy work ourselves."

From a modern perspective it seems a strange thing that man-hauling, that epitome of suffering, would be embraced by these men who had already suffered

"At the start of the Southern Journey, a mileage of nine geographical miles a day was attained [with the ponies] and after the day and night's rest at One Ton Depot, the mileage was increased to an average of 11 geographical miles" (Lyons 1924: 66). This photo records the situation at the start of the journey; as the mountains were approached, sledging conditions and the weather deteriorated, and so did the ponies. The last animals were put down on December 9, 1911. "Poor beasts! they have done remarkably well," Scott wrote, "considering the terrible circumstances under which they worked" (Jones 2006: 342).

much and knew they would suffer more. As expedition leaders, Wilson and Scott may have written their journals under the assumption that posterity would always be looking over their shoulders, and that they therefore had to say all the stalwart, adversity-accepting things expected of British explorers. But their apparent near-pleasure at the anticipation of certain pain in the traces was not unique: Bowers, Cherry-Garrard, Lashly, and physicist Charles "Silas" Wright, to name only a few whose journals mirror their authors' very different positions within the prevailing class structure, said much the same thing. It was as though they were all reciting a formula, a catechism within a larger "ministry of suffering," to use David Crane's evocative phrase, that could both justify their torment and strengthen their belief that things would come out all right in the end. At least that is how it was at the beginning; as the days and weeks wore on, Scott's mood became more and more somber. The days during which they could simply plod along, when nothing disturbed the unrelieved monotony of putting one foot in front of the other, became "the best part of the business, they mean forgetfulness and advance."

Because of the delays and slow going in early December, Scott had already found it necessary to start on S (summit) rations, the food that was supposed to sustain his party for the trek across the plateau to the pole and back. It is here, perhaps, that it first becomes inescapably clear that Scott's plans had begun to

Crampon used during the *Terra Nova* expedition. "A most useful type was evolved during the expedition. . . . The lower sole was of an aluminium alloy studded with thick quadrate pointed nails and a piece of thick leather fixed the sole to a metal heel similarly studded. Around this leather a rough shoe of storm-canvas was sewn" (Lyons 1924: 36).

INSET: A pair of crampons hangs from Day and Nelson's bunkbeds at Cape Evans in 2003.

terminally unwind. At some level, Scott certainly understood that polar weather, just like his food supply and the shortness of the sledging season, was a crucial limiting factor. Seemingly, he thought that the conditions of Antarctic wind, temperature, and snow he experienced during the *Discovery* expedition could be regarded as normal, and were therefore a sufficient guide to the weather he might expect on his present run toward the pole. But the reality was sharply different, and his journals are filled with expressions of puzzlement concerning the circumstances that he actually encountered, as though Nature in this awful place was somehow intentionally perverse. At the very end, in his last camp, he would write in a last letter to Sir George Egerton, "There is no accounting for [the unexpectedly cold weather], but the result has thrown out my calculations." With Antarctic weather it is not the average that is uniquely dangerous, but the variance—the less usual but still fundamentally predictable phenomena that can nowadays be estimated to occur with a one-year, ten-year, or hundred-year probability. Without adequate data on Antarctic weather extremes, Scott relied on his restricted experience and hoped for the best. But, by so doing, he underestimated the effect that bad-weather days would have on his progress, and set in motion a cascade of events that would leave him with an ever-narrowing series of options.

Amundsen, not a catechist at Scott's church, thought man-hauling an absurdity, to be avoided at all costs. Leaving the Butchery, he estimated that his team was three weeks, perhaps less, from the pole.

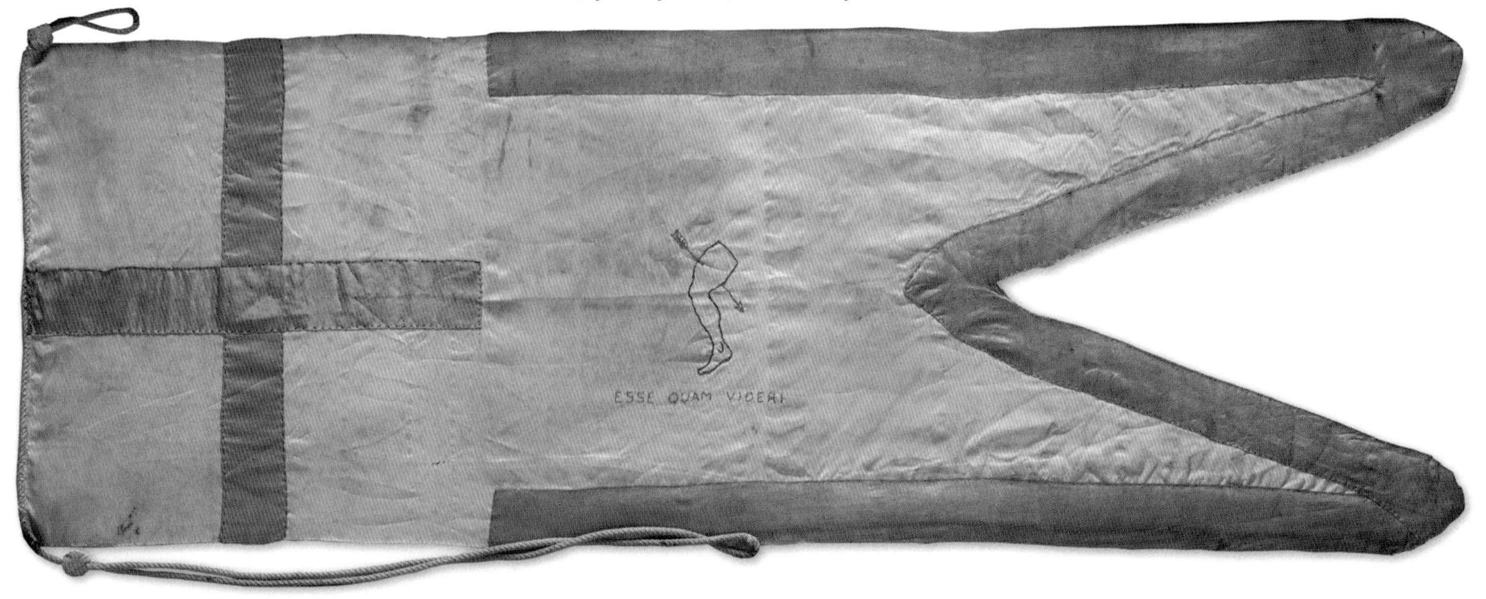

Bowers's sledging flag, found at the last camp. His own flag was late in arriving, so he made his own out of an available blank. The inscription reads "Esse quam videri," or "To be, rather than to seem to be." The symbolism of a leg with an arrow passing through it is a play on the original meaning of the surname Bowers or Bower (that is, maker of bows).

Wilson would regularly spend hours in uncomfortable cold sketching his surroundings. On December 22, 1911, a few days after having finally reached the top of the Beardmore Glacier, Scott wrote, "Now it is perfectly clear, and we get a fine view of the mountain behind which Wilson has been sketching" (Jones 2006: 357).

DEUTSCHE UHRENFABRIKATION
GLASHÜTTE i/S
A. LANGE & SÖHNE
10

CHAPTER 12

December 1911–January 1912

Cigars and Black Flags

Once the men had reached the head of the Axel Heiberg Glacier, Bjaaland posed the Norwegian team for a photograph. They hoped that the worst was now behind them, but on December 1 they entered the area they dubbed The Devil's Ballroom: "We saw nothing, absolutely nothing. The ground below us was hollow, and it sounded as though we were walking on the bottom of empty barrels." After several days they left the mountains far behind and stood on the polar plateau—on nothing but frozen water, thousands of feet above the rocks of East Antarctica. "The surface at once became fine and even," Amundsen wrote, "with a splendid covering of snow everywhere, and we went rapidly on our way south with a feeling of security and safety."

Still, it was not easy going. All of them were suffering from frostbite, and the dogs were becoming hungry, devouring anything edible left unguarded—whip handles, ski-bindings, boots. On December 6 (in fact December 5), they reached the highest point they registered on the plateau, 10,750 feet (3,275 m); on the following day, they passed Shackleton's farthest point south, prompting Amundsen to mark the occasion:

> [Now] 88°23' was past; we were further south than any human being had been. No other moment of the whole trip affected me like this. The tears forced their way to my eyes; by no effort of will could I keep them back. It was the flag yonder that conquered

FACING PAGE: In order to calculate longitude from a sextant reading, it was critical to know the exact difference between Greenwich Mean Time (now Universal Time) and the local time when an observation was made. For that purpose, expeditions in the heroic age carried several chronometers (highly accurate watches) to ensure accuracy. The chronometer pictured here, marked "10," was one of three that Amundsen took to Antarctica.

On the Devil's Glacier, November 29, 1911: "In the foreground, below the high snow-ridge that forms one side of a wide but partly filled-up crevasse, the marks of ski can be seen in the snow. . . . Close to the tracks can be seen an open piece of the crevasse; it is a pale blue at the top, but ends in the deepest black—in a bottomless abyss" (Amundsen 1912, 2: 86).

> me and my will. Luckily I was some way in advance of the others, so that I had time to pull myself together and master my feelings before reaching my comrades. We all shook hands, with mutual congratulations; we had won our way far by holding together, and we would go further yet—to the end.

And he was effusive in his praise of his predecessor:

> We did not pass that spot without according our highest tribute of admiration to the man, who—together with his gallant companions—had planted his country's flag so infinitely nearer to the goal than any of his precursors. Sir Ernest Shackleton's name will always be written in the annals of Antarctic exploration in letters of fire. Pluck and grit can work wonders, and I know of no better example of this than what that man has accomplished.

They built a depot on the spot, leaving 200 pounds (90 kg) of provisions; the next morning, with the wind blasting into their ravaged faces, they set out to cover the remaining distance to the pole, estimating that it should take less than a week. As they raced toward their goal, all the while they dreaded sighting some indication of Scott's presence—what would it be? "Shall we see the English flag—God have mercy on us, I don't believe it," Bjaaland wrote the evening before the final push.

On the afternoon of December 14 (December 13), 1911, with Amundsen in the lead sled, there was a sudden cry from behind.

"Halt!"

The sledges came to a stop. The race had been won; Roald Amundsen had reached the geographical South Pole. Wisting, Hassel, Hanssen, and Bjaaland joined Amundsen in holding up a pole with the Norwegian colors. They looked around them, but they could see nothing from horizon to horizon, just snow and ice, and nothing other than their eyes and their instruments to tell them that, yes, they were at The End. And that they were first.

For the next three days Amundsen fussed: They had reached the *area* of the pole, but his instruments were not capable of giving an absolutely precise position. Amundsen being Amundsen, he wanted to leave nothing to chance or later criticism. He got the men up at 11 P.M. to take sextant readings; because the sun hardly varied in altitude during its course at this time of year, it is not surprising that their calculations were not in agreement: "[I]t clearly shows how unreliable and valueless a single observation like this is in these regions." So Amundsen sent out Bjaaland, Wisting, and Hassel 12 miles (20 km) in three different directions, thinking that one of them at least would cross the invisible point of approximation of all meridians. Then, Amundsen checked his observations once more and pitched a tent—Polheim—"as near to the Pole as humanly possible with the instruments at our disposal," and named the local part of the polar plateau for his king, Haakon VII. Inside the tent he placed some letters and other things that Scott would discover nearly five weeks later.

The Daily Mirror

THE MORNING JOURNAL WITH THE SECOND LARGEST NET SALE.

No. 2,672. FRIDAY, MAY 17, 1912 One Halfpenny.

CAPTAIN AMUNDSEN PLANTS THE NORWEGIAN FLAG AT THE SOUTH POLE AND PHOTOGRAPHS A MEMBER OF HIS EXPEDITION STANDING BESIDE IT.

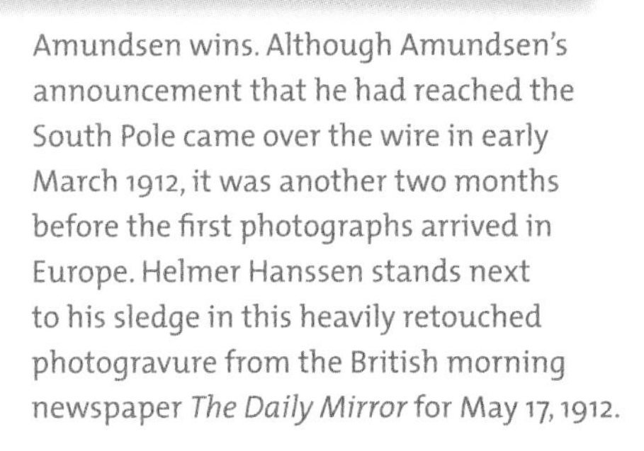

Amundsen wins. Although Amundsen's announcement that he had reached the South Pole came over the wire in early March 1912, it was another two months before the first photographs arrived in Europe. Helmer Hanssen stands next to his sledge in this heavily retouched photogravure from the British morning newspaper *The Daily Mirror* for May 17, 1912.

ABOVE: Polheim, December 16 or 17, 1912 (l to r): Amundsen, Hanssen, Hassel, and Wisting. The Norwegian flag flies above a homemade banner marked "*Fram*."

RIGHT: During the three days the Norwegians spent in the vicinity of the South Pole, Amundsen and his men worked strenuously to ensure that there would be no room for anyone to doubt that they had actually stood at exactly 90°S. The problem was that sextants—their only instruments for establishing their location—could not be relied on to provide highly accurate positions on land. In this posed shot, Amundsen is sighting and Hanssen is bending over a tray, presumably filled with mercury and functioning as an artificial horizon. By aligning the true image of the sun with the virtual one provided by its reflection in the mercury, one could compensate for the lack of a true horizon (which could only be provided by the sea). This scene would be repeated many times over before Amundsen was satisfied that the job was done.

By the end of the day on December 17 (December 16) they had done everything they could to certify their victory and were ready to start back. Bjaaland had secreted cigars in his gear, which he proffered to the others that night. The men smoked and chatted; some appropriate words were said, and they had a little seal meat. The next day they left without further ceremony.

When Scott and his men reached the top of the Beardmore, they were six days behind the pace set by Shackleton. Scott fretted about this, but he was also wrestling with a decision: Who would go on with him to the pole, and who would be sent back? He made his choices in two stages, keeping counsel only with Wilson. On December 20, the first "supporting party," consisting of Atkinson, Cherry-Garrard, Wright, and Patrick "Patsy"

Sledging at the base of Beardmore Glacier in mid-December, with Mt. Kyffin in the background. "[A]fter being delayed for five days by a blizzard . . . progress was further delayed by soft snow on the lower reaches of the glacier. Here the rate of travel on some days fell as low as 1/4 mile per hour or less, due to the sledges sinking in so far that the crosspieces rested on the snow" (Wright 1924: 41).

Three Degree Depot was set up at 87°S on December 31, 1911; Scott's pole party returned to it exactly one month later. It was here, on the outward journey, that Taff Evans (seen here in December, holding the cooker) injured his hand, which later turned septic and may well have contributed to his demise.

Keohane were told how things stood; they left for the north two days later. Atkinson, the silent man, quietly accepted the decision; Cherry was heartbroken; Wright was angry and didn't hide it; Keohane, a P.O. used to following orders without questioning them, said nothing. Scott excused the second supporting party on January 3, but it consisted of three men rather than four—Teddy Evans, Crean, and Lashly. Evans took it hard, but he was an officer and put a good face on, as Scott expected he would. Like Keohane, the bluejackets Crean and Lashly followed orders, but Crean wept nonetheless. The party selected to go on to the South Pole would thus be Scott, Wilson, Oates, Taff Evans—and Bowers, added seemingly at the last minute from Teddy Evans's group.

Scott thought that Teddy's team would have a comparatively easy 750-mile (1,200 km) haul back to Hut Point and Cape Evans. It was, after all, still summer. But their return journey was a transit through cold hell. Evans and Lashly had been man-hauling without letup since the breakdown of the last tractor near Corner Camp. Evans rapidly developed scurvy on the way back, becoming increasingly incapacitated and

eventually semicomatose. He was close to dying. The two seamen decided that, to save their officer, Lashly would stay with him at their camp, about 35 miles (56 km) from Hut Point. Crean would walk the remaining distance to seek help, taking no tent or anything else besides a few biscuits. On February 19 he made the trip in eighteen hours, nonstop; Teddy Evans was rescued the next day by Atkinson and Demetri, the Russian dog driver, who happened to be staying at Hut Point. The gods were evidently pleased: Evans went on to become a war hero, admiral, member of parliament, and, eventually, a life peer.

For his journey to save Evans, widely regarded as "the greatest single-handed act of heroism and fortitude in the entire Heroic Age of Polar exploration," Crean was awarded the Albert Medal. Undaunted by his experiences on the *Terra Nova* expedition, this extraordinarily tough Irishman later shipped out once more to Antarctica, in order to accompany Shackleton on the *Endurance* expedition. Fate had another life-saving job for him: It was Crean, together with Shackleton and Worsley, who made the crossing of the spine of South Georgia in May, 1916, to bring news that their shipmates were alive but stranded on Elephant Island.

Much has been written about Scott's decision-making at this juncture, and how he should have chosen this man over that. Such evaluations benefit from the mirror of hindsight; Scott had nothing to go on but what he had seen of the men's individual performances, and what he thought he needed in manpower to make the last push for the pole. The decision to include Birdie Bowers was understandable from the standpoint of increasing hauling power, as Bowers was one of the strongest members of the team. But by taking Birdie along as a fifth man, Scott added to the complications he was already facing. Since rations had been organized in units for four-man sledging teams, the men had to perform a hasty redistribution of provisions on the ice. Food would now loom even larger as a critical factor for the journey ahead. Fuel was another problem. Heating water for "hoosh"—the stewlike concoction of pemmican and biscuit made for every meal, with the occasional extra treat—took appreciably longer now that they were cooking for five instead of four. Bowers didn't even have skis at this time because a few days earlier, in a moment of utter misjudgment, Scott had ordered Teddy Evans's sledge team to depot their skis in an apparent effort to reduce sledge weight and proceed on foot. There were other, less obvious problems with the fitness of the pole party. Though he wasn't letting on, Oates was hampered by an increasingly bad foot, and his old Boer War injury was starting to cause him pain. Despite his enormous strength, Taff Evans was visibly beginning to tire. Perhaps he was already suffering from the first effects of scurvy, or perhaps from a serious infection; he had cut his thumb quite badly when working on one of the sledges, and within a few days it was suppurating. The gathering of fate and circumstance was taking an ominous turn.

On January 4, when the second supporting party finally split off to the north, Scott and his remaining men were still some 150 miles (240 km) from the pole. They had hoped that the terrain ahead would be much less dreadful than the Beardmore had been, but each day forward seemed worse than the last. Some days the snow was so soft that the sledge runners simply sank into it, greatly increasing the effort required to pull the load. On other, very cold days the snow surface turned into crystalline sand, which also severely impeded hauling. Sastrugi, the wind-hardened ridges, were a different problem. Because they were sculpted by prevailing winds, they were valuable as directional guides, but their razorlike edges cut into the sledge runners and the men's footwear. Yet, once every so often, the sledges roared along, gliding almost friction-free and sending the men's spirits soaring.

Despite fierce winds and yet another blizzard, Scott finally passed Shackleton's farthest south on January 9, three years to the day after Shackleton had had to turn around. In large capital letters, Scott wrote "RECORD" in his diary; one rival down, he must have thought, one to go. But of course the race was already over.

Another menace was beginning to threaten. Despite temperatures in the –20°F (–29°C) range—cold but not intolerable to men in good condition—Scott and his companions were beginning to feel an abnormal chill. "It is most unaccountable why we should suddenly feel the cold in this manner" Scott wrote; it must be due "partly the exhaustion of the march, but partly some damp quality in the air." But there was more to it than that. Because Scott took ponies instead of confining himself to dogs, he was forced to start his journey later than Amundsen. Although daytime temperatures on the Plateau were about the same as the Norwegians had experienced a month earlier, overnight temperatures would eventually begin to plunge as Antarctica entered winter. Recent thought is that, in addition to other factors, vitamin deficiency increased their susceptibility to cold, and was at least partly to blame for the failure of Evans's hand to heal properly.

As famished men often do, they dreamt of food, of dinners past and ones yet to come, with groaning tables piled with every kind of delicacy. Bowers imagined gathering together all the poor children of London at Christmastime, and feeding them with all the sweets they could eat. If asked, Scott's men would have said they were merely a bit peckish; a little dodgy in the gut, perhaps a little concerned about their gums and feet, but no worries once they got to the next depot and fed to repletion. In fact, they were already far down a path leading to serious malnutrition and starvation, suffering

In the letter left at Polheim for King Haakon VII of Norway, Amundsen noted that he reached the vicinity of the South Pole on December 14 (actually December 13) with four companions and dogs. He proudly mentioned that he named the region of the South Pole "King Haakon VII Plateau"—overlooking the fact that Shackleton had named much the same area after his own monarch in 1909. The letter was almost overlooked by the relief party: Silas Wright noted in his diary that it was found while the last of the gear from Scott's tent was being gathered together, "among bumph, must remember to give it to Atch" (Bull & Wright 1993: 349).

a cascade of damage to their bodies and minds that eventually affected not only their strength but also their judgment. By contrast, Amundsen and his men actually gained weight on their polar journey because they had planned rations so that they could increase their calorie intake on the return trip. Indeed, there was so much food for man and dog alike that the word "rations" hardly applies.

As late as mid-January the British team still had not seen any man-made tracks leading south; they permitted themselves the hope that this meant they had beaten the opposition. But on January 16, as they slogged closer to 90°S, Bowers spotted something in the distance. A black speck—a mirage? But "[s]oon we knew," Scott wrote, "that this could not be a natural snow feature." Whipping in the light wind was a black flag on a discarded sledge runner—a symbol startling in its incongruity and unambiguous in its meaning. The flag was one of several that had been set out by Amundsen's men on their survey runs to ensure that they had actually intersected the pole. "This told us the whole story . . . . The Norwegians have forestalled us and are first at the Pole. It is a terrible disappointment, and I am very sorry for my loyal companions."

"Our poor slighted Union Jack": a swatch of the flag hoisted by Scott and his companions at the South Pole, January 18, 1912, and found at the last camp. In his last letter to Kathleen, Con told her that a piece of the flag should be looked for in his kitbag; he encouraged her to send a piece to King George, another to Queen Alexandra, and to keep the rest.

Scott and his men reached the close environs of the South Pole the next day, January 17, 1912. Amundsen had beaten them by thirty-four days. Scott's words were blunt: "The POLE. Yes, but under very different circumstances from those expected. We have had a horrible day—add to our disappointment a head wind 4 to 5, with a temperature –22°, and companions labouring on with cold feet and hands. . . . Great God! this is an awful place and terrible enough for us to have laboured to it without the reward of priority."

After taking some theodolite readings to confirm the Norwegians' work, the next day they headed toward a partly snow-covered tent spotted by Bowers. It was, of course, Amundsen's Polheim. Scott entered; inside were a number of discarded items, a letter for King Haakon, and another in English addressed to "Captain Scott":

> Dear Captain Scott,
> As you probably are the first to reach this area after us, I will ask you kindly to forward this letter to King Haakon VII. If you can use any of the articles left in the tent please do not hesitate to do so. With kind regards I wish you a safe return.
> Yours truly,
> Roald Amundsen

Tryggve Gran's Impressionistic painting of one of the black flags seen by Scott and his companions, based on a sketch by Dr. Wilson.

BELOW: One of Amundsen's black flags, on which has been placed a copy of the first volume of Amundsen's best-selling *The South Pole*. The flag was collected by Wilson and found at Scott's last camp. Amundsen wrote that "three small bags were made . . . and in each of these was placed a paper, giving the position of our camp. In addition, each of [the men] carried a large square flag [to attach to a pole or a spare sledge runner]" (Amundsen 1912, 2: 126).

Years later, Raymond Priestley, one of the geologists on the expedition, observed scornfully—or perhaps whimsically—that at this moment Scott "was degraded from explorer to postman" by Amundsen, which is surely unfair to both men. Amundsen was merely taking precautions against the chance that he might perish on his return; Scott would have asked the same thing of him, had he been first.

Wilson, always the collector, wanted a souvenir: "I took some strips of blue-grey silk off the tent seams—it was perished [disintegrated]." The pieces were found with his other effects at the last camp, a mute reminder of all they had suffered only to come in second.

After leaving his own note, Scott asked Bowers to photograph the party, with "our poor, slighted Union Jack" flying. Birdie took ten exposures at the South Pole; the film was recovered at the last camp and developed at Cape Evans months later. Viewing them at the time, Cherry thought that "all the party look fit and well, and their clothes are not iced up," but this is a matter for the beholder to judge.

Those of Bowers's photos that are reproduced here (see pages 166–67) are among the most famous in exploration history. At one level they are simply record shots, to prove that they did what they set out to do; there is no effort at composition beyond having the men exchange places and replant their sledging flags. At another, the images stand as both testament and icon: Everyone looks exhausted and listless, no one more so than Scott. His gaze is downcast, blank, away from the camera; of all of them, he seems the most physically changed, the least recognizable. But of course one sees what one wants to see where spin is everything. To Scott's biographer George Seaver, writing in 1933, the photos show that "[t]here is no hint of any 'collapse of morale' here—'We have done what we came for.'" He especially commented on the image that shows Wilson and Scott with their mouths open, "heads thrown back, roaring with laughter, evidently at some remark of the photographer. That men could laugh at all under such conditions is something that calls for more than a passing comment." It certainly does, especially if one believes that Seaver's interpretation does not ring true. In this photograph (top, page 167) Scott looks more as though he is shouting, and Wilson seems to be in mid-sentence, not mid-laugh. If it was all so funny, why is Oates looking at his feet?

The Norwegian home Polheim
is situated in 89°58' S Lat
SE by E (comp) 8 miles
15 Decbr. 1911
Roald Amundsen

Wilson noted in his journal for January 18, 1912 that Scott sent him to fetch another sledge runner with a black flag: "I found a note tied to it showing this was the Norskies' actual final Pole position [sic]. I was given the flag and the note with Amundsen's signature [by Scott]. . . ." (Seaver 1933: 280). Actually, Amundsen's note fixes the position of Polheim—not the pole—relative to the flag: "The Norwegian home Polheim is situated in 89[°]58'S Lat SE by E (comp[ass]) 8 miles. 15 Decbr. 1911 Roald Amundsen."

The march back would be joyless, something to be endured rather than celebrated. Both weather and food supply played on Scott's mind; problems with either—or worse, both—could have disastrous consequences. Scott's last dairy entry (with expurgated words reinstated) before turning back incorporates all of this: "Well, we have turned our back now on the goal of our ambition with sore feelings and must face 800 miles of solid dragging—and goodbye to most of the day-dreams!"

All that now remains of the tent at Polheim: fragments of silk pulled from the tent's seams by Wilson while at the pole on January 18, 1912.

These four photographs are from a group taken by Bowers while at the South Pole. The first two have been frequently reproduced, but the third and fourth very rarely because of their poorer quality and, perhaps, a certain disturbing element they exhibit.

TOP LEFT: (l to r) Scott, Oates, Wilson, and Taff Evans at Polheim.

BOTTOM LEFT: Wilson, Scott, Evans, Oates, and Bowers in front of their own tent near the pole, flags flying.

TOP RIGHT: (standing l to r) Wilson and Scott, (seated l to r) Oates and Evans—laughing, shouting, or doing something else?

BOTTOM RIGHT: Wilson, Scott, Evans, and a blurry Oates—is Oates already starting to disappear?

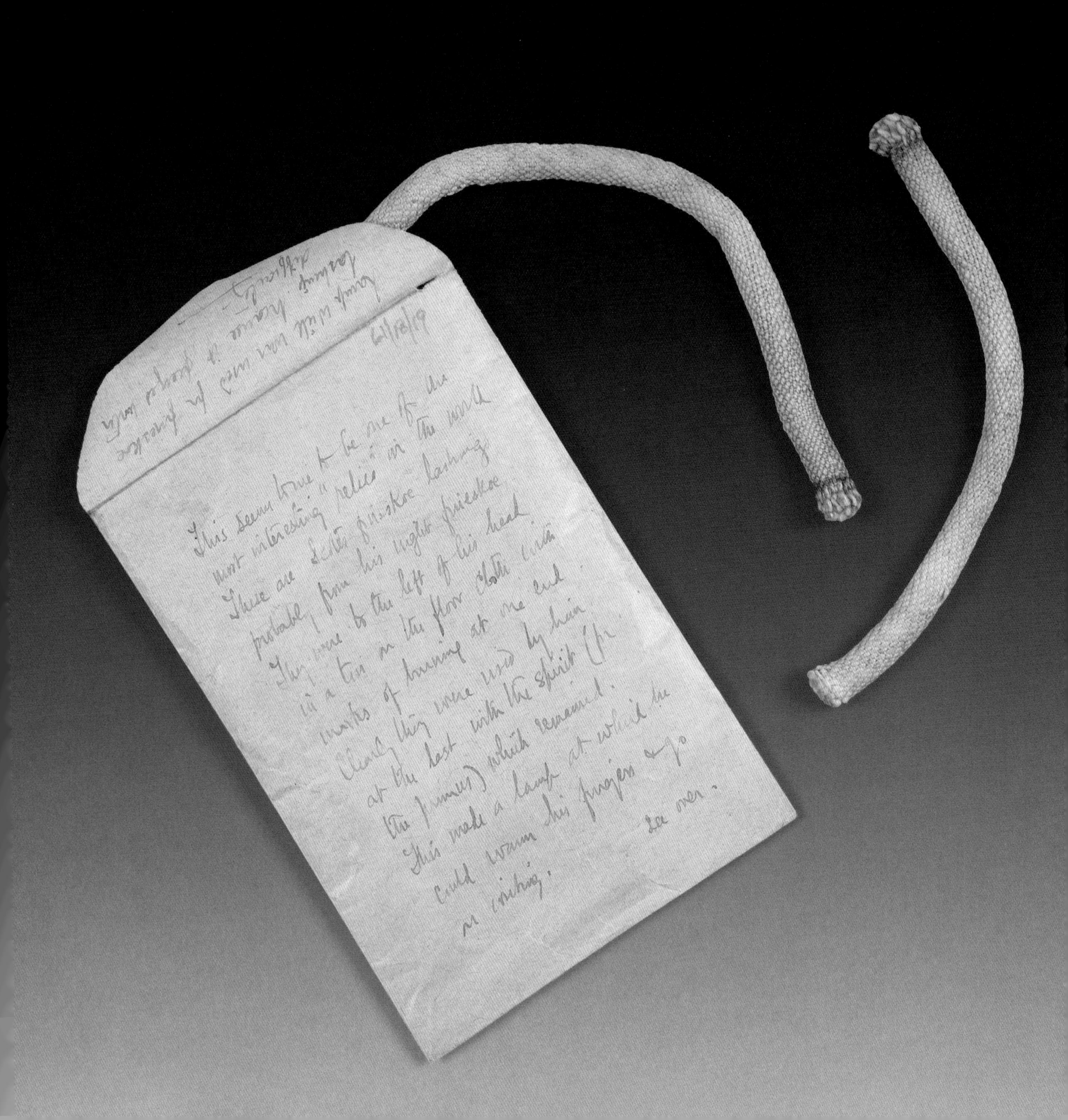
6/1/19
This seems to me to be one of the
most interesting "relics" in the world.
These are Scott's finnesko lashings
probably from his right finnesko.
They were to the left of his head
in a tin on the floor cloth with
marks of burning at one end.
Clearly they were used by him
at the last with the spirit (for
the primus) which remained.
This made a lamp at which he
could warm his fingers & go
on writing. See over.

CHAPTER 13

February–March, 1912

"It is finished"

Although he had carefully stocked his depots and felt confident that the weather would not seriously hamper him, Amundsen still had some worries. He was especially concerned that Scott might arrive at the pole within the next few days and somehow get the news out to the world first. Their return had little of the drama that Scott and his men would experience: There was calm weather, sunshine, and the monotony of covering an average of 15 miles (24 km) a day, followed by eating, sleeping, and getting up to do it all over again. The Norwegians traveled on the plateau at night, with the sun behind them, in order to avoid the problem of snowblindness. Because Amundsen did not want to exceed his average daily distance while at high altitude, he would order the men to spend extra hours in their sleeping bags to conserve their strength.

FACING PAGE: Pieces of lampwick used as laces (lashings) for finnesko boots, found at Scott's last camp. On the envelope in which they were contained, Cherry-Garrard wrote of the importance of these seemingly useless bits of material: "This seems to me to be one of the most interesting 'relics' in the world. These are Scott's fineskoe [sic] lashings probably from his right fineskoe. They were to the left of his head in a tin on the floor cloth with marks of burning at one end. Clearly they were used by him at the last with the spirit (for the primus) which remained. This made a lamp at which he could warm his fingers & go on writing. See over. [Text continues on reverse side of envelope:] Lamp wick was used for fineskoe lashings because it frayed with difficulty. I saw them when I first entered the tent with Atkinson & we examined the bodies: and Atkinson said to me 'I told you the Owner would not last'—this because we mistook his body for that of Seaman Evans. When we were finally leaving these lashings of lamp wick were lying on the snow by the grave & Atkinson said I might keep them."

Amundsen built large cairns (like this one at 83°S) on the Barrier at regular intervals, to serve as guideposts to depots on the way back. Together with other safety measures, it worked, because he didn't miss a single depot on the return journey to Framheim. Scott built cairns also, but not as elaborately, and a number were missed. Remarkably, some of Amundsen's dogs that escaped during the course of the journey south managed to travel back to the Barrier depots, obviously looking for food. Only the one at 82°S was successfully broken into; of the runaways themselves, nothing was ever seen again.

The paucity of good images of the Norwegians during their journey to the South Pole and back underlines the fact that Amundsen, normally the meticulous planner, had not given adequate attention to one matter that he really should have. Before leaving Norway, Amundsen asked professional photographer Anders Beer Wilse to give some of his men photography and darkroom lessons, but he himself couldn't be bothered. He felt that all he needed to do was cover a suitable range of f-stops when he photographed a subject, and presto! at least one exposure would be adequate. He was wrong; most of his shots turned out to be completely unusable. Even the ones that could be retrieved were, to put it mildly, awful. After Amundsen's return, Wilse tried hard to doctor his images enough so that they could be used for lantern slides, but he ruefully concluded that Amundsen had lost "many thousands of kroners' income" in reproduction rights because of the "hopeless amateur material he had produced."

Once they had broken through the mountains, Bjaaland saw to it that the trek home became a race of a different kind, and he amused himself by always trying to stay ahead of the dogs on his skis. They were covering more than 20 miles (32 km) a day and, because they were hitting their well-stocked depots, they were eating heartily (chocolate and double rations), if only to lighten their sledges. Once they reached the Barrier, Amundsen, still nervous that the British were not far behind, decided to sprint in the mild weather. By January 25, 1912, they were doing 30 miles (48 km) a day. The following day, the Norwegians would skate across the ice of the Bay of Whales and arrive at Framheim at four in the morning, with eleven dogs and two sledges remaining. Their trip to the pole and back had taken ninety-nine days and covered almost 1,860 miles (3,000 km). Now they were home, ten days ahead of schedule.

Three members of the Japanese Antarctic expedition visit *Fram* in January 1912, just before Amundsen's return from the pole and the ship's departure for Europe. The intent of the leader, Nobu Shirase, was to explore King Edward VII Land, but poor conditions and bad weather prevented him from carrying out most of his plan.

Amundsen had planned his entrance into Framheim so that he would catch Lindstrom sleeping. Stepping inside the hut, he roused the cook. "Good morning, my dear Lindstrom," Amundsen said, "Have you any coffee for us?"

Surprisingly, *Fram* had had another visitor just before Amundsen and his men arrived. On January 16, 1912, *Kainan Maru*, the vessel carrying the Japanese Antarctic expedition under Nobu Shirase, swung into view in the Bay of Whales. It was far too late in the year to do much; the Japanese made a brief foray onto the Barrier, traveling 160 miles (260 km) to 80°05'S before horrendous conditions caused them to turn around. Although little of lasting significance was achieved, Shirase and his men demonstrated that Antarctic exploration was not for Europeans alone.

Loading *Fram* took only a couple of days because most of the expedition's expendable equipment was left behind. Amundsen cast off for Hobart, Tasmania, on January 30, 1912.

For Scott and his men, a successful march home depended on decisions that had been made months ago, with virtually no room for error. Heading north in blizzard season meant that their depots would have to be located and reached in a timely manner, and Scott had not made allowance for injuries to any of his men, which would and did slow them down. For the first part of their return, at high altitude on the plateau, the pole party would be man-hauling with a full S-ration per man of 16 ounces (453 g) of biscuit, 12 ounces (340 g) of pemmican, 2 ounces (57 g) of butter, 0.57 ounces (16.2 g) of cocoa, 3 ounces (85 g) of sugar, and 0.86 ounces (24.4 g) of tea. These rations would provide each with 4,600 calories a day, but it has been calculated that they probably burnt more than 5,500 each day. It was no wonder that Bowers, in his diary, noted that he and the others were becoming noticebly thinner. They were slowly starving to death.

Unlike Amundsen, Scott was never able to solve the problem of paraffin "creeps" or serious leakages that occurred when the fuel was stored in stoppered tins in the depots. This often led to losses of one-quarter to one-half of the contents. To prevent such loss, Amundsen hermetically sealed his tins by soldering them shut.

In addition to the loss of fuel, the weather was wearing the British team down. Scott reported poor conditions on January 19, the day they started on their return: "[F]ine crystals spoil the surface; we had heavy dragging during the last hour in spite of the light load and a full sail." Earlier in the day, when they passed by the black flag that had first signaled the presence of the Norwegians, they decided to collect it as a souvenir and to use the staff on which it hung as a yard for their sail. Poor conditions, with sastrugi, blizzards, and obliterated tracks, made going very difficult for the next several days.

Evans showed persistent signs of deep frostbite on his cheeks and nose, according to Wilson's diary, and Oates's feet were "very cold." The distance between depots was pushing them on; some days they hauled for as much as 19 miles (30 km). But making such distances did not come without its price. Evans's hands were in increasingly bad condition, and Scott noticed that there "is no doubt that Evans is a good deal run down."

By January 24, Scott was worried: "Things beginning to look a little serious," he wrote. The bright sun in their eyes and the strong winds forced them to stop frequently because they had a hard time keeping to their old tracks. On that day, after covering only 7 miles (11 km), "cold fingers all around" were slowing them down. "This is the second full gale since we left the Pole. I don't like the look of it," Scott wrote. "Is the weather breaking up? If so, God help us, with the tremendous summit journey and scant food."

On the next day they reached Half-Degree Depot and were able to replenish their supplies, but there was no fresh meat. It had been six weeks since they had last consumed pony meat and what little vitamin C it contained. Wounds were slow to heal, and the workload at 10,000 feet (3,050 m) each day was accompanied by nosebleeds, dehydration, and severe headaches.

Toward the end of January, conditions improved and they made good progress. On the last day of the month they picked up Bowers's skis; he had been without them for the last 350 miles (560 km), since December 31, when Scott had ordered them cached with those of the other members of Teddy Evans's sledge party. Scott had previously noted that "I'm afraid [Bowers] must find these long marches very trying with short legs"; he did not, however, see fit to spell Birdie off by rotating the available skis among the men.

By this time Evans's fingers were in bad shape from frostbite and the knife gash inflicted weeks before, and even Wilson and Scott were suffering from painful injuries that made man-hauling ever more difficult. Oates was suffering as well, but stoically. On February 4, both Scott and Evans fell into a crevasse—Evans for the second time in a few days. This time it seemed to have a serious effect on the seaman, because Scott observed he was becoming "dull and incapable." Two days later, Scott wrote in his diary that "Evans is the chief anxiety now; his cuts and wounds suppurate, his nose looks very bad, and altogether he shows considerable signs of being played out." On February 7 they reached the Upper Glacier Depot, only to find that the rations were less than expected. "First panic," Scott wrote, "certainly that biscuit-box was short. Great doubt as to how this has come about, as we certainly haven't over-issued allowances. Bowers is dreadfully disturbed about it."

The next day was warmer, and after pulling in the morning, Scott decided to geologize for the rest of that day and the next under the shadow of Mt. Buckley. Among the interesting rocks they recovered was coal "with beautifully traced leaves in layers," and they also saw ripple marks on rocks from some ancient beach. He ended that day's notes with a heartfelt plea: "We deserve a little bright weather after all our trials . . . "

He got a bit of better weather for a time, but worse conditions overall. Navigating the ice and crevasses of the Beardmore proved difficult, as old tracks were lost along

Linen bags for small provisions—this one originally contained tea—were repurposed as sample bags. Wilson used them to collect interesting rocks during the southern journey, including the famous erratics from the Beardmore glacier that contained fossilized plant remains.

Sledging medicine chest used on the *Terra Nova* Expedition: "Dr. Wilson designed a case for a unit of four men of which the contents were estimated to be sufficient for such needs as might arise. It was light and easy of transport, weighing 4 lbs. when full. It was constructed with square covers fitting into each other, and secured by a strap and buckle which passed round both compartments" (Lyons 1924: 51).

with precious time. They were miles from the next depot, and a desperate Scott was forced to reduce rations, stretching three days of pemmican meals to four. Then, on February 13, Wilson saw the flag that marked the location of the Mid-Glacier Depot. "[W]e were soon in possession of our 3 ½ days' food," Scott wrote almost pathetically; this "was the worst experience of the trip and gave a horrid feeling of insecurity. . . . In future food must be worked [out] so that we do not run so short if the weather fails us." And more ominously still: "Evans has no power to assist with camping work."

On the next day, February 14, Scott observed, "[T]here is no getting away from the fact that we are not going strong." Evans's condition had been deteriorating, as Scott noted, "from bad to worse"; two days later he was "nearly broken down in brain, we think." Oates was less tactful, writing that Evans "has lost his guts and behaves like an old woman or worse." With 400 miles (640 km) to go, Oates pondered, "God knows how we are going to get him home. We could not possibly carry him on the sledge."

They were "pulling for food" at this point, with two days' march to go before reaching the Lower Glacier Depot and only barely enough food left. On February 17, Evans dropped out of harness and shambled along behind the sledge. By noontime he had fallen far behind, causing Scott and the others to go back on skis after him. They found him on his knees, his "clothing disarranged, hands uncovered and frostbitten, and a wild look in his eyes." Slurring his speech and unable to walk, Evans waited with Oates while the others went back for the sledge. They had scarcely gotten him into the tent when Evans became unconscious. Wilson believed that Evans had injured his head in a fall, but dehydration, incipient scurvy, hypothermia, malnutrition, cerebral edema, and perhaps other factors could have contributed to his condition at the time. As the largest of the men in the group, he was, in effect, starving at a faster rate than the others, and his injuries had no doubt exacted a severe mental strain. Evans never regained consciousness, and died later that night in the tent. "It is a terrible thing to lose a companion in this way," Scott wrote, " . . . but calm reflection shows that there could not have been a better ending to the terrible anxieties of the past week."

On the same night as Evans's death, Scott and the others made a dash for the depot, which they reached easily. The next day they marched to the place where the last ponies had been shot, Shambles Camp, and for the first time in a long while they enjoyed full meals and a holiday from straight pemmican and biscuit. But the terrible downturn in their fortunes continued. The men were still in poor physical condition, despite the addition of pony meat to their diet, and the weather was turning progressively colder. Worse—much worse—was the agonizing man-hauling over terrible surfaces: "Like pulling over desert sand, not the least glide in the world," Scott observed. Although the number of miles they covered per day varied, overall they were going at half the pace they needed to achieve in view of the lateness of the season. And the men were being affected in other, more subtle ways. They gradually wrote less and less in their journals, eventually stopping altogether—except for Scott, who never gave up writing no matter how badly things went.

At times uncertain of their position, they missed an important depot of pony meat on February 22, although on February 24 they did manage to find the Southern Barrier Depot and the line of snow cairns that told them they were on the correct bearing. There were messages from Meares, Atkinson, and Teddy Evans, showing that the supporting parties had successfully gotten down from the plateau and onto the Barrier.

Cherry-Garrard included a number of Wilson's paintings and sketches in the two-volume editions of *Worst Journey*, but most had to be dropped from later "cheap" editions. This sketch, from the first British edition, is entitled *Where Evans Died*; the scene depicted is the area below Mt. Fox, on the western margin of the Beardmore Glacier. Wilson sketched it on December 11, 1911, during the ascent of the glacier; Evans died there two and a half months later, on February 17, 1912.

However, there was to be no meat: The carcass of Christopher, the pony that had been shot and buried there, had turned rotten. They still had more than 300 miles (480 km) to go, and yet again the fuel they found in the depot was "woefully short," Scott observed. "Pray God we have no further set-backs."

In late February, night temperatures were plummeting to –40°, which made it excruciatingly difficult to get on their boots and clothes each morning. Nothing dried out; the wet items merely turned into polygons of frozen leather and fabric overnight. "It is a race between the season and hard conditions and our fitness and good food." By March 3, they were achieving just 4 miles (6.5 km) a day over a surface of crystals that created much friction on the runners. "God help us," Scott wrote, "we can't keep up this pulling, that is certain . . . . [W]hat each man feels in his heart I can only guess." The paraffin oil was practically spent; for heating their hoosh they tried to rig up a lamp that would burn the methylated spirit (denatured alcohol) used as starter fuel for their primus stove, but they didn't think it would be of much use because spirit burns too fast.

Oates had become their other worry. Because he never complained, the others had no idea how badly his feet had been affected by frostbite and, now, probably gangrene. As early as January 25, he noted in his journal that his big toe had turned black; he hoped that "it is not going to lame me for marching," revealing either ignorance about his condition or willful disregard. He soldiered on through February, his feet inert blocks. By March 6, he was unable to pull and merely stumbled alongside the sledge. Also, Scott's mood swings had become more obvious in his daily entries: A merely good day is bruited as truly exceptional and portentous ("we are wonderfully fit considering . . . "), but a few sentences later, despair erupts with "I should like to keep the track to the end."

On March 7, Scott wrote, "[o]ne feels that for poor Oates the crisis is near." Clearly, though not recorded in any of the diaries, the expectation was that Oates would do the right thing: He should march as long as he could; when he could march no longer, he must not slow down the others. Scott had hoped against hope that, by this time, as previously agreed, Atkinson, Cherry-Garrard, and Meares would be heading south with the dogs, to replenish the remaining depots. But in fact Scott had left conflicting messages with the men—at one point ordering that the dogs not be exposed to any unnecessary risks, as they were to be saved for the next season. Incredibly, Cherry had been at One Ton Depot with Demetri since March 4, waiting for the pole party to come over the Barrier so he could hurry them back to Cape Evans in time to catch *Terra Nova* before it sailed, assuming that would be what Scott wanted to do. He waited a week, but with Demetri seriously ill, dog food low, and Scott's apparently clear instruction that the dogs not be placed in harm's way, he felt he had no choice but to turn back, which he did on March 10. On that date, Scott's party was confined "in a comfortless blizzard camp, wind quite foul," slightly more than 50 miles (80 km) away—no more than a two- to three-day trip with the dogs in good weather. Cherry would have to live with that knowledge for the rest of his life.

On that same day, Scott recorded in his journal that "poor Titus is the greatest handicap. He keeps us waiting in the morning [trying to put his boots over his terribly damaged feet] until we have partly lost the warming effect of our good breakfast, when the only wise policy is to be up and away at once." Scott "practically ordered" Wilson to distribute sufficient opium tablets to permit each man to decide when to end it if circumstances became unbearable. Just days later, on March 14, Oates asked to be left behind in his sleeping bag, but the others urged him on. Oates managed to keep going, but that night, he decided it was his time. In Scott's diary, for either March 16 or 17 (he had lost track of dates), he wrote:

Snow knife made by Chief Stoker William Lashly, lying on fur mittens belonging to Acting Leading Stoker Edward MacKenzie. Knives like this were used to cut blocks of hardened snow for pony shelters and for weighing down tent skirts. "The particular virtue of the large fur mittens was the fact that they were wind-proof" (Lyons 1924: 36).

> Should this be found I want these facts recorded. Oates' last thoughts were of his Mother, but immediately before he took pride in thinking that his regiment would be pleased with the bold way in which he met his death. We can testify to his bravery. He has borne intense suffering for weeks without complaint, and to the very last was able and willing to discuss outside subjects. He did not—would not—give up hope to the very end. He was a brave soul. This was the end. He slept through the night before last, hoping not to wake; but he woke in the morning—yesterday. It was blowing a blizzard. He said, 'I am just going outside and may be some time.' He went out into the blizzard

and we have not seen him since. . . . [T]hough we tried to dissuade him, we knew it was the act of a brave man and an English gentleman.

If the date was indeed March 17, Oates had intentionally limped out of the tent to his death on or just before his thirty-second birthday. The others knew that, for them as well, the end was near, although according to Scott's journal they remained "unendingly cheerful." Daytime temperatures had plunged in the last several days, and they were plagued with serious frostbite. Even Scott, whose "best feet" had been a source of pride, was now hobbling along. His right foot had become so bad that "amputation is the least I can hope for now."

Scott could no longer pull, but at this juncture it is unlikely that the others could have done much even if they had left him behind. On March 21, Bowers and Wilson planned to set off for the next depot with the hope of bringing food and fuel back to where Scott lay. They never left. They may have been stopped by the weather, as a storm blew in. Or perhaps they were simply too weak to carry on. Instead, they stayed in the tent and wrote their last letters. Bowers wrote to his mother:

Cherry-Garrard's helmet and goggles. The helmet "comprised a hood fitting over the head, with a projecting funnel surrounding a narrow opening shaped to the face, and widening to the outer border which was attached to a soft copper wire" (Lyons 1924: 33).

> I should so like to come through for your dear sake. It is splendid to pass however with such companions. . . . There will be no shame however and you will know that I have struggled to the end. . . . Oh how I do feel for you when you hear all. You will know that for me the end was peaceful as it is only sleep in the cold. Your ever loving son to the end of this life & the next where God shall wipe away all tears from our eyes.

Wilson, who had promised to visit Titus Oates's mother, could only write to her now, telling her that he had never seen a man show as much courage as her son. He also wrote to his own wife, telling her (in Seaver's condensed transcription):

> [W]e have struggled to the end and we have nothing to regret. Our whole record is clean, and Scott's diary gives the account. . . . The Barrier has beaten us—though we got to the Pole. . . . All the things that I had hoped to do with you after this Expedition are as nothing now, but there are greater things for us to do in the world to come. . . . Your little testament and prayer book will be in my hand or in my breast pocket when the end comes. All is well.

Wilson had taken a dogeared copy of *The Book of Common Prayer* with him on all his sledging trips, including this one. The flyleaves and pastedowns—indeed, most spare surfaces—are covered with religious meditations in his tiny, spidery hand. Many inscriptions are no longer fully legible, but those that are tell of a man for whom death and the hereafter held nothing but wonder and promise. None is dated, but there is one passage on the front flyleaf that may serve, as much as anything can, to give an insight into his state of mind during his last days on the Barrier. The meditation is on Christ's last utterance (underlined words) on the cross, when he receives a drink of vinegar, then gives up his spirit:

> It is finished. This teaches us that everything is ready, that we can come to the marriage feast of the Lamb, that we haven't to save ourselves, that we haven't to make our atonement—that it is done. All is ready for us.

Unlike Bowers and Wilson, Scott was not a religious man except in the most conventional, observe-the-proper-form way. He did not expect to see his wife or son again in the afterlife, and was keenly aware that the end—a permanent end—was near. Now he was writing for his unseen audience, shaping his story and attempting to explain the now-inevitable tragic outcome. His letters display the tones of one who was stepping into his role as martyr. "I was *not* too old for this job," he wrote in a letter to his last commanding officer, Admiral Sir Francis Bridgeman. "It was the younger men that went under first . . . We are setting a good example to our countrymen, if not by getting into a tight place, but facing it like men when we get there." In letter after letter, Scott trumpeted the courage and dignity of his fellow Englishmen, who "still die with a bold spirit, fighting it out to the end." And in letter after letter, he blamed weather, debilitation, and misfortune—but not faulty organization—as the cause of the disaster.

According to Scott's last entries, they stayed in the tent for nine days and nights, unable to go farther because of the terrible weather, helplessly waiting for the weather to break as food and fuel grew less each day. Susan Solomon's evaluation of available meteorological records for the past century indicates that Barrier temperatures in the late fall or early winter of 1912 were indeed significantly colder than the long-term average. On the other hand, the evidence is mixed at best for a continuous, raging nine-day storm. Perhaps any unsettled weather was too much for the men to face now; perhaps in the end they preferred to die in their tent rather than in their traces. In any case, Scott used his last days to write once more to his wife Kathleen, composing letters she would read months later after she had sailed for New Zealand in the hope of meeting her husband upon his glorious return from the South Pole. "I wasn't a very good husband," Scott wrote, "but I hope I shall be a good memory. Certainly the end is nothing for you to be ashamed of, and I like to think that the boy will have a good start in his parentage of which he may be proud. It isn't easy to write because of the cold—40 below zero and nothing but the shelter of our tents. You must know that quite the worst aspect of this situation is the thought that I shall not see you again. The inevitable must be faced, you urged me to be a leader of the party, and I know you felt it would be dangerous. I have taken my place throughout, haven't I?" The question is rhetorical, but says something about the swirl of uncertainties that always plagued him. His entire polar journey had been conducted as an interrogative, and the answer was now in.

In his most famous missive, his "Message to the Public," Scott concluded by avowing that, "Had we lived, I should have had a tale to tell of the hardihood, endurance and courage of my companions which would have stirred the heart of every Englishman. These rough notes and our dead bodies must tell the tale, but surely, surely, a great rich country like ours will see that those who are dependent on us are properly provided for."

Scott and his companions knew they were just 12.7 miles (20.4 km) away from the plenitude of supplies awaiting them at One Ton Depot, but distance was now an irrelevancy. They shared what little food remained, waiting for the end. Perhaps they managed to gain a little comfort from the opium pills that had been distributed earlier. "I do not think we can hope for any better thing now," Scott wrote in his last diary entry on March 29. "We shall stick it out to the end, but we are getting weaker, of course, and the end cannot be far. It seems a pity, but I do not think I can write more. R. Scott. Last entry: For God's sake look after our people."

It was quiet in the tent now. The winds continued to whip up the fine snow, coating the canvas in a thin white rime.

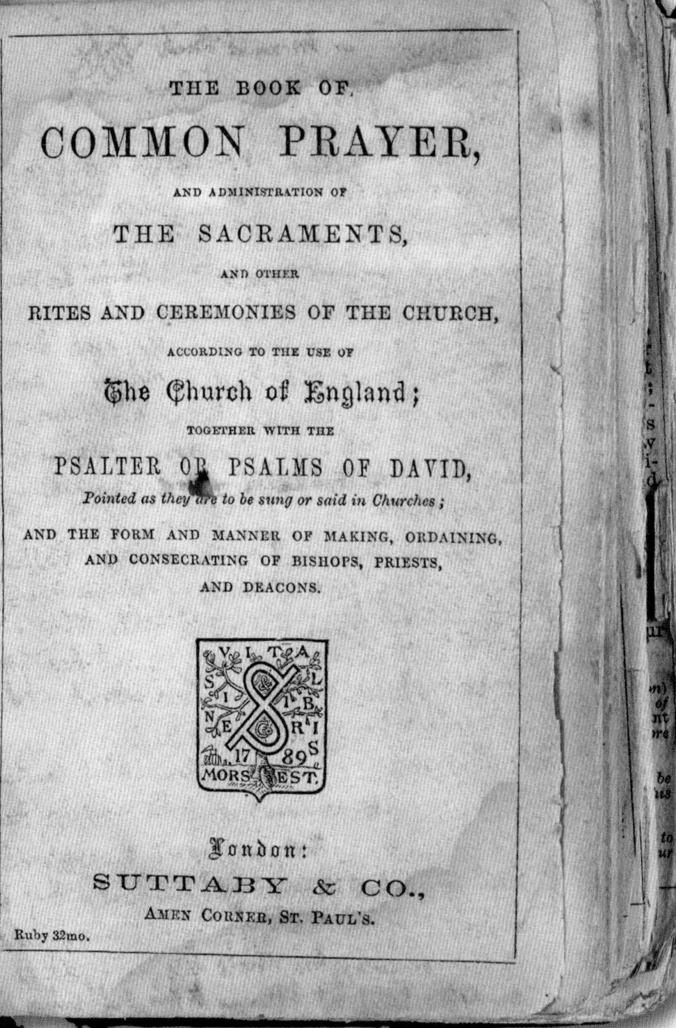
THE BOOK OF

COMMON PRAYER,

AND ADMINISTRATION OF

THE SACRAMENTS,

AND OTHER

RITES AND CEREMONIES OF THE CHURCH,

ACCORDING TO THE USE OF

The Church of England;

TOGETHER WITH THE

PSALTER OR PSALMS OF DAVID,

Pointed as they are to be sung or said in Churches;

AND THE FORM AND MANNER OF MAKING, ORDAINING, AND CONSECRATING OF BISHOPS, PRIESTS, AND DEACONS.

London:

SUTTABY & CO.,

AMEN CORNER, ST. PAUL'S.

Ruby 32mo.

Front flyleaf of Wilson's copy of the *Book of Common Prayer*, found at the last camp. Wilson noted on the pastedown that this volume had been on all his sledging journeys. His copy of the New Testament, which he also took on the southern journey, was left with his body by the search party.

Scott at The End

Perhaps the clearest example of Scott's self-discipline, harshly viewed by some recent authors as merely self-justification, is the manner in which he conducted himself during his last days. We shall never know how the decision to stay on in the tent at the last camp was made. Was it really due to a severe storm? Did Scott ask Wilson and Bowers to stay with him, or did they decide on their own that they could not abandon their leader and friend? We do have evidence, however, that even as he and his companions felt the wind of the wings of death brush against them, Scott never gave up on one thing: his writing. Writing was his way of dealing with the numerous pressures that crowded in on him during his Antarctic expeditions, whether these came from the environment or from people; now writing was his way of fighting fate to the last minute, creating something that would persist after he was enfolded by death. Except for Taff Evans, the others had kept private journals, but they stopped, one by one, during the return over the Barrier—Bowers on January 29 (except for occasional meteorological notes), Oates on February 24, Wilson on February 27. In the last camp during late March they wrote their final letters, Bowers to his mother, Wilson to his wife, Oriana, and a few others to whom he felt a special obligation, such as Oates's mother and his old friend Reginald Smith. But that was it; having transmitted to paper their final, loving thoughts to those closest to them, they could now pass in the hope that these documents would eventually be retrieved and read by those to whom they were addressed. From at least March 16 onward, Scott, by contrast, wrote a whole flock of letters and directives—to the wives and mothers of those dying with him, to those in charge of the financial details of the expedition, to his backers and old friends, to the British public, to Kathleen. And these were not shakily written, sad one-liners; in these last days his writing was as fluid and elegant as anything he had written in better times. Yes, he was writing for posterity, making sure that his voice would be heard regarding why he had failed in one sense but morally succeeded in so many others, and had, in any case, done the best anyone could have under the circumstances. If there was hubris at the end, there was also the strength to insist that his own views be heard by those who would judge him.

Scott's last journal has been on permanent public display since 1914; now in the British Library's new building, it shares gallery space with other major works in the English language.

Birdie Bowers's last journal and the wallet in which he kept it, found at Scott's last camp.

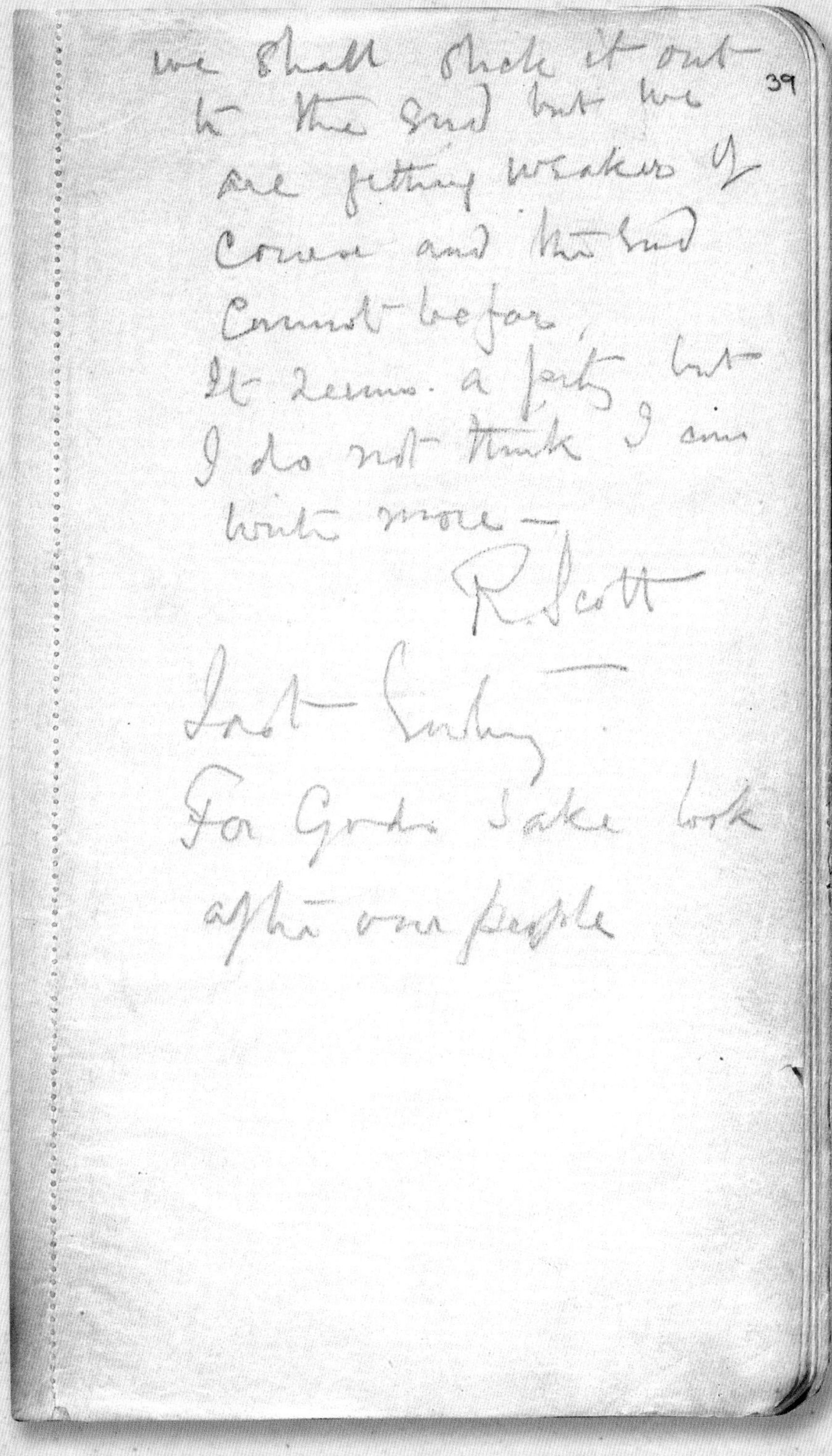

39

We shall stick it out
to the end but we
are getting weaker of
course and the end
cannot be far.
It seems a pity but
I do not think I can
write more —

R. Scott

Last entry —
For God's sake look
after our people

"For God's sake look after our people": Scott's last entry, written sometime in late March 1912 as he, Wilson, and Bowers lay in their tent just 12.7 miles (20.4 km) from One Ton Depot. Scott's last expressed thought was thus not about failure or fault or Englishmen dying nobly, but about how those left behind would fare once he was gone.

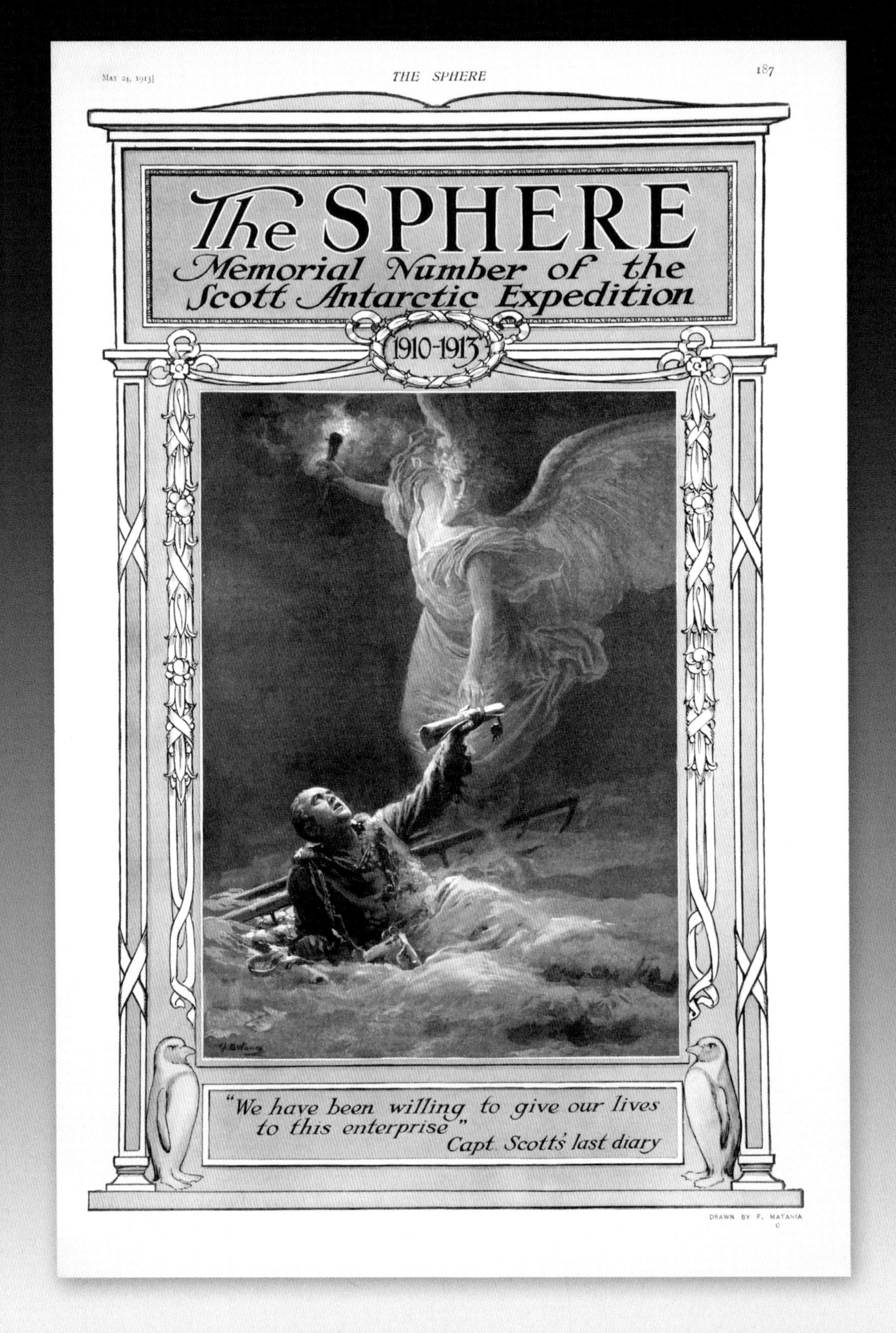

May 24, 1913]
THE SPHERE
187
The SPHERE
Memorial Number of the
Scott Antarctic Expedition
1910-1913
"We have been willing to give our lives
to this enterprise"
Capt. Scott's last diary
DRAWN BY F. MATANIA

CHAPTER 14

November 1912

"It is the tent"

On March 7, 1912, as Scott and his men were nearing their end on the Barrier, Roald Amundsen brought *Fram* into the harbor of Hobart, Tasmania. He was still worried that the British aboard *Terra Nova* somehow might have beaten him back from Antarctica and stolen his thunder by being first to announce a successful journey to the South Pole. Amundsen knew that the race was not won until the world was informed, and when he learned that his rival's ship had not been seen, he set about announcing his news.

The first telegram he sent, in private code to prevent the news from leaking out, was to his brother Leon. Others soon followed, including coded cables to Nansen and King Haakon so that they'd be informed before the general public learned of the Norwegian's coup. Leon Amundsen had arranged for both the London *Daily Chronicle* and the *New York Times* to publish exclusive stories, and for a heady three weeks, as *Terra Nova* sailed for New Zealand, the conquest of the South Pole belonged to Amundsen alone. The *Times* commissioned Ernest Shackleton to write a commentary on Amundsen's feat, and the Irishman observed, "I must say that throughout the journey Amundsen got more out of his dogs than any British expedition could hope to have done. I personally pin my faith on ponies, but the Norwegians, as I have said before, are so used to driving dogs and Amundsen had such vast experience in this method of traveling that he undoubtedly took full advantage of it."

FACING PAGE: *Dulce et decorum est pro patria mori:* The dying Scott passes his journal to an allegorical figure, presumably Knowledge, in the Scott memorial number of *The Sphere,* May 24, 1913.

Despite acceptance of Amundsen's victory, the world seemed to hold its breath, intent on waiting for *Terra Nova* to come back from McMurdo Sound so that the whole story might be known. An article in the March 16, 1912, edition of *Harper's Weekly*, an American magazine, sounded a note of either doubt or impartiality, depending on one's viewpoint:

> Captain Amundsen knows nothing of the whereabouts of Captain Scott [but] England has not abandoned the hope that her flag was planted first at "the pole"—for the exact location of this geographical point cannot, of course, be determined absolutely by means of a sextant and artificial horizon. . . . [T]here would be room for two flags to wave, so far apart as to be invisible each from the other, yet each approximating to the site of the pole.

But when the ship arrived in New Zealand on April 1, she brought no news of victory, or even of accomplishment. All that could be said was that Scott's party had not returned in time to meet *Terra Nova* before she sailed. This was not an immediate cause for alarm, as Scott had said all along that the pole party might be late returning. Privately, the Norwegians were convinced Scott had made it to the South Pole, but they were not so sure he had survived the journey home, given the season.

Meanwhile, with Teddy Evans invalided back to New Zealand, Surgeon Atkinson was now senior officer in command at Cape Evans. A critical day arrived: March 27, 1912, the latest date by which the southern party should have returned, according to Scott's calculations the previous year. Despite poor weather, Atkinson headed south with Patsy Keohane, man-hauling into brutal gales and snowstorms to look for Scott and his companions. On March 30 they reached a point just south of Corner Camp—about 40 miles (65 km) beyond Hut Point, but more than 100 miles (160 km) away from where Scott and his companions were then lying—when Atkinson called it quits. The weather was terrible and the season far advanced; there was little chance of seeing anyone along the way except at depots. After leaving an additional food cache, Atkinson and Keohane turned back for Hut Point, pondering whether it was still possible that Scott and the others were alive. It was the day after Scott's last dated diary entry.

Also worrying Atch Atkinson and the depleted Cape Evans group was the whereabouts of Campbell's northern, ex eastern, party. After leaving news at Cape Evans in January concerning the presence of the Norwegians in the Bay of Whales, *Terra Nova* beat northward and dropped the northern party on Cape Adare on February 20, 1911. The team spent a modestly successful year amassing collections and observing wildlife; on January 3, 1912, the returning *Terra Nova* picked them up and deposited them, with their gear and a six-week supply of provisions, a few days later at a new site near Terra Nova Bay, 200 miles (320 km) north of Cape Evans. This was meant to be a short prospecting trip, with pickup scheduled for no later than mid-February. But sea ice conditions grew increasingly worse and, even though the ship tried time and again to get through to the rendezvous point, it never got closer than 35 miles (56 km). By early March it was clear that Campbell's team could not be reached that year, and *Terra Nova* steamed away to New Zealand.

The stage was now set for an epic survival story. When it became clear to Campbell and his five men that they were not going to be relieved before the austral winter began in earnest, they set about trying to preserve their lives. Over the next nine months, the northern party would suffer privations that would only be exceeded by those who went all the way to the pole—with the difference that all of Campbell's party survived, albeit barely. To escape the worst effects of the winter season they constructed an "igloo"—actually more of an ice cave—on Inexpressible Island, composed themselves as best they could, and waited. "[I]f ever men knew each other inside and out," wrote Raymond Priestley, "it was the six of us who had dwelt together for seven months literally 'in a hole in the snow'."

Atkinson felt responsible for the northern party, even though it was objectively mad to make a rescue attempt in this season. Indeed, he didn't even know if they

Norges Statsbaner.
Form. nr. 407.

TELEGRAM.

Til Fridtjof Nansen
Lysaker

NORSK JERNBANE-TELEGRAF.

Signal fra Hobart

Amundsen

(VI. 1911)

A.S. DIDRIKSEN, CHRISTIANIA.

Amundsen used codes to ensure that only those entrusted with the key would be able to understand the content of his cables. This one, sent March 7, 1912 to Fridtjof Nansen from Hobart, Tasmania, reads (in translation) "Thanks for everything mission accomplished all well." The "mission" was the achievement of the South Pole; Amundsen wanted to let Nansen know before the newspapers did.

Page 10 THE DAILY MIRROR, MAY 21, 1913 Page 15

THE LITTLE TENT OF DEATH WHERE CAPTAIN SCOTT WROTE HIS IMMORTAL MESSAGE TO THE NATION.

The tent of death as the search party found it after clearing away the snow. It was on November [illegible], 1912, eight months after the hand of death had gripped the gallant little band, that the search party sighted it. It was five miles away, but only a yard of it was visible above the snow which was slowly covering it. Another eight months, and all trace of it would have been lost. From the records inside the party learned the terrible truth, for it was here, while waiting for death, that Captain Scott wrote his last immortal message, in which the leader appealed to "our countrymen" on behalf of their dependents.—(Copyright in England. Droits de reproduction en France réservés.)

The text accompanying this image from the May 21, 1913, edition of the *Daily Mirror* runs, "The tent of death as the search party found it after clearing away the snow." This is somewhat misleading because only the inner tent is depicted; the outer tent had evidently already been removed to shroud the bodies before the snow cairn was built over them. In any case, the tent is seemingly completely empty, suggesting that it was probably repositioned away from the bodies for the purpose of this photograph.

needed rescuing: Perhaps *Terra Nova*'s last attempt to relieve them had been successful, and they might be now spending a relaxing winter in New Zealand. Even so, Atkinson, together with Keohane, Williamson, and Wright, set out in mid-April to look for Campbell and his team. Lack of light, the capriciousness of the sea ice, and the fact that they were simply "done up" ended their effort, and they returned to Hut Point on April 23.

At Cape Evans the men spent the winter period obsessively turning one question over and over. Come spring, should they head for the Barrier to try to find Scott and his men, almost surely dead, in order to recover diaries and records—any proof that the southern party had made it to the Pole? Or should they instead look for the northern party, who, they believed, had a better chance of still being alive? But what if they missed either, or both, along the way? What if Campbell and his men were already dead? In midwinter the matter was finally put to a vote, and, with one anonymous abstention, the men in the hut voted unanimously to look for the pole party. Wright wondered in later years whether the abstainer was Cherry.

The decision to look for the probably dead over the possibly quick may seem callous—if not absolutely inexcusable—to modern sensibilities, but the men remaining at Cape Evans felt a crushing responsibility to answer the question everyone would ask: Who won the race? Silas Wright, a member of the search party, wrote in his memoirs years later that the "first object of the expedition had been the Pole. If some record was not found, their success or failure would forever remain uncertain. Was it due not only to the men and their relatives, but also to the expedition, to ascertain their fate if possible?" As for Campbell and his companions, well, it was hoped that they could get themselves out.

In late October of 1912, Atkinson, Wright, Gran, Cherry-Garrard, Keohane, and several others comprising the inaptly named "relief expedition" headed south, proposing to

The Scott Polar Research Institute (SPRI) was organized in 1926 at the University of Cambridge to advance the scientific investigation of polar regions, in commemoration of the heroic efforts of Robert Falcon Scott to make research an integral part of the exploration of high-altitude exploration. SPRI acquired its first independent building (above) in 1934; since then, the much-enlarged institute has become a leading force in many areas of Arctic and Antarctic research. INSET: Lady Scott's bust of Scott in polar costume, positioned above SPRI's main entrance.

track the line of cairns and depots that Scott and his companions would perforce have followed. How far they would have to go was anybody's guess; they were prepared to be gone three months, and even to surmount the Beardmore onto the plateau if they had to. They took dogs and seven Indian Army mules, brought to Cape Evans by the returning *Terra Nova* as part of the base's resupply the previous summer. Nothing was found at Safety Camp, or Corner Camp, or One Ton Depot; the pole party clearly had not made it this far, so where could they be? Then, on November 12, only a few miles south of One Ton Depot, Wright spotted something in the distance and went over to get a closer look. The others, noticing this, came over as well; he turned and said, simply, "It is the tent." Cherry-Garrard, who related the discovery of Scott's last camp in *Worst Journey*, noted that it was not immediately recognizable as such

Frank Debenham was judged to be the best among the amateur photographers at Cape Evans. When Ponting left Antarctica on *Terra Nova* in March 1912, he gave Debenham several cameras and various other pieces of equipment so that the photographic record of the expedition could be continued. This panoramic shot (above) is entitled "Start of the search party from Cape Evans"—the party that was sent out in late October 1912 to look for the bodies of Scott and comrades. The draft animals are Indian Army mules, not ponies; they were brought to Cape Evans by *Terra Nova* on its first return visit in early 1912.

Trail gear from the *Terra Nova* expedition: Nansen cooker, bamboos and ski pole, inner tent, pair of skis marked with Scott's initials, and Cherry-Garrard's sledge. Cherry used this sledge on the trip to One Ton Depot in early March 1912 to see if he could intercept Scott en route to McMurdo Sound; he also used it on the relief party journey that found the last camp in November 1912. "The most useful type of sledge in man-hauling for a four-man unit is the 12-foot sledge with hickory runners of Nansen type" like this one (Lyons 1924: 37).

Oates's reindeer sleeping bag. The bag was entered by moving aside the large flap. The small flap, turned to one side, has clearly been cut away from the rest of the skin. It has been suggested that someone, perhaps Wilson, made the small flap with his knife so that Oates could more easily get his horribly swollen, frostbitten foot into and out of his bag. It has also been suggested that it was one of Oates's finnesko, not the bag, that was cut open for this purpose. Unfortunately there is no allusion in any of the diaries to either action (Scott alone was keeping a diary at the time of Oates's decline).

because snow had drifted over the tent to such an extent that it looked like a cairn. Wright recalled that he ordered that the tent "should not be touched until Atkinson and the dog party came up. I think this was about an hour later." A few swipes of the hand revealed cloth and bamboo, and there was no remaining doubt. "There was nothing to do but dig the tent out," Cherry wrote. The tent, consisting of inner and outer components, was well tethered and everything was properly stowed inside. The three men were in their sleeping bags, Scott flanked by Bowers and Wilson. Cherry thought that The Owner had died last. In his report Atkinson noted that, after the tent was opened, "[e]ach man of the Expedition recognized the bodies," meaning, apparently, that because of the condition of the dead it was not immediately evident who was who, and their identities had to be confirmed by consensus. (Indeed, he and Cherry first thought that the body in the middle was Taff Evans', not Scott's.)

As detailed in essentially similar descriptions of the day's events by several of the relief party's members in later years, Atkinson retreated to the search party tent to read Scott's diary. As requested by Scott in a note left for those who would eventually find their bodies, Atkinson read pertinent entries to the men assembled around him. Following prayers from Corinthians, the relief party buried Scott, Wilson, and Bowers in their sleeping bags, draping them with the fabric of the outer tent in which they took their last breaths. Crossed skis were placed over the cairn; on a separate bamboo they left an inscription, signed by all members of the relief party, which stated that "[i]nclement weather and lack of fuel was the cause of their death."

The relief party gathered up the pole party's belongings, instruments, letters, and diaries, as well as the rock samples, flags, and other equipment that had been removed from the tent, and loaded them on sledges. Then they pushed south to look for the body of Titus Oates. His sleeping bag was found some miles away, where it had been left by Scott,

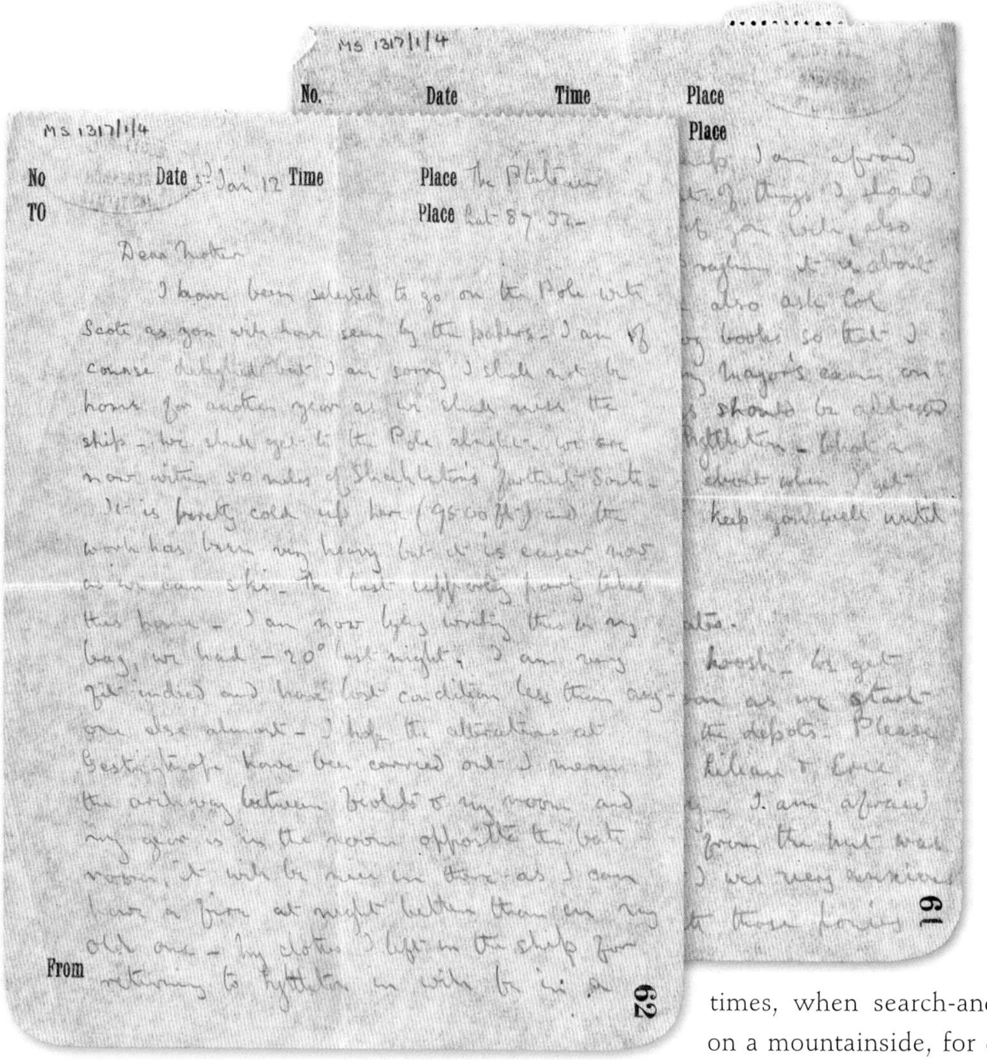
MS 1317/1/4

No Date 3rd Jan 12 Time Place The Plateau

TO Place Lat. 87 32

Dear Mother

I have been selected to go on the Pole with Scott as you will have seen by the papers. I am of course delighted but I am sorry I shall not be home for another year as we shall miss the ship. We shall get to the Pole alright. We are now within 50 miles of Shackleton's furthest South. It is pretty cold up here (9500 ft) and the work has been very heavy but it is easier now as we can ski. The last supporting party takes this home. I am now lying writing this in my bag, we had −20° last night. I am very fit indeed and have lost condition less than anyone else almost. I hope the alterations at Gestingthorpe have been carried out I mean the archway between Bobbie's & my room and my gun is in the room opposite the bath room, it will be nice in there as I can have a fire at night better than in my old one. My clothes I left in the ship for returning to Lyttelton in will be in a

From

62

Oates's last letter to his mother was written on January 3 and 4, 1912, just as the second supporting party, led by Teddy Evans, was about to depart for the north. The letter reads in part: "Dear Mother, I have been selected to go on the Pole [journey] with Scott. . . . I am of course delighted but I am sorry I shall not be home for another year as we shall miss the ship. We shall get to the Pole alright. We are now within 50 miles of Shackleton's furthest south. . . . I am very fit indeed and have lost condition almost less than anyone else. . . . I am afraid the letter I wrote to you from the hut was full of grumbles [especially about Scott] but I was very anxious about starting off with those ponies." Less than two and a half months later Oates would be dead.

but his body could not be located. The relief party erected another cross near the spot where Oates left the tent to meet his death.

The leaving behind of the bodies of Scott and his men raises some nagging questions. In our times, when search-and-rescue teams encounter bodies on a mountainside, for example, unless there are unusual circumstances every effort is expended to bring the dead back home. There are many reasons for this, but the simplest is that, from a hundred different perspectives, it is considered proper to do so. In the heroic age it would have been no different. In 1922 Sir Ernest Shackleton's corpse was taken all the way to Montevideo after he died aboard his last vessel, *Quest,* as it was standing off South Georgia. And when Lady Shackleton said, no, his remains ought not to be brought back to England, but instead buried at the place of his greatest accomplishment, his body was taken back to South Georgia and interred in the little cemetery above Grytviken. (His gravesite, later adorned with a magnificent sculptural headstone, is now a place of pilgrimage and contemplation.)

The decision to leave the bodies of the last members of the pole party where they died cannot have been made from any considerations of weight or difficulty in transport. The relief party was only 150 miles (240 km) from Cape Evans, with provisions for three months, and they had mules for heavy hauling. It has, however, been suggested that the bodies were not removed because the men were covered with the hideous sores and other stigmata of advanced scurvy—the evidence of which might be counted another mark against Scott's leadership if the dead were returned. That seems unlikely on several grounds, including the fact that Dr Wilson, who assiduously nursed his companions all the way along, made no mention of symptoms of scurvy in his detailed notes on the men's condition up to the end of February. Atkinson also stated that he saw no sign of scurvy, although how he could have made a truly satisfactory examination of their frozen, ravaged bodies is difficult to imagine. This is where the matter has to be left. Atkinson—who was in command and the only one who could have made the decision to leave the bodies—put only one sentence into his otherwise dry official report that suggests a reason: "alone in their greatness they will lie without change or bodily decay, with the most fitting tomb in the world above them."

The relief party headed back to Hut Point, reeling with grief and uncertainty about what to do next. Along the way, the topic of the northern party came up once again; if they couldn't have saved Scott, could they at least rescue Campbell and his men? Cherry recorded on November 17 that "I think we are all going crazy together. . . . The latest scheme is to try and find a way over the plateau to Evans Cove [where the northern party had been dropped], trying to strike the top of a glacier and go down with it." The plan was dangerous, if not suicidal, but their feelings of helplessness to prevent tragedy had indeed made them crazy, and they were willing to consider anything to end their confusion and sorrow. Fortunately, when they pulled into Hut Point on November 25, they found that they would not have to undertake another trip over the ice; Campbell and his men were safe, all alive (although some not well in mind and body), having arrived at Cape Evans by their own efforts on November 6, 1912.

The expedition was nearly at an end. Priestley, Gran, and others spent some time on Mt. Erebus, undertaking geological studies and making a successful ascent to the crater rim. Wright continued with his glaciological studies and took care of the meteorological instruments. Cherry collected a good series of embryos of the Adelie penguin, completing work that he had started with Wilson. It was now mid-January of 1913, high summer, but still no ship had arrived. The men began to prepare for another winter. Then, on January 18, *Terra Nova* was seen entering the sound. Cherry recollected that he heard the standard greeting as the ship drew near:

The northern party on the eve of their return to Cape Evans (l to r): George Abbott, Victor Campbell, Harry Dickason, Raymond Priestley, Murray Levick, and Frank Browning. Priestley entitled this photo, "After nine months without a wash or change of clothes" (Priestley, 1914: facing 340). Campbell and his men had spent the winter of 1912 in difficult circumstances because *Terra Nova* was unable to get through the sea ice off South Victoria Land to relieve them. What had been intended as a few weeks' camp ended up lasting from March to November. With inadequate gear and few provisions, they survived in a cave they had dug into the ice on Inexpressible Island, about 200 miles (320 km) north of Cape Evans. At the beginning of the 1912 summer they managed to walk back to Cape Evans unaided, to the great relief of Atkinson, who thought they might have perished in the same manner as Scott and his men.

"'Are you all well,' through a megaphone from the bridge.

'The Polar Party died on their return from the Pole; we have their records.' A pause and then a boat."

After working nonstop for twenty-eight hours loading the ship, the remnants of the British Antarctic Expedition assembled themselves, ready for departure. Cherry wrote in his diary, "I leave Cape Evans with no regret: I never want to see the place again. The pleasant memories are all swallowed up in the bad ones." On January 20, a nine-foot-tall wooden cross had been raised on Observation Hill, a local prominence on Hut Point Peninsula, and dedicated to the dead of the pole party. The inscription cut into the jarrah-wood cross included the last line of Tennyson's *Ulysses*: "To strive, to seek, to find, and not to yield."

Three weeks later, at 2:30 A.M. on February 10, 1913, *Terra Nova* arrived at the port of Oamaru, New Zealand. The ship stood out from land so that no prying newspaper men would get the story before they were ready to release it. Atkinson went ashore by launch to send the press telegram that would announce the tragic news to the public. Traveling up the coast, on February 12 *Terra Nova* entered its old provisioning port, Lyttelton. The men were astounded at what they saw: Flags were at halfmast, and a pall cast over the town. "We landed to find the Empire—almost the civilized world—in mourning," Cherry wrote in some amazement.

Roald Amundsen was lecturing in Madison, Wisconsin, when he learned of Scott's fate. The following day in Chicago, a journalist described Amundsen's emotional reaction to the news. "Horrible, horrible!" a genuinely distraught Amundsen exclaimed. "And to think that while these brave men were dying . . . in the waste of ice, I was lecturing in warmth and comfort in Australia."

Amundsen, who had held the stage for nearly a year as the victor in the race to the South Pole, began to experience a seismic shift in public opinion. With some success he had beaten back the attitude, popular in Britain, that he was simply lucky to have made it to the South Pole before Scott. Over the next few months, the mass media devoured the letters and diary entries written during Scott's last days, and hefty special numbers of illustrated magazines rolled out the story of the pole party in obsessive detail. Amundsen, the iron man who had planned for everything, had not imagined that Scott would eclipse him by dying in Antarctica in a way that would make the gods weep. Had Scott and his companions not conducted themselves like soldiers in a frightful, mortal battle, never giving way and taking tender care of their wounded until the end? Had the men of the pole party not revealed, in their persons and by their acts, that the doughty qualities that had fashioned the Empire still existed in the etiolated, self-doubting Britain of 1913? Had Scott not dragged photographic evidence as well as Amundsen's letter to the King of Norway across the Barrier ice to *prove* that the Norwegian had beaten him to the Pole?

Amundsen had to wonder if Scott wasn't the true hero after all. "It's quite a coup: he wins at the last," recites Sverre Anker Ousdal, cast in the role of Amundsen in Central Independent Television's 1985 dramatization of Huntford's book, *Last Place on Earth*; "he wins."

When the death of Scott and his companions was announced in early February of 1913, newspapers and illustrated magazines—the mass media of the day—produced special numbers and thick, detailed spreads on the British Antarctic Expedition and the tragedy of the last camp. For ease of public comprehension, as well as to provide opportunity for editors' patriotic asides, The Expedition was reduced to The Race—wrapped in the Union Jack and delivered up as a *roman* of rivalry and deliverance for modern times. Some of the newspaper art is particularly telling in this regard. In this illustration from *The Sphere*, Scott and his party stand resolute in the lighted foreground, looking boldly into the distance; Amundsen's party is relegated to the shaded margin, stooped and glowering in their heavy beards.

Un numero arretrato centesimi 70
PER GLI ABBONAMENTI indirizzare vaglia alla Amministrazione in TORINO, via IV Marzo, 12.
ITALIA e COLONIE: Anno L. 18; Semestre L. 9,50
:: ESTERO: Anno L. 36 - Semestre L. 19 ::

ILLUSTRAZIONE DEL POPOLO

Sedici pagine - Centesimi 35
PER GLI ANNUNCI a pagamento rivolgersi alla *Unione Pubblicità Italiana*, via Santa Teresa, 2, TORINO, ed alle sue Succursali. - Tariffa: L. 10 il mm. di colonna; una pagina intiera L. 10.000.

Koald Amundsen, coi suoi audaci compagni, è ritornato nella capitale della Norvegia a bordo dell'apparecchio « Dornier Wal 25 », reduce dal volo polare. Le terrazze e i tetti di Oslo erano gremiti di cittadini che diedero all'ardito esploratore il saluto della patria *(Disegno di Alfredo Ortelli)*.

CHAPTER 15

1913–1928

Amundsen Agonistes

Amundsen outlived Scott by sixteen years, dying a month before his fifty-sixth birthday, on or about June 18, 1928, somewhere between the Norwegian mainland and Bear Island. On that date he was flying to Svalbard to help in efforts to rescue the crew of the downed airship *Italia*. His plane, not designed for Arctic conditions, evidently came down hard, either crashing or capsizing after landing; it seemed very heavily laden to those who watched it take off from Tromsø, which might have been a contributing factor. There was no reason for Amundsen to risk his life in this way—two years earlier he had announced his retirement from active exploration—and certainly he had no reason to look for a man whom he detested, *Italia*'s captain Umberto Nobile. But he did it anyway, for his own reasons, and as a result may be said to have died a real hero—and not just as the man who made a career of going to the coldest, most isolated places on earth.

Roald Amundsen in 1928.

As documented by his biographer Tor Bomann-Larsen, Amundsen conducted much of his emotional life in secret; it was not an easy life, for him or anyone around him. Those closest, by relationship or interest, were alternately embraced or pushed away, depending on whether they had fulfilled expectations or were in any way found to

FACING PAGE: The safe return of all members of Amundsen's aerial North Pole expedition in 1925 received worldwide attention. The cover of this Italian periodical depicts his triumphant flight over Oslo on July 5. However, here his plane, a Dornier Wal, has gained cabin windows and a racing stripe that it lacked in reality.

be deficient, mutinous, or of an independent frame of mind. He never married, but engaged in serial relationships with women who were. He had no acknowledged children of his own, but in Siberia during the *Maud* expedition he adopted one girl and "borrowed" another to be the child's companion, in an "experiment" to show that native people could benefit from education just as much as whites could. Some years later, during a period of financial turmoil, he returned the companion, Camilla, to her parents, and sent his adopted daughter, Kakonita, to live with the Wistings for a while before she was sent back to Siberia. He never saw either of them again, and, other than incidental contact with Camilla's father, there is no evidence that he maintained a relationship or helped them in any way. The "experiment" was all very irregular and peculiar, but very much Amundsen: He wanted what he wanted, until he didn't anymore.

One might think that, having achieved the South Pole, Amundsen deserved a period of rest and reflection in which he could ponder his future and devote himself to the necessary tasks of book-writing and lecture-giving to secure money for future enterprises. In fact he did exactly that, writing much of his book *Sydpolen* (appearing in English translation as *The South Pole*), destined to be a best-seller, while returning to Europe. But he worked under the weight of an unfulfilled obligation to Nansen and his financial backers, which included the government of Norway. The obligation was to undertake the *real* "Third *Fram* Expedition," the promised voyage of Arctic exploration and scientific research that he had abandoned in 1910 to go south. He himself had portrayed the race to the South Pole as merely an "extension of the original plan of the expedition," a diversion for the purpose of raising both public interest and cash. Having now completed the diversion, to preserve honor he had to go forward—immediately, some of his contemporaries thought—with the long-delayed trip to the north. The Third *Fram* Expedition was consciously designed as a successor to Nansen's original *Fram* experiment of 1893–96, in which the scientist-explorer demonstrated that there was a clockwise drift of the Arctic sea ice. Amundsen intended to start at a position different from Nansen's in order to ensure that his ship would drift over the North Pole—something Nansen had wanted to do, but in the end could not.

After many other diversions, including extensive lecture tours, Amundsen was finally ready to go to the Arctic in July of 1914, but the guns of August ended this phase of the expedition before it even started. Although the First World War dampened polar exploration, it was a financial boon to many in Norway, including Amundsen. As a neutral country, Norway was in a position to use its large shipping capacity to carry goods to and from ports in the war zone. This arrangement ended in much tragedy in 1917, when Germany resumed unrestricted war at sea, but by that time the ship-owning Amundsen brothers had made a great deal of money.

Amundsen invested his profits in attempting to build what he hoped would be the ideal craft for high-latitude exploration, an updated version of *Fram*. *Maud*—named after the Queen of Norway—was finally launched in 1918, after eating through most of Amundsen's recently acquired fortune. The expedition would formally last until 1925—but without Amundsen, who left the ship for good in 1922. In part he left because he realized he was accomplishing nothing: The vessel had mostly been locked in Siberian ice since entering the Northeast Passage, and the hoped-for transit of the North Pole was not going to happen. But the central reason that he left was because he was in hot pursuit of a new idea: He was going to fly across the North Pole from Wainwright, Alaska, to West Spitsbergen, the largest of the islands comprising Svalbard. In June, 1914, he had acquired the first civilian pilot's license to be granted in Norway, but realized that the aircraft of the time were not up to a polar crossing. In fact, they still weren't in 1923, when he made his attempt anyway. His plane, a Junkers JL-6, overturned on a test run near Nome, Alaska, and ended up a total wreck. Amundsen was not in the aircraft at the time, which was providential; he wanted to try again, but a new reality had taken over. His creditors were

Maud, which Amundsen built with his own money, was intended as a successor to *Fram*, and had a similarly rounded hull for withstanding pressure ice. Here it is seen in the ice at Maudhaven, near Cape Chelyuskin on the north end of the Taimyr Peninsula. *Maud* finally escaped the ice and completed the transit of the Northeast Passage (only the second vessel to do so), but her end was an unhappy one: In 1925, with Amundsen bankrupt, *Maud* was impounded and sold.

legion and unsympathetic. His financial health, always precarious, was now in a state of total collapse. Within a year he was bankrupt.

The early 1920s were dark days for Roald Amundsen. He had a catastrophic falling-out with his brother Leon, who had run his affairs for years and did all the things that Amundsen couldn't, or wouldn't, do for himself. Hereafter Amundsen was like a man without a compass in a polar snowstorm. He made a number of bad financial and personal decisions, often because of poor advice from those who sought to profit from his notoriety. He was out of money, out of favor, and his career as an explorer seemed over. "I was closer to giving up in desperation than at any other time in my 53-year-old life."

Then a remarkable thing happened. In late 1924 he gained a new supporter, an American from a wealthy background, who was willing to put up the money so Amundsen could continue to explore—as long as he could join in. Lincoln Ellsworth and Roald Amundsen were opposites in most ways, but converged in one crucial respect: All that mattered was to be involved in great things. Ellsworth was willing to commit his fortune—actually, his father's fortune—and remain in the background, leaving ample room for Amundsen's considerable ego to perform as expedition leader. Ellsworth went on, after Amundsen's death, to conduct further explorations in the Antarctic during the 1930s. He was long associated with the American Museum of Natural History as a trustee and benefactor. The museum's archives contain a large collection of objects connected with his travels, including several items illustrated in this book that Amundsen gave to him as mementos.

The expedition they planned in concert with the Norwegian Aeronautical Association was based on using two Dornier "Wal" (Whale) floatplanes, which would take off from King's Bay, West Spitsbergen, circle the pole, and return. The planes were technical marvels of the day. Constructed of duralumin, and thus light but strong, they were powered by dual Rolls-Royce engines in a tractor-pusher configuration (one engine mounted directly behind the other). The pilots were Hjalmar Riiser-Larsen, who was destined later on to have a substantial career of his own as an aerial Antarctic explorer, and Leif Dietrichson, who would have a different destiny, bound up with Amundsen's at the very end. The planes, named simply *N24* and *N25* after their production numbers, took off on May 21, 1925. Amundsen acted as navigator for *N25*; Ellsworth, after a crash course given by the pilots, was made navigator of *N24*.

After eight hours in the air, they thought that their estimated speed should have put them at or near the North Pole. The radioless planes landed close together but initially out of each other's sight. Amundsen determined their position to be 87°43', far short of their goal. The two crews eventually made contact over the ice, and now

King's Bay, May 1925: A small army of men helps to reposition Amundsen's Dornier Wal *N25* by pushing on its tailpiece. The plane's design featured two axially mounted motors, producing a push-pull effect.

had to establish what courses were open to them. There were only two choices: walk out, across 460 miles (750 km) of sea ice to Cape Columbia in eastern Greenland, where a supply depot for the *Maud* expedition had been laid down some years earlier; or fly out, all six men traveling on the remaining Dornier, *N25* (*N24* had been damaged on landing). Realistically, the first option was certain death; it was summer, and the floes were breaking up and in motion. Trying to fly out carried substantial risks, but it was not hopeless. *N25* was in good shape, and one of the men on board, Karl Feucht, was a Dornier mechanic. The most serious problem they faced was lack of a suitable runway. There was too much ice to attempt a takeoff from the water, but, after several unsuccessful starts, they were eventually able to move *N25* onto a large, long floe that could be adapted to the purpose—given time and adequate tools. They had neither. Amundsen mapped out their strategy: Beginning on 9 June, on low rations of 10.5 ounces (300 g) of food per man per day, they would use picks, ski poles, wooden shovels, and even their own feet as compactors to fashion a 1,300-foot (400 m) runway. And they had to be finished by June 15, just a week away, before the

N25 down on the ice at 87°43'S, at the start of a three-week survival adventure that almost cost Amundsen and his companions their lives. Here the men are seen fashioning the runway that would permit their plane to take off.

food ran out. Working up to the last minute, they got into the craft, the men arranged along the fuselage floor, Riiser-Larsen at the controls. There was no provision for disaster—all superfluous equipment, such as tents, had been left behind. Describing the events of this day, Amundsen wrote that "[w]e saw nothing where we sat, could only feel the speed by the movements. Suddenly it started to judder, as though it wanted to leave the ground. At last it gave a final jerk and we felt we were airborne. The feeling of release was indescribable."

The plane touched down on clear water near Nordaustlandet, the large island forming the northeast corner of Svalbard. A passing whaler picked them up and carried them over to King's Bay, and to pandemonium. Amundsen and his men had been judged lost and perhaps already dead, and rescue/retrieval efforts were underway. But now it was clear that all had been saved, and by their own efforts. It was Amundsen's best, his Shackleton, moment. Flying in the now-famous *N25* to Oslo, he returned an acknowledged hero, and for the moment all was forgiven. The resulting book—in English, *Our Polar Flight*—on the aerial attempt on the North Pole and the ensuing struggle to get

The heroes return (l to r): Oscar Omdal, Hjalmur Riiser-Larsen, Amundsen, Leif Dietrichson, Karl Feucht, and Lincoln Ellsworth pose after flying *N25* from their forced camp on the sea ice back to Svalbard, June 15, 1925.

everyone back safely, was released in October; ten thousand copies were sold in the first hours of the first day of sale.

One may think that it is stories of tragedy that attract people to the history of polar exploration. It is not, or it is not merely so; it is the stories of *overcoming* looming tragedy that people remember best. The race for the South Pole had a tragic aspect, but obviously not for Amundsen. The fact that he won the prize, handily, with rather meager resources, and without losing men along the way, was given the respect it deserved among professional explorers, but his story lacked emotional resonance when stacked against Scott's. In effect, there was no dreadful misfortune that he had to overcome. Amundsen simply worked by the numbers to get to the South Pole and

The first undisputed attainment of the North Pole occurred when the semidirigible *Norge* passed over it while flying from Svalbard to Alaska, May 11–14, 1926, carrying Amundsen, Wisting, Ellsworth, Nobile, and a team of airshipmen. The entire trip took only seventy-two hours.

back; no muss, no fuss, no heroics. By contrast, the almost miraculous return of the Dornier expedition was every bit as emotionally fraught as Shackleton's voyage from Elephant Island to South Georgia, and the public devoured the story.

His new-found fame aside, Amundsen still needed to attain the North Pole, to get back on the trajectory of accomplishment that provided him with the life and attention he craved. Dornier offered to build a new, larger plane for that purpose, but he had his eye on a different method of travel, the airship. In the 1920s, lighter-than-air equipment was enjoying its heyday: Dirigibles could go much farther—and considerably more safely, judging from contemporary accident records—than airplanes of the day. A little over a month after Amundsen's return from the ice, he was already making plans to use an Italian-built semidirigible to cross the pole from Svalbard and perhaps travel on to Alaska. In this endeavor, in addition to Ellsworth and his money, he would have a new, enthusiastic backer who was not interested in polar discovery as such, but was keen on projects that offered advantageous publicity for his budding New Roman Empire. His name was Benito Mussolini.

Then a shock: The American explorer Richard Byrd sailed into King's Bay with a Fokker monoplane on board and a scarcely concealed ambition to be the first to fly over the North Pole—which he accomplished (or said he did) on May 9. In a way this incident was a reprise of the race for the South Pole, with Amundsen now in the role of the also-ran. A further irony is that Amundsen said he didn't mind that Byrd had claimed the prize, because his goal was different, to explore unknown parts of the Arctic Ocean—in effect, to do science.

The airship, rechristened *Norge,* finally started poleward on May 11, 1926 amid much internal dissent among expedition members. In addition to Amundsen and his men, including Ellsworth and Riiser-Larsen, it had been agreed that there would be a large complement of Italian airshipmen who would actually run things. In Amundsen's eyes, the *Norge*'s designer, Colonel Umberto Nobile, was simply another hired hand who was brought along because of his specialist knowledge—and because the Italian government required it. In Nobile's eyes, he had a status that was on par with Amundsen's, and he was therefore entitled to play a leading role in the conduct of the expedition. Given the personalities involved, flashpoint was reached early, and often. The expedition was itself "one huge balloon, pumped up by American dollars, unashamed Norwegian nationalism and ready-to-burst fascist ambitions."

This expedition, destined to be Amundsen's last professional venture, was anticlimactic in every way and almost without incident. There was literally nothing for the great explorer to do. In the gondola he was placed in a chair next to a side window, so that he could survey what passed beneath with binoculars. He hoped to see land, but of course there wasn't any. When 90°N was reached, the engines were muted, Norwegian, American, and Italian flags were dropped, fine words said, and that was the end of it: job done. Of all of his old companions from the South Pole expedition, only Oscar Wisting was with him on the airship; they shook hands, the only two humans to have been at (or over) both poles.

Because to this point there had been no operational difficulties with *Norge,* the decision was made to continue as planned over the Arctic Ocean in the direction of Alaska, to fill in the last remaining blank spots on the map, just in case there was something over there that needed discovering. Nothing was seen except water and ice. The airship came in over the northern Alaskan coast in windy conditions, and to avoid risk, made a landing at Teller, a village near Nome, on May 14, 1926. The entire trip over the polar sea had taken seventy-two hours.

The only moments of drama came when *Norge* lost wireless contact with its West Spitsbergen base a few hours after the pole was reached. Thus nothing was heard of the airship until the news of its arrival was spread from Nome on May 15. In the day preceding there had been much speculation about the fate of the expedition. Had disaster struck again? When the happy ending was announced, newspapers in Norway and Italy acclaimed the indisputable success of their countrymen in revealing the last of the great geographical unknowns. It was a day to submerge, or rather integrate, nationalistic feelings: Along with the Italian flag, the American and Norwegian flags flew outside Mussolini's window in Rome. But good relations were shattered almost immediately when it became clear that the team was riven by bickering and mutually hostile feelings, arising as much from Amundsen's behavior as Nobile's. As far as the Italian colonel was concerned, he was a co-leader who deserved the same respect and press attention that Amundsen and Ellsworth were enjoying. As far as Amundsen was concerned, Nobile was merely a "salaried airship commander on a Norwegian ship, which belongs to an American and myself." Nobile reacted angrily and held his own press conferences. And so it went, month after month, as expedition

Aeronauts of the North Pole (l to r): front row, Amundsen, Ellsworth, and Nobile; standing, Riiser-Larsen (far left) and Oscar Wisting (fourth from left, only partly visible), the only man other than Amundsen who had been to both poles. The other individuals are members of the Italian-Norwegian airship crew.

members were conveyed separately across the continent from Seattle to New York, and thence to their respective homelands in Europe. Along the way they were met with enthusiastic crowds, in front of whom they blatantly played their nationalistic cards. In all it was a rather sordid display of triumphalism, since neither group could have done without the other.

At the conclusion of the expedition, Amundsen announced that he was not going exploring again. Although he was hardly aged, it was time. He had passed about as much of his life in the twentieth century as he had in the nineteenth. In parallel with the succession of centuries, he started with dogs and ended with airplanes and airships, a metaphor for technological progress in methods of travel. However, his style of polar exploration, which was all about making new geographical discoveries and then moving on to the next big thing, was already anachronistic. In the future, polar expeditions would be run increasingly by governments rather than individual operators, and would be concerned with an ever-widening array of scientific inquiries, not simply getting to a place on—or off—the map.

In retirement Amundsen's personality took on a disturbing new aspect. Nansen thought he had become mentally unstable. In late 1927 he published his memoirs under the title *My Life as an Explorer*, a slim volume that was less concerned with what made him what he was than with settling accounts. He flailed out, almost indiscriminately, against Nobile, his brother Leon, fellow Arctic explorer Vilhjalmur Stefansson, the Norwegian Aeronautical Association, his old companions from *Fram* days, Lord Curzon and the Royal Geographical Society, and many others, cataloging their perceived insults, slights, and misrepresentations. To his admirers in Norway and abroad, it was staggering that this great man could harbor so vast an array of petty, obsessive grievances and, worse, disgorge them all at once in what should have been the literary capstone of his career. In short, as Bomann-Larsen has noted, *My Life* was "more of a suicide bid than an autobiography."

In the months following, his actions became increasingly erratic. Without explanation he canceled a lecture tour in America, less than a month into a scheduled five-month commitment. He fired old retainers and sparked a demeaning fight with the Royal Geographical Society over a silly incident which may or may not have occurred years before. Nansen, asked his opinion, could only state that this sort of thing had happened to other polar explorers, possibly because the enormous physical suffering they experienced affected not only their bodies but also, eventually, their minds. In Amundsen's case there was nothing that could be done, he said; one could only hope that people would see that he was now to be pitied rather than censured.

IL MATTINO ILLUSTRATO

Anno V. - NAPOLI - N. 21
21 - 28 Maggio 1928 (Anno VI)
Prezzo Cent. 40
SI PUBBLICA OGNI SETTIMANA

A mezzogiorno del 6 maggio, marinai e alpini italiani, a bordo della "Città di Milano" bloccata dai ghiacci dello Spitzbergen avvistano entusiasti il dirigibile "Italia" col gen. Nobile, che giunge alla King's bay, penultima tappa verso il Polo

(Disegno di F. De Nicola)

Flag-waving sailors aboard the Italian support ship *Città del Milano* cheer Nobile's airship *Italia* as it arrives in King's Bay on May 6, 1928, for its polar flight later that month. In actuality, despite the fact that Nobile requested the crew's help to land their huge craft, the ship's captain said his men could not be spared from their regular duties!

And so it might have continued to the end of Amundsen's days, his reputation and achievements turning to bitter ashes, had fate not intervened once more. Nobile, with Mussolini's somewhat muted agreement, had mounted a new dirigible expedition to continue the aerial exploration of the Arctic Ocean, once more using West Spitsbergen as a base. On May 25, 1928, radio contact with his airship, *Italia*, was lost. Amundsen was called in for his views on what might be done, and with others he suggested that Norway begin a search-and-rescue mission if that seemed the proper course. Mussolini declined; only Italians could save other Italians. Yet, strangely, the Italian government did nothing except manufacture excuses for their inaction. But since nobody knew where the airship might be stranded, talk of an all-Italian rescue effort was a bit premature in any case.

Then on June 7, weak radio signals were received from surviving members of the airship's crew; they had gone down on the ice north of Svalbard, and they were now trying to survive on the floes until they could be located and brought back. With the fascists persistently inert, rescuing Nobile now became an international free-for-all, with dozens of ships and planes converging on King's Bay to take part in the adventure of the year. Amundsen had been sidelined, probably because he was viewed as a liability rather than an asset, but now he found a new patron in the form of a wealthy Frenchman who bought him a plane, a Latham 47 equipped with floats. This aircraft was not the best choice for the task because it could handle neither ice nor rough water, but it was what was available, and Amundsen took it. He and a crew of five, including three French airmen and one of the pilots from the Dornier Wal expedition, Leif Dietrichson, set off from Tromsø on June 18, 1928, bound for King's Bay. Radio contact was lost, permanently, at 6:45 P.M. Roald Amundsen, who had come back from beyond time and again, had passed into the irremeable mists cloaking the Norwegian Sea.

It is uncertain what happened. Several search and rescue efforts were mounted (one of which was led by Tryggve Gran, by then a major in the Royal Norwegian Air Force), but they saw nothing. Three months later, a float clearly belonging to the Latham was found off Tromsø; later, a fuel tank from the plane was also recovered. The prevailing speculation is that the plane was forced down on water in bad weather and was damaged. Whether death came to Amundsen and his crew immediately, or after some attempt to save themselves, is impossible to say. In late 2009, a Royal Norwegian Navy expedition used a robot submersible to see if any wreckage could be located on the sea floor. Although the expedition was unsuccessful, it was a fitting thing to do in memory of Amundsen, as the centenary of the Race to The End approaches.

Norway had lost its polar hero, who had once fallen from grace but now took his place among the immortals. Later that year, the Norwegian government declared December 14, 1928, as South Pole Day, in memory of Amundsen, the Arctic explorer who went the distance, to glory. An outpouring of affection and remembrance erupted throughout the land for this hard, remote man who had given his young country so much to be proud of. Nansen's eulogy was simple: "[W]hen his work was done he returned to the icy wilds, where his life's work lay. He found an unknown grave under the clear sky in the world of ice."

This is the last known photograph of Roald Engebreth Gravning Amundsen, standing in front of the engine cowling of his Latham 47. The plane disappeared shortly after takeoff on June 18, 1928, taking him and five others to their deaths somewhere between Norway and Svalbard.

CHAPTER 16

After The End

Apsley Cherry-Garrard, the anguished participant-observer who wrote his generation's definitive testament concerning Scott's last expedition and the heroic age, spent much of his later life trying to come to terms with his experiences in Antarctica. In *The Worst Journey in the World,* Cherry attempted to provide an honest account of the British expedition and the heroism and sacrifice that he witnessed. While there is no question that some of the incidents he lived through—such as the winter journey to collect emperor penguin eggs—were exceedingly traumatic and dangerous, his biographer Sara Wheeler shows that the years he spent on the *Terra Nova* expedition were the most exhilarating and consequential of his life.

The deep significance of his time at Cape Evans, however, did not come to him immediately. He needed, especially, distance and time from the events of 1912 to come to terms with the things that bothered him most, such as what he should have or could have done as he waited for some sign of the pole party at One Ton Depot, or why Scott failed while Amundsen succeeded so brilliantly. Near the end of *Worst Journey* he collected his thoughts on what makes a polar explorer, or, more precisely, what such an explorer must be prepared to face. It is not a detailed, sophisticated discussion, but more an outpouring of raw emotion in which he raced from topic to topic, only half finishing one idea before launching into another. It is, in effect, what he himself went through, although couched in the third person. Cherry suffered a great

FACING PAGE: *Sledging in April—Camping after Dark*, by E. A. Wilson, probably 1902. Pencil. The image relates to a depot trek made by Scott, Wilson, and ten others during April 1–4, 1902, during the *Discovery* expedition; they encountered extremely bad weather and turned back after going only 12 miles (19 km).

deal from psychosomatic and depressive illnesses in his later life, and it is not surprising that his perspective is internal. Polar explorers, Cherry insisted, must be able to contemplate loss with equanimity (even to the point of suicide, if one suffers a serious, disabling accident in the field). They must accept starvation as part of the price of admission to an exclusive club, not only with regard to food, but also sexual and social starvation. And they must determine what they can physically withstand: "[T]here is precious little shirking in Barrier sledging: a week finds most of us out." Cherry found out: He discovered that he could surmount his physical limitations—even his wretched eyesight—and stride along with the best of his *Terra Nova* mates. But overall the price he paid was emotionally and physically bankrupting. It is fitting that the chapter in which these observations are presented is entitled "Never Again."

In another telling passage Cherry asked, "'Is it worth it?' What is worth what? Is life worth risking for a feat, or losing for your country?" In framing these questions Cherry had, of course, Scott in mind, for whom, he thought, the feat of getting to the pole was not enough; there had to be more, which in Scott's case was the acquisition of knowledge. That may be true of Scott's purpose for the *Terra Nova* expedition as a whole, but the point requires some dissection.

Cherry-Garrard's instant classic, *The Worst Journey in the World*, has been published in several editions, with many reprintings, since its original appearance in 1922. Depicted here (l to r) are the first two-volume British edition (Constable & Co.), the first two-volume American edition (Doran), and one of several printings of the one-volume "cheap" edition issued by Chatto & Windus.

Both Scott and Amundsen understood that, to most people, a spot on a map such as the South Pole is of interest only if something of undoubted significance can be attached to it. For Amundsen, significance always came from the difficulty of attaining the goal, or, more precisely, succeeding where others had failed; easy or twice-visited goals sold no books, garnered no financial support. For Scott, significance was a more complex matter. Being first mattered, but that was not the only or even the most important goal. Cherry argued that, for The Owner, there had to be a suitable motive that went beyond merely grabbing the brass ring, and this was provided by the advancement of science.

But here we must ask, what was the nature of the scientific information that Scott could gain only by going all the way to the South Pole? Could it not have been purchased at much lower cost, human and otherwise, on the section of the plateau that lay only 100 miles (160 km) to the west in South Victoria Land? Properly speaking, apart from some geological observations and the famous weight of rocks man-hauled all the way from the Transantarctic Mountains to the last camp, Scott's direct contributions to the scientific understanding of the polar plateau were not much more extensive than Amundsen's, or Shackleton's for that matter. He carried no special instruments other than those connected with determining position, bearing, altitude, temperature, and the like, because such devices were required for survival. So did Amundsen, and both parties took extensive meteorological and altitude records. Dr. Wilson had biological training, but it would be misrepresentative to call him a research scientist in the league of Wright, Simpson, or Nelson. It takes nothing away from Wilson's reputation as a naturalist to observe that, like Scott, he was interested in everything around him, but in most respects lacked the specialist training that would have provided a basis for making significant scientific discoveries. (Although in research much depends on opportunity; had Wilson lived and maintained his interest in diseases of wildfowl, he might well have been able to use his medical background to make important discoveries.) On the southern journey, Scott could have chosen to take a young, vigorous scientist interested in ice physics—Silas Wright— with him to the pole, but he sent Wright back, just as he did the slightly older and less fit Atkinson. While there is no point in second-guessing Scott's choices—and Wright would certainly have died with the rest of them—it is nevertheless the case that having a professional scientist at the pole did not rank in importance with having a seaman or a soldier.

Even so, there remains an important difference between Scott and Amundsen in their attitude to research. It was vitally important to Scott to have his expedition recognized as primarily scientific in purpose, and to that end he invited scientists to join the expedition at significant expense to his program. The observations and collections they made during the course of the *Terra Nova* expedition formed the basis for an extensive body of scientific literature that is still consulted today. But if their Antarctic investigations are not well remembered, even in their respective disciplines, this is at least partly because of the conditions under which they worked. Field scientists working in Antarctica today are supported by elaborate infrastructures that are funded and maintained by national polar programs. If their work enjoys continuing funding they can travel to Antarctica as often as needed. For studies that require ongoing data collection, such long-term access to study sites is critical. By contrast, with very few exceptions, the scientists of the heroic age had one chance, and one only, to go to Antarctica; if they didn't get what they needed in their sole throw of

the dice, they were out of luck. Frankly, it is a tribute to the enormous industry of Scott's scientific staff that they accomplished as much as they did.

For Amundsen, such considerations were of course beside the point; his South Pole expedition had one purpose only, and personnel selection was made exclusively on the basis of who could further his ambition to stand first at 90°S. (In fairness to Amundsen's record it should be noted that he arranged for *Fram* to undertake a major oceanographic cruise in the South Atlantic during the winter of 1911, while he was preparing for his assault on the South Pole.) Some of Amundsen's men wrote their memoirs in later years, but none had the educational or experiential background to produce much more than a collection of yarns and personal reminiscences. The handful of scientific reports that were generated from data collected by Amundsen's team or *Fram*'s crew were written by researchers in Europe, none of whom had the experience or the insight that comes from being on Antarctic ice.

The tragic half of Scott's reputation will always dominate any treatment of his legacy, but anyone who knows the sweep of his entire story, and not merely his overexposed, miserable ending, recognizes that, by encouraging scientific investigation of the Last Continent as a desirable goal unto itself, he did something that few and perhaps no other participant in the heroic age was willing or even in a position to do. This was his fundamental contribution, and every scientist who has worked in the Antarctic since then owes something to him for it.

Scott, Amundsen, and Shackleton were among the most successful of what we may call the celebrity explorers of the early twentieth century. Like celebrities today, their fame was only partly due to accomplishment; the rest comes from whatever aspects of society's desires and ambitions they reflected back, like so many animate mirrors. But fashions change in choice of heroes just as they do in other areas, and for this reason it is hardly surprising that popular views of each of these men have undulated with the beat of the times, now rising, now falling. And, just as with modern celebrities, in the successive popular views of these men there is much that is manufactured, much complicating detail that is left out, much that is modified to fit a preferred image, good or bad. Thus there will never be *the* story of Scott or of Amundsen or of Shackleton, but only versions thereof, and the version adopted by one generation may be quite different from that preferred by another.

In the late 1990s, for example, in no small measure due to the *Endurance* exhibition prepared by the American Museum of Natural History, Ernest Shackleton, regarded

Scott Memorial Fund

APPEAL TO AMERICANS TO HELP!

"We have never heard of greater heroism not even among the ancients who made an art of dying nobly." Vide American Press.

PRESIDENT:
ADMIRAL PEARY

VICE-PRESIDENT:
CLARENCE H. MACKAY

"The story will serve as an example to our youth. It will become one of our national stories." Vide London "Times."

HENRY CLEWS,
TREASURER
15 BROAD ST., N. Y.

PERCY S. BULLEN,
SECRETARY
1524, 30 BROAD ST., N. Y.

THE British Government has undertaken to pension the widows of Captain Scott and Petty Officer Evans and voluntary provision will be made by the countrymen of the dead heroes for the benefit of other dependents.

A minimum sum of $150,000 will be needed to relieve Captain Scott's estate of the liabilities he incurred for the expedition upon which he met his death. This will be subscribed in England.

It is felt that something more remains to be done to fittingly commemorate the great Tragedy of the Antartic.

In response to wishes expressed on all sides that a **Permanent Memorial** in honour of Captain Scott and his dead comrades be inaugurated definite steps are now being taken. To assist in establishing the **Permanent Memorial, American Aid is Invited.**

In cordial cooperation with the Mansion House Fund, of which the Lord Mayor of London is President, the "Daily Telegraph" of London has started a fund the proceeds of which will be devoted to the **Memorial** scheme and meantime, pending the completion of the government and voluntary provision the "Daily Telegraph" has undertaken the task of rendering immediate help to dependents, and, if deemed advisable supplementing the government pensions.

The Mansion House and the "Daily Telegraph" will combine their resources in establishing the Permanent Memorial and a **Branch of the Joint Fund has now been opened in New York to which subscriptions are herewith invited.** It is believed many Americans will appreciate the opportunity of joining with the countrymen of Scott on the other side of the Atlantic in providing a permanent memorial and urgent appeal is now made for their generous support.

No details can be given thus early regarding the precise form of the Permanent Memorial except that it will undoubtedly embody the universal wish that the heroism of Scott's gallant band shall be fittingly commemorated.

The American Geographical Society and other American Societies devoted to scientific exploration have sent messages indorsing the Scott Memorial Fund and so also have many prominent and representative American citizens.

Rear-Admiral Peary has headed the list with a donation of $100 and sent a telegram warmly indorsing the Memorial Fund. Dr. Henry Fairfield Osborn, President of the American Museum of Natural History has sent us $100 and expressed satisfaction that a memorial scheme is afoot. Hon. Joseph H. Choate also sends a donation of $100. Another friend who wishes that his name remain anonymous has given $500. **Capt. Amundsen, discoverer of the South Pole, has donated $100.**

The Names of American Donors unless otherwise desired will be published in the New York newspapers and in the daily subscription lists of the London "Daily Telegraph".

All sums, big and small, will be gratefully acknowledged by **Mr. Henry Clews, of Henry Clews & Co., bankers, and should be addressed to Mr. Henry Clews, Treasurer of the American branch of Scott Memorial Fund, 15 Broad St., N. Y. City.**

Honoring Scott's last wish that "our people" be taken care of, a fund (originally named The Lord Mayor's Fund) was started to provide pensions for the widows and families of *Terra Nova*'s heroic dead. Eventually, £75,000 (£2.1–2.5 million or US$3.3–4.0 million in today's currencies) was raised, about half of which went to dependents. The broadside illustrated here canvassed for American donors, which, it was noted, already included Captain Amundsen and Henry Fairfield Osborn, president of the American Museum of Natural History. Funds remaining in the trust were later spent, in part, to build the Scott Polar Research Institute in Cambridge, England.

by many of his contemporaries as a man of unreliable character, was carried aloft by a mighty storm of popular opinion into the emotional space we reserve for those we perceive to be the best among us. By emulating the apparent inner strengths of such people, it was said, you too could find it in yourself to act like a Shackleton in, say, business or political life. But how much do most people really know, or really want to know, about these men of the heroic age? If you think Shackleton was your kind of hero, does it matter that he was an acknowledged womanizer whose business dealings were sometimes shady? Or, in Amundsen's case, that he was an adulterer who made a practice of evading his creditors? If Bowers was a saint in your eyes, are you concerned that, by modern standards, he was a thoroughgoing racist and religious bigot? If Petty Officer Evans was a working-class hero, does this excuse the fact that he was also a loutish binge drinker? Most egregious of all: what, if it is true, as biographer Michael Smith contends, that in 1900 Oates fathered a child on an eleven-year-old girl? My point is that these were real people, with real lives and personal histories, in which things happened sometimes that were far from commendable or praiseworthy. If one seeks to understand them they first have to be accepted for what they were, free of notions concerning what is or is not a proper heroic personality. Those who are attracted to the strenuous life are, after all, rarely slaves to convention.

The view from a century later allows some aspects of the contest for the South Pole to be seen more clearly than was the case at the time. Scott and Amundsen faced similar challenges; each had to solve an enormous variety of logistical and practical problems, akin to sorting through pieces of a jigsaw puzzle to find the correct, successive fits that will make the entire picture appear. But their methods were quite different.

Amundsen knew exactly how he wanted to achieve his single goal, to get to the pole and back, and to do it first. Of course, not all of the pieces of the puzzle were known to him prior to his landing on the ice: Some decisions had to be made on the spot, and some of these were bad. He almost brought his expedition to disaster during the abortive September journey because he did not understand the relationship between the exceptionally low temperatures he experienced on the Barrier and the coreless winter of the Antarctic. But in the main there was no second-guessing, no major, poorly thought-out changes in plan at the last minute, no departures from what he knew from experience would work. His approach was spare, practiced, narrowly focused, matter-of-fact.

Scott was none of that; intellectuals rarely are. Despite the enormous amount he learned on the *Discovery* expedition about living and working in the Antarctic, almost a decade later he was still frequently unsure whether he was making the right decisions. He burdened himself further by, in effect, trying all possible fits to his puzzle-pieces simultaneously. Thus, in the matter of transportation, he did not trust dogs but took some anyway. Ponies made some, but not much, sense as disposable draft animals in the Antarctic, but since Shackleton had used them, and since Shackleton had almost made it to the pole, so . . . we take them. The motor sledges, untested in extreme cold or in the ice conditions found in the Antarctic, represented to Scott's fertile analytical mind a technological fix that could ease the job of crossing the Great Ice Barrier; so they came, each costing the equivalent of a thousand pre-1914 pounds, and they accomplished little before failing. In the end, the only way left to him was the Royal Navy way, man-hauling, justified in *Discovery* days with the ringing phrase that "no journey made with dogs can approach the height of that fine conception which is realised when" men do all the work, which seems to mean no more than it is a fine thing to use men as dogs. Unlike the case with Amundsen, there were many bad decisions: allowing Wilson, Cherry-Garrard, and Bowers to almost kill themselves for science on the winter journey to Cape Crozier, trumpeting it as a "test" of the proper proportion of fats, carbohydrates, and proteins in sledging rations; taking a fifth man to the pole, seemingly on the whim of an idea that does not seem to have been discussed with anyone, even Wilson; and never managing to think about little, obvious things, such as setting up enough cairns or planting signal flags across a line of march so that depots would be found easily in any weather.

While doubts have often been expressed about Scott's level of preparation, it was not until Roland Huntford's *Scott and Amundsen* appeared in 1979 that Scott as a moral as well as practical failure became a matter of intense discussion. Much of Huntford's criticism is justified; much isn't. In Antarctica Scott was not blatantly foolhardy, but he seems to have been insufficiently conscious of how close he persistently scraped along the rasp edge of disaster. This is not about his confidence level or his taking chances as such; Amundsen took chances as well. The difference between them is that Amundsen tried to tilt the probabilities in his favor by careful forethought and overcompensation. By contrast, Scott was "[c]ontinually on the panic," thought Charles Royds, one of the officers on the *Discovery* expedition, "expecting everything to be done at once and rows if nothing is done." By "panic" Royds meant that any matter, trivial to monumental, that blocked Scott in some way had to be dealt with immediately; if not, he would enter a persistent state of nervous excitement that could be relieved only by taking action—any action. Thus there was the time in March 1911, after depot-laying, when he and others were forced to stay at Hut Point for more than a month because stable sea ice between the peninsula and Cape Evans was still forming. Scott became extremely fretful and impatient, and told

"Wilson and [Cherry] to prepare for an attempt to reach Cape Evans by crossing the icefalls on Erebus: but this was given up after a talk with Bill." This trek would have entailed an extremely dangerous crossing of a heavily crevassed area that he *knew*, from fearful accidents occurring during the *Discovery* expedition in similar terrain, should be avoided at all costs. As Cherry noted, "the land that joins the two [capes] has never yet been crossed by a sledge party owing to the great ice falls which cover the slopes of Erebus." It was fortunate that Wilson prevailed.

There often seems to be no proper scale to Scott's reactions to things, no correlation between the size of the issue at hand and how he dealt with it. During the winter of 1911 at Cape Evans he seemed to be out of sorts almost constantly, and small things would set him off horribly. Those who were less given to having their hands conspicuously occupied—such as the scientists—while The Owner was on the prowl for slackers were the subject of some of his most hypercritical asides.

A persistent vein of opinion concerning Scott's leadership is that he knew, or should have known, that the race—whatever one thinks that consisted of—was over the moment he learned that Amundsen, his dogs, and his methods were securely ensconced on the Barrier above the Bay of Whales. But what could Scott have done in any case? He couldn't just cede the prize—that would have been professional suicide. All he could do was say, publicly, that he didn't care so very much, because Britain was in Antarctica for the science, not the laurel-gathering. He may have secretly hoped that something would happen to Amundsen's team along the way so that the Norwegians would come in second, or not at all, but on the surface he stuck to his objectives.

Would it have been a bad thing for Scott and the last remnant of his polar party to have come in second *and* to have survived? The view that Britain demanded that explorers either win through or be brought back on their shields is Kiplingesque nonsense. Scott, Wilson, and Bowers did not choose to die because of the unbearable shame of losing a contest that was, in the scheme of things, of no greater significance to the world than that middies' cutter race off St. Kitts so long ago, when Markham had first taken note of the young Scott. In any case, survival after the end of March would have meant, probably for each of them, numerous operations and amputations—feet, noses, fingers—and a lifetime of having to deal with other kinds of scars, including emotional and mental ones. The British public would have tsk-tsked in compassion for their suffering, and there would have been medals and anodyne speeches. But because men had died, there also would have been an official inquiry. All the poor decisions, inadequate foresight, disgruntled expedition members—all this and more would have come out for public inspection and delectation. Scott would have hated it.

Yet for all of his obvious, documented failings there is a full measure of countervailing evidence concerning Scott's strength of character, his sense of justice, his willingness to do anything and everything he asked his men to do. It is just not conceivable that this man, who conducted not one but two expeditions to Antarctica, who had veterans and novices alike clamoring for positions on his team, was the blubbering, unstable incompetent that some authors have made him out to be. Scott may never receive the level of approbation that Shackleton has recently enjoyed, in part because Shackleton's apotheosis came for him comfortably late, long after the chief participants in his expeditions had died. Scott comes with much more baggage, and with a list of virtues that were considered exemplary in upper-class, prewar Britain, but which have little resonance today. Nevertheless, one expects that the wheel will turn again, when new attitudes take hold or old ones are reinterpreted.

Scott was an essential part of the heroic age of Antarctic exploration; indeed, it would be hard to imagine why that age would deserve its sobriquet were it not for Scott's matchless chronicling of his participation in it. He wrote like no one else has ever written of the experience of being there, of the landscapes and the seasons and the cold embrace of the ice, of his participation in the last of the great races for geographical discovery, of exhilarating accomplishment as well as bitter defeat. In the English-speaking world, Amundsen is sealed in the aspic of popular remembrance as Scott's machinelike nemesis and competitor for the achievement of being first to the South Pole, but his story is much richer, as well as more human, than this limited acquaintance with the man provides. Scott was in love with words, Amundsen with deeds; it is this opposition of types that provides not only much of the drama of the Race to The End, but also its moments for contemplation. A century later, their inseparable stories of striving, seeking, finding, and never yielding still provide inspiration to all wanderers on the face of the Earth.

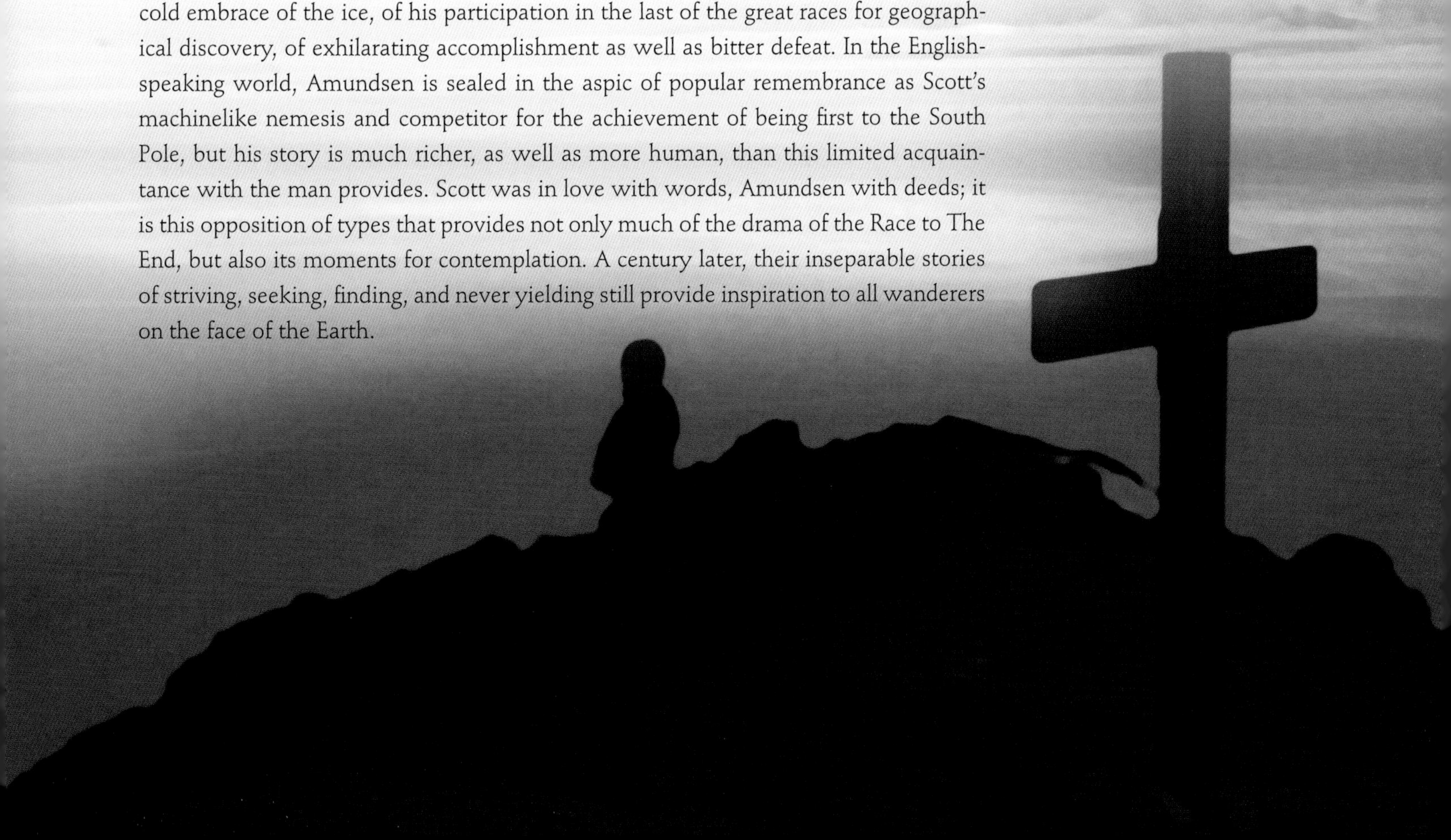

Cross of jarrah-wood (seen here in 2003) erected on Observation Hill January 20, 1913, commemorating the loss of Scott, Wilson, Oates, Bowers, and Evans.

Selected Biographies

Terra Nova Expedition

THE POLE PARTY

Henry R. Bowers ("Birdie"; 1883–1912): Lieutenant in the Royal Indian Marine with no previous polar experience; he was taken onto Scott's pole party after demonstrating extraordinary organizational skills, physical strength, and resourcefulness. He died with Scott on the return journey from the South Pole.

Edgar Evans ("Taff"; 1876–1912): Career petty officer in the Royal Navy (hence "P. O. Evans" in diaries, to distinguish him from the officer with the same surname, "Lieutenant Evans"). Taff was on both of Scott's expeditions. A favorite of Scott because of his great strength and practical skills, he was selected for the pole party. For unexplained reasons he became severely disoriented and then disabled early in the return trip; he slipped into unconsciousness and died in February 1912.

Lawrence E. G. Oates ("Titus," "Soldier"; 1880–1912): Captain in 6th Inniskilling Dragoons, a British Army cavalry unit. Of independent means, he donated £1000 to acquire a place on the *Terra Nova* expedition. He was placed in charge of the ponies and was a member of the final pole party. Having developed severe, disabling frostbite of the feet, Oates famously sacrificed himself in early March 1912 in order not to impede the others in their desperate effort to reach Cape Evans.

Robert F. Scott ("The Owner"; 1868–1912): Royal Navy officer who led both the *Discovery* (or National Antarctic) Expedition, 1901–04, and the ill-fated *Terra Nova* (or British National) Expedition, 1910–1913. He died with four others, probably at the end of March, on the return journey from the South Pole, which he and his companions had attained on January 17, 1912.

Edward A. Wilson ("Uncle Bill"; 1872–1912): Physician, painter, and naturalist, Wilson's drawings and watercolors form lasting visual tributes to the *Discovery* and *Terra Nova* expeditions, on both of which he served. He did not survive the return from the pole, dying at the last camp with Scott and Bowers.

OTHER PARTICIPANTS IN THE BRITISH SOUTHERN JOURNEY 1911–1912

Edward L. Atkinson ("Atch"; 1881–1929): A Royal Navy surgeon and trained parasitologist, Atkinson was a member of the first support party that accompanied Scott onto the polar plateau. In command at Cape Evans after the departure of Lt. Teddy Evans in March 1912, he led the relief party that found Scott's last camp.

Apsley G. B. Cherry-Garrard ("Cherry"; 1886–1959): At twenty-four years old, the second-youngest member of the expedition, Cherry was, like Oates, a paying customer, having donated £1000 to its coffers. He would later write *The Worst Journey in the World*, a work that is not just an adventure story about egg-hunting in the middle of the austral winter, but also a complex, dark meditation on the significance of exploration.

Thomas Crean (1876–1938): Petty officer, Royal Navy. On the return from the polar plateau, his incredible solo march to Hut Point to bring back help for the gravely ill Teddy Evans earned him the Albert Medal. Crean also served on the *Endurance* expedition and, with Shackleton and Worsley, made the heroic crossing of South Georgia in May 1916, which resulted in the eventual rescue of the men marooned on Elephant Island.

Bernard C. Day ("Rivets"; 1884–1965): Day was an electrician and mechanic; he drove the first car in Antarctica (on Shackleton's *Nimrod* expedition). On the *Terra Nova* expedition, he drove one of the motor sledges; after it broke down he man-hauled with others in support of Scott's southern journey almost to the Transantarctic Mountains.

Edward R. G. R. Evans (usually "Teddy" in diaries, sometimes "Teddie"; 1880–1957): Eventually retiring as an admiral, Evans was a Royal Navy lieutenant when he was selected as Scott's second-in-command. In charge of the second supporting party, Evans developed scurvy but was saved by his heroic sledgemates, Crean and Lashly. He was sent home aboard *Terra Nova* in March of 1912 to recover, but returned the next year to relieve the expedition.

Demetri Gerof (properly, Dmitriy Girev; variously "Dmitri," "Dimitri" in diaries and the literature (1888–1932?): Brought from Siberia as a dog driver by Meares. He went as far as the base of the Beardmore Glacier with the southern party, and later accompanied Cherry-Garrard in March 1912 to One Ton Depot, looking for Scott's party.

Tryggve Gran ("Trigger"; 1889–1980): Norwegian brought on to train the men to ski, Gran stayed until the end of the *Terra Nova* expedition and was a member of the relief party that found Scott's final camp in November 1912. After the *Terra Nova* expedition, Gran returned to Norway and became a pilot. He participated in the search for Amundsen when the explorer's airplane went down in 1928.

Patrick Keohane ("Patsy"; 1879–1950): Petty officer and member of the first support party. He participated in the search for Scott's last camp.

William Lashly (also spelled Lashley; 1867–1940): Chief Stoker, Royal Navy. Accompanied Scott onto the polar plateau, returning in early January 1912 with Teddy Evans and Crean. Noted for his modesty, loyalty, and dependability—the "Wilson of the lower deck." He stayed with Evans while Crean went for help; if Crean hadn't reached Hut Point, all in the party would probably have died. Received Albert Medal for his heroism.

Cecil H. Meares ("Mother"; 1877–1937): Certainly an adventurer and probably at least once in his career a British spy, Meares was brought onto the *Terra Nova* expedition as an expert dog handler. He accompanied Scott as far as the base of the Beardmore Glacier, then returned to Cape Evans to leave on *Terra Nova* in March 1912.

Charles S. Wright ("Silas"; 1887–1975): Canadian physicist on the scientific staff and member of the first support party. He participated in the search for Scott's last camp.

OTHER PERSONNEL

Victor L. A. Campbell ("The Wicked Mate"; 1875–1956): Royal Navy lieutenant who was appointed to lead the eastern party to King Edward VII Land, which was then completely unexplored. Finding *Fram* uncomfortably close to his target, he switched to South Victoria Land and his expedition became the northern party. Because of difficulties with the ice, his team was not relieved by ship and had to spend the winter of 1912 with inadequate supplies and shelter.

Frank Debenham ("Deb"; 1883–1965): Australian geologist on the scientific staff; later, first director of the Scott Polar Research Institute in Cambridge, UK.

Herbert G. Ponting ("Ponco"; 1870–1935): The expedition's official photographer, Ponting documented many aspects of life on Cape Evans and vicinity in still photos and movie film. Some of the most famous photographic images of the heroic age came from Ponco's cameras.

George C. Simpson ("Sunny Jim"; 1878–1965): British meteorologist in the Indian meteorological service, assigned to Scott's *Terra Nova* expedition. His assignment ended in March 1912, and he returned to Simla, India.

T. Griffith Taylor ("Griff"; 1880–1964): Australian geomorphologist on the scientific staff, worked extensively in South Victoria Land.

Fram Expedition

Roald E. G. Amundsen (1872–1928): Norwegian explorer with many firsts, including the South Pole. He is acknowledged as one of the greatest, if not the greatest, polar travelers of all time. Amundsen and his men arrived at the South Pole on December 15, 1911, more than a month before Scott's party; all returned safely to their camp (Framheim) on the Bay of Whales after sledging 1860 miles (2990 km) over the course of ninety-nine days.

Olav O. Bjaaland (1873–1961): Norwegian ski champion and one of the five men on Amundsen's team to reach the South Pole.

H. Fredrik Gjertsen (1885–1958): Lieutenant in Norwegian navy; officer on *Fram*.

Helmer J. Hanssen (1870–1956): One of five members of Amundsen's party to reach the Pole, Hanssen was in charge of navigation. He later joined the *Maud* expedition as captain.

Sverre H. Hassel (1876–1928): Expert dog driver and one of the five men in Amundsen's party to reach the Pole.

F. Hjalmar Johansen (1867–1913): Experienced polar trekker who had traveled with Nansen aboard *Fram* in 1893–1895, the only one to accompany the great explorer on his ski trip to Franz Josef Land. Amundsen dismissed him from the pole party for criticizing his leadership in front of the other men. Depressed and out of money, Johansen committed suicide in January 1913.

Adolph H. Lindstrom (1866–1939): Accompanied Amundsen on *Gjøa* as well as *Fram* as cook. Maintained Framheim while the polar and eastern parties went exploring.

Thorvald Nilsen (1881–1940): Lieutenant in Norwegian navy and captain of *Fram*. He commanded the ship during its oceanographic survey of the South Atlantic while Amundsen and his team made their pole journey.

Kristian Prestrud (1881- 1927): Lieutenant in Norwegian navy who joined the shore party at the Bay of Whales. He nearly froze to death during Amundsen's first try for the South Pole in September 1911, but was saved by Hjalmar Johansen. Later participated in the eastern party.

Jørgen Stubberud (1883–1980): An Oslo carpenter who constructed the "observation hut" that became Framheim, he asked Amundsen if he could join his polar expedition. Participated in eastern party sent to explore King Edward VII Land.

Oscar Wisting (1871–1936): One of Amundsen's longest-serving compatriots, he went with him to both poles. Wisting assumed command of the *Maud* expedition when Amundsen left in 1922. On a 1936 sentimental visit to *Fram*, then undergoing restoration in Norway, he passed away while sleeping on his old bunk.

Others

Leon H. B. Amundsen (1870–1934): Roald Amundsen's brother, business manager, and impresario before they had a falling out over property matters in 1923–1924, which ended their relationship.

Clements R. Markham (1830–1916): President of the Royal Geographical Society from 1893 to 1905, Markham oversaw the organization of the National Antarctic (*Discovery*) expedition and was a strong supporter of Scott's second or British Antarctic (*Terra Nova*) expedition.

Fridtjof Nansen (1861–1930): The great Norwegian explorer, statesman, and humanitarian who was Amundsen's sometime benefactor and mentor.

Kathleen Bruce Scott (1878–1947): Wife of Robert Scott, she was on her way to New Zealand to meet her husband when she learned that he had died, with his men, some nine months earlier. She went on to have a successful career as a sculptor, remarrying and eventually assuming, as her second husband's consort, a title (Lady Kennet).

Ernest H. Shackleton (1874–1922): Accompanied Scott on the southern journey during the *Discovery* expedition, but was sent home early for health reasons. In 1907 he again set out for the South Pole as leader of the *Nimrod* expedition, but was forced, due to the weather, to turn around just 112 statute miles from the Pole. After the famous *Endurance* expedition of 1914–1916, he went south once more, on the *Quest* in 1922, and died while anchored off South Georgia.

Notes

These notes concern attribution of matter quoted in the text; the list of sources is provided in the bibliography. All of the more recent works noted here provide excellent, extensive bibliographies for those interested in additional reading. For convenience, edited published diaries are listed under the names of the editor(s). Scott's *Terra Nova* diaries, including formerly expurgated material, have been republished in a new scholarly edition by Jones (2006); I have usually quoted from this compilation in preference to *Scott's Last Expedition,* edited by Huxley (1914, 4th ed.). Excerpts from other sources, including diaries and letters, are noted by the published source in which they may be found; origination dates are given if known or reported by published sources. Major figures (see Selected Biographies page 222) are identified by surname only.

CHAPTER 1

The End Observed

"anyone to see him sad" Lady Kennet [Kathleen Bruce Scott Young], November 29, 1910, in Crane (2005: 393).

"to reach the South Pole . . ." From Scott's printed appeal for funds, in Crane (2005: 356).

"With a queer elation . . ." Lady Kennet (1949: 90).

"Scott at South Pole . . ." Lady Kennet (1949: 90).

"I've got some news . . ." Lady Kennet (1949: 120). The total dead were five, including Scott. See also Pound (1966: 311).

"one who is still . . ." Evening Standard, February 16, 1913, in Fiennes (2005: 382).

"a million and a half children . . ." New York Times, February 15, 1913.

"will be strongly stamped . . ." New York Times, February 15, 1913.

"The worst has happened" Scott, diary, January 17, 1912, in Jones (2006: 376).

"awful place" Scott, diary, January 17, 1912, in Jones (2006: 376).

"It's a glorious record . . ." Kathleen Scott to Sir George Egerton, in Huntford (1980: 558).

"gladly forego any honour . . ." Daily Chronicle, February 12, 1913, in Huntford (1980: 561).

"a Country doomed . . ." James Cook, in Horwitz (2002: 220).

"England had ever *led . . ."* James Clark Ross, (1847, 1: 117).

"we might with equal chance . . ." James Clark Ross (1847, 1: 219).

"the greatest piece . . ." Sixth International Geographical Congress, in Rosove (2000: 67).

"purposely made edible . . ." Evans in Huxley (1914, 2: 491)

"was particularly well put . . ." Evans in Huxley (1914, 2: 492)

CHAPTER 2

November–December 1910: Scott Sails South

"A day of great . . ." Scott, diary, December 2, 1910, in Jones (2006: 15).
"the ship all the time rolling . . ." Wilson, diary, December 2, 1910, in Tarver (2006: 103).
"It was a sight . . ." Evans (1952: 52).
"incapable" Scott, diary, May 5, 1911, in Jones (2006: 463 [app. 3]).
"terrible slow to learn" Scott, diary, May 5, 1911, in Jones (2006: 463 [app. 3]).
"greatest lot of crocks . . ." Oates, in Smith (2006: 116).
"additional risk" Wheeler (2002: 60–61).
"I have lively recollections . . ." Cherry-Garrard (1937: 51).
"crystalline continent" Solomon (2001: 69).
"The scene was incomparable . . ." Scott, diary, December 10, 1910, in Jones (2006: 24).
"My father was idle . . ." Scott, in Gwynn (1929: 163).
"I was much struck . . ." Scott, in Fiennes (2003: 13).
"seawater analysis" Fisher and Fisher (1957: 26–27).
"entertainments" Fisher and Fisher (1957: 26–27).
"another two days' . . ." Bomann-Larsen (2006: 76).

CHAPTER 3

June–September 1910: Amundsen's "Small Excursion South"

"Dear Professor Fridtjof Nansen . . ." Trans. in Kløver (2009: 201).
"The idiot! Why . . ." Nansen, in Huntford (1980: 318).
"his most dangerous rival . . ." Bomann-Larsen (2006: 78).
"There are many things . . ." Fredrik Gjertsen, in Huntford (1980: 298).
"Hurrah. That means . . ." Bjaaland, in Huntford (1980: 299).
"as everybody knew . . ." Bjaaland, in Huntford (1980: 300).
"At first, as might . . ." Amundsen (1912, 1: 128–29).

CHAPTER 4

October–December 1910: Challenge Served

"ship behaved splendidly . . ." Scott, diary, in Jones (2006: 58).
"61 tons in forcing . . ." Scott, diary, December 30, 1910, in Jones (2006: 56).
"Amundsen is acting suspiciously . . ." Gran, in Huntford (1980: 322).
"What do you think . . ." Oates to mother, November 23, 1910, in Smith (2006: 111).
"The last we had heard . . ." Cherry-Garrard (1937: 42).
"how Amundsen can . . ." Ernest Shackleton, in Huntford (1980: 320).
"no more sailing qualities . . ." Clements Markham, in Crane (2005: 383).

"If, as rumour . . ." Gran, in Huntford (1980: 320).
"the Pole was the main objective" Scott, in Crane (2005: 356).
"Ponting cannot face . . ." Scott, diary, December 1, 1910, in Jones (2006: 15).
"The sun also . . ." Scott, diary, December 30, 1910, in Jones (2006: 58).
"never seen a party . . ." Scott, diary, December 30, 1910, in Jones (2006: 60).
"So we were glad . . ." Wilson, diary, in Huxley (1914, 1: 614).
"Fortune would be . . ." Scott, diary, December 30, 1910, in Jones (2006: 60).
"the whole seventeen . . ." Scott, diary, January 4, 1911, in Jones (2006: 71).
"The great trouble with . . ." Scott, diary, January 4, 1911, in Jones (2006: 72).
"comfortable quarters for the hut . . ." Scott, diary, January 4, 1911, in Jones (2006: 72).
"3 motors at £1000 each . . ." Oates, diary, November 7, 1911, in Smith (2006: 176). Interestingly, Motor Sledge No. 2 is listed as a donation, evidently paid for by the Royal Masonic School, Bushey, Herts (cf. Jones 2006: 437).
"The hut is becoming . . ." Scott, diary, January 19, 1911, in Jones (2006: 96).
"but they only take . . ." Scott, diary, January 6, 1911, in Jones (2006: 77).
"Everyone declares that . . ." Scott, diary, January 6, 1911, in Jones (2006: 77).
"remarkable headpiece" Scott, diary, January 8, 1912, in Jones (2006: 369); cf. Solomon (2000: 163).

CHAPTER 5

October 1910–January 1911: Last of the Vikings

"For the first twenty-four hours . . ." Amundsen (1912, 1: 166).
"no terrors to oppose us" Amundsen (1912, 1: 166).
"I saw and understood . . ." Amundsen (1927: 26).
"would rather die . . ." in Huntford (1980: 64).
"The sun finishes its wandering . . ." Amundsen, diary, June 20, 1898, in Decleir (1999: 113–14).

CHAPTER 6

January 1911: Making Ready

"does not go back sick . . ." A. B. Armitage to H. R. Mill, 1922, in Preston (1997: 68).
"If we had not achieved . . ." Scott (1905, 2: 125).
"You shall go to the Pole . . ." Kathleen Bruce to Scott, in Preston (1997: 98).
"I may say that this . . ." Amundsen (1912, 1: 370).
"Scott seems very . . ." Cherry-Garrard (1937: 96).
"They are supposed . . ." Cherry-Garrard, diary, January 11, 1911, in Huntford (1980: 334).
"Well, if they are planning . . ." in Fiennes (2003: 215).
"I did not think . . ." Scott, diary, January 5, 1911, in Jones (2006: 73-74).

CHAPTER 7

January–April 1911: The Road to One Ton

"Curses loud and deep . . ." Wilfred Bruce to Kathleen Scott, February 27, 1911, in Huntford (1980: 342).
"The Englishmen [were] absolutely . . ." Fredrik Gjertsen, in Huntford (1980: 343).
"did not look very inviting" Thorvald Nilsen, in Huntford (1980: 344).
"One of them . . ." Victor Campbell, in Huntford (1980: 345).
"But my head doesn't seem . . ." Scott, diary, January 19, 1911, in Jones (2006: 97).
"Well, we're in . . ." Reported conversation, George Simpson to H. R. Mill, in Huntford (1980: 362).
"[we] shall I am sure . . ." Oates to mother, January 22, 1911, in Huntford (1980: 363).
"real good" Scott, diary, January 24, 1911, in Jones (2006: 104).
"with such extraordinary . . ." Scott, diary, January 24, 1911, in Jones (2006: 104).
"I cannot have much sympathy . . ." Scott, diary, February 2, 1911, in Jones (2006: 111).
"kept silent fearing . . ." Scott, diary, February 2, 1911, in Jones (2006: 459 [app. 3]).
"they go through in lots . . . ." Scott, diary, January 24, 1911, in Jones (2006: 104).
"A more unpromising lot . . ." Oates, in Fiennes (2003: 204).
"magical" Scott, diary, January 30, 1911, in Jones (2006: 110).
"If we had more of . . ." Scott, diary, February 3, 1911, in Jones (2006: 113).
"Raging chaos" Cherry-Garrard (1937: 113).
"Fight your way . . ." Cherry-Garrard (1937: 113).
"Suddenly, we heard . . ." Scott, diary, February 14, 1911, in Jones (2006: 123).
"for not supervising . . ." Scott, diary, February 14, 1911, in Jones (2006: 124).
"I have had more . . ." Gran, in Hattersley-Smith (1984: 59).
"I was running . . ." Wilson, in Seavers (1933: 224).
"had been considerably mauled . . ." Cherry-Garrard (1937: 126).
"thin as rakes . . ." Scott, diary, February 22, 1911, in Jones (2006: 134).
"Hunger and fear . . ." Scott, diary, February 3, 1911, in Jones (2006: 116).
"the day pales . . ." Scott, diary, February 22, 1911, in Jones (2006: 135).
"possessed with an insane sense . . ." Cherry-Garrard (1937: 128).
"the arrival of . . ." Bowers, in Cherry-Garrard (1937: 142).
"the Killers were too . . ." Bowers, in Cherry-Garrard (1937: 144).
"What about the ponies . . ." As reported in Mason (1979: 138).
"Poor trustful creatures! If . . ." Bowers, in Cherry-Garrard (1937: 146).
"These incidents were . . ." Scott, diary, March 3, 1911, in Jones (2006: 141).
"Have exercised the ponies . . ." Scott, diary, April 16, 1911, in Jones (2006: 162).

CHAPTER 8

February–March 1911: 42,000 Biscuits

"We could not tell . . ." Amundsen (1912, 1: 209).
"flag at the mainmast . . ." Amundsen, in Huntford (1980: 347).
"Cannot understand what . . ." Amundsen, in Huntford (1980: 347).
"One thing only fixes . . ." Scott, diary, February 22, 1911, in Jones (2006: 135).
"If we reach the Pole . . ." Gran, diary, February 26, 1911, in Hattersley-Smith (1984: 63).
"is now known . . ." Williams (2008: 136).
"so genuinely upset . . ." Bowers, in Fiennes (2003: 220).
"Amundsen's enterprise falls far . . ." Gran, in Fiennes (2003: 220).
"over-taxing . . . these fine animals" Amundsen (1912, 1: 237).
"All sentimental feeling . . ." Amundsen (1912, 1: 242).
"rectal complaint" Huntford (1980: 353).
"Of the 42,000 biscuits . . ." Amundsen, 1912 RGS lecture, in Kløver (2009: 118).

CHAPTER 9

Winter 1911: Taking Stock

"to lay down . . ." Scott's May 1911 lecture as summarized in *South Polar Times* 3, no. 2: 24.
"Everyone was interested, naturally" Scott, diary, May 8, 1911, in Jones (2006: 189).
"without any plan worthy . . ." Huntford (1980: 394).
"I have asked everyone . . ." Scott, diary, May 8, 1911, in Jones (2006: 189).
"Amundsen's chances . . . are rather . . ." Debenham, diary, in Huntford (1980: 394).
"need very careful organization . . ." Debenham, diary, in Speak (2008: 34).
"everyone was enthusiastic . . ." Scott, diary, September 14, 1911, in Jones (2006: 286).
"would not only bring failure . . ." Simpson, in Huntford (1980: 396).
"as if Amundsen did . . ." Debenham, diary, May 8, 1911, in Huntford (1980: 395).
"inclined to chuck . . ." Comment attributed to Scott by Debenham, in Huntford (1980: 395).
"I for one am . . ." Bowers to Kathleen Scott, October 27, 1911, in Preston (1997: 158).
"I don't know whether . . ." Debenham, diary, in Huntford (1980: 396).
"Our plan is one . . ." Amundsen, diary, April 18, 1911, in Huntford (1980: 380).
"we were living on the Barrier . . ." Amundsen (1912, 1: 347).
"Considerably better than . . ." Huntford (1980: 381).
"The thought of the English . . ." Hassel, diary, August 13, 1911, in Huntford (1980: 393).
"I'd give something to know . . ." Amundsen (1912, 1: 378).
"a tale for our generation . . ." Scott, diary, August 2, 1911, in Jones (2006: 259).

CHAPTER 10

Spring 1911: The Race Begins

"To risk men and animals . . ." Amundsen (1912, 1: 384).

"I told you so!" Hanssen, diary, in Huntford (1980: 409).

"I don't call it an expedition . . ." Hassel, diary, September 17, 1911, in Huntford (1980: 410).

"It is already evident . . ." Scott, diary, October 27, 1911, in Jones (2006: 309).

"motor programme is not . . ." Scott, diary, October 27, 1911, in Jones (2006: 309).

"So here end the entries . . ." Scott, diary, October 31, 1911, in Jones (2006: 311).

"I had rather a horrid day . . ." Lady Kennet (1949: 100).

"I dislike Scott intensely . . ." Oates to mother, October 24–31, 1911, in Smith (2006: 171).

"The dream of great help . . ." Scott, diary, November 4, 1911, in Jones (2006: 315).

CHAPTER 11

November–December 1911: Barrier to Plateau

"we had reason to be . . ." Amundsen (1912, 2: 13).

"we never had to move . . ." Amundsen (1912, 2: 29).

"The task we had . . ." Amundsen (1912, 2: 47).

"The wildness of the landscape . . ." Amundsen (1912, 2: 56).

"In four days they had . . ." Huntford (1980: 449).

"Come and say dogs . . ." Amundsen, diary, November 21, 1911, in Huntford (1980: 450).

"One might think . . ." Hassel, diary, December 12, 1911, in Bomann-Larsen (2006: 108).

"There was depression . . ." Amundsen (1912, 2: 63).

"A year's care . . ." Bowers, in Mason (1979: 177).

"[A]t every step . . ." Scott, diary, December 10, 1911, in Jones (2006: 344).

"Thank God the horses . . ." Wilson, diary, December 8, 1911, in Huxley (1914: 627).

"ministry of suffering" Crane (2005: 59).

"the best part of the business . . ." Scott, diary, December 29, 1911, in Jones (2006: 363).

"There is no accounting . . ." Scott to George Egerton, no date, in Jones (2006: 418).

CHAPTER 12

December 1911–January 1912: Cigars and Black Flags

"We saw nothing . . ." Amundsen, 1912 RGS lecture, in Kløver (2009: 140).

"The surface at once . . ." Amundsen (1912, 2: 106).

"88°23′ was past . . ." Amundsen (1912, 2: 114).

"We did not pass . . ." Amundsen (1912, 2: 114).

"Shall we see the English . . ." Bjaaland, diary, in Huntford (1980: 486).

"Halt!" Amundsen (1912, 2: 121).
"[I]t clearly shows . . ." Amundsen, in Kløver (2009: 150).
"as near to the Pole . . ." Amundsen (1912, 1: xvii).
"the greatest single-handed act . . ." Smith (2006: 198).
"RECORD . . ." Scott, diary, January 9, 1912, in Jones (2006: 370).
"It is most unaccountable . . ." Scott, diary, January 12, 1912, in Jones (2006: 373).
"[s]oon we knew . . ." Scott, diary, January 16, 1912, in Jones (2006: 376).
"The POLE. Yes . . ." Scott, diary, January 17, 1912, in Jones (2006: 376, 470 [app. 3]).
"Dear Captain Scott . . ." Evans (1952: 232).
"was degraded from explorer . . ." Priestley, ms. cited by Huntford (1980: 516).
"I took some strips . . ." Wilson, diary, January 18, 1912, in Seaver (1933: 280).
"our poor, slighted Union Jack" Scott, diary, January 18, 1912, in Jones (2006: 377).
"all the party . . ." Cherry-Garrard (1937: 495).
"[t]here is no hint . . ." Seaver (1933: 281).
"heads thrown back, roaring . . ." Seaver (1933: 281).
"Well, we have . . ." Scott, diary, January 18, 1912, in Jones (2006: 378, 470 [app. 3]).

CHAPTER 13

February–March 1912: "It is finished"

"many thousands of kroners' . . ." Anders B. Wilse, in Lewis-Jones (2009: 56).
"Good morning, my . . ." Huntford (1980: 526).
"[F]ine crystals spoil . . ." Scott, diary, January 19, 1912, in Jones (2006: 380).
"very cold" Scott, diary, January 25, 1912, in Jones (2006: 384).
"is no doubt that Evans . . ." Scott, diary, January 23, 1912, in Jones (2006: 383).
"Things beginning . . ." Scott, diary, January 24, 1912, in Jones (2006: 383).
"cold fingers all around . . ." Scott, diary, January 24, 1912, in Jones (2006: 384).
"This is the second . . ." Scott, diary, January 24, 1912, in Jones (2006: 384).
"I'm afraid [Bowers] must find . . ." Scott, diary, January 20, 1912, in Jones (2006: 382).
"dull and incapable" Scott, diary, February 4, 1912, in Jones (2006: 390).
"Evans is the chief anxiety . . ." Scott, diary, February 6, 1912, in Jones (2006: 391).
"First panic . . ." Scott, diary, February 7, 1912, in Jones (2006: 391).
"with beautifully traced . . ." Scott, diary, February 8, 1912, in Jones (2006: 392).
"We deserve a little . . ." Scott, diary, February 8, 1912, in Jones (2006: 392).
"[W]e were soon in possession . . ." Scott, diary, February 13, 1912, in Jones (2006: 395).
"Evans has no power . . ." Scott, diary, February 13, 1912, in Jones (2006: 395, 471 [app. 3]). Sentence continues, Evans "is a great nuisance and very clumsy" (expurgated).
"[T]here is no getting away . . ." Scott, diary, February 14, 1912, in Jones (2006: 396).
"nearly broken down in . . ." Scott, diary, February 16, 1912, in Jones (2006: 396).

"has lost his guts . . ." Oates, diary, February 17, 1912, in Crane (2005: 494).
"God knows how . . ." Oates, diary, February 17, 1912, in Huntford (1980: 524).
"pulling for food" Scott, diary, February 15, 1912, in Jones (2006: 396).
"clothing disarranged . . ." Scott, diary, February 17, 1912, in Jones (2006: 397).
"It is a terrible thing . . ." Scott, diary, February 17, 1912, in Jones (2006: 398).
"Like pulling over desert . . ." Scott, diary, February 19, 1912, in Jones (2006: 399).
"woefully short . . ." Scott, diary, February 26, 1912, in Jones (2006: 403).
"It is a race between . . ." Scott, diary, February 24, 1912, in Jones (2006: 402).
"God help us . . ." Scott, diary, March 3, 1912, in Jones (2006: 405).
"it is not going . . ." Oates, diary, in Smith (2006: 209).
"we are wonderfully fit . . ." Scott, diary, March 7, 1912, in Jones (2006: 407).
"I should like to . . ." Scott, diary, March 7, 1912, in Jones (2006: 407).
"One feels that . . ." Scott, diary, March 7, 1912, in Jones (2006: 407).
"in a comfortless blizzard . . ." Scott, diary, March 10, 1912, in Jones (2006: 409).
"poor Titus is the greatest . . ." Scott, diary, March 10, 1912, in Jones (2006: 408).
"practically ordered" Scott, diary, March 11, 1912, in Jones (2006: 409).
"Should this be found . . ." Scott, diary, March 16 or 17, 1912, in Jones (2006: 410).
"unendingly cheerful" Scott, diary, March 16 or 17, 1912, in Jones (2006: 410).
"best feet" Scott, diary, March 18, 1912, in Jones (2006: 411).
"amputation is the least . . ." Scott, diary, March 18, 1912, in Jones (2006: 411).
"I should so like to come . . ." Bowers, in Huntford (1980: 544).
"[W]e have struggled . . ." Wilson to Oriana Wilson, no date, in Seaver (1933: 294).
"It is finished. . . ." On flyleaf of Wilson's *Book of Common Prayer* (London: Suttaby & Co., no date). SPRI MS 984
"I was not *too old . . ."* Scott to Admiral F. C. Bridgeman, no date, in Jones (2006: 417).
"It was the younger . . ." Scott to Admiral F. C. Bridgeman, no date, in Jones (2006: 417).
"still die with a bold . . ." Scott to Sir J. M. Barrie, no date, in Jones (2006: 416).
"faulty organization" Scott, "Message to the Public," no date, in Jones (2006: 421).
"I wasn't a very good . . ." Scott to Kathleen Scott, in Gwynne (1929: 163).
"Had we lived . . ." Scott, "Message to the Public," no date, in Jones (2006: 421).
"I do not think . . ." Scott, diary, March 29, 1912, in Jones (2006: 412). Although it has been doubted that a single storm could have kept the men from leaving camp for as long as nine or ten days, in mid-June 1912 Cherry-Garrard (1937: 446) experienced one that lasted eight days, with high winds the whole time. However, it is not clear from Scott's description of his last days what the temperature was, or whether the "blizzard" was principally a snow- or a windstorm.

CHAPTER 14

November 1912: "It is the tent"

"I must say that throughout . . ." Ernest Shackleton, *The New York Times*, March 9, 1912

"Captain Amundsen knows . . ." *Harper's Weekly*, March 16, 1912.

"[I]f ever men knew . . ." Raymond Priestley (1914: 376).

"done up" Cherry-Garrard (1937: 433).

"It is the tent." Wright, in Cherry-Garrard (1937: 481).

"should not be touched . . ." Wright, in Bull and Wright (1993: 346).

"There was nothing to do . . ." Cherry-Garrard (1937: 482).

"[e]ach man of the Expedition . . ." Atkinson, in Huxley (1914, 2: 346).

"[I]nclement weather and lack . . ." Cherry-Garrard (1937: 483).

"I think we are all going crazy . . ." Cherry-Garrard (1937: 488).

"'Are you all well' . . ." Cherry-Garrard (1937: 565).

"I leave Cape Evans with no regret . . ." Cherry-Garrard (1937: 565).

"To strive, to seek . . ." Cherry-Garrard (1937: 566).

"We landed to find the Empire . . ." Cherry-Garrard (1937: 573).

"Horrible, horrible! . . ." *Daily Chronicle*, February 12, 1913, in Huntford (1980: 561).

CHAPTER 15

1913–1928: Amundsen Agonistes

"experiment" Bomann-Larsen (2006: 246).

"extension of the original plan . . ." Amundsen (1912, 1: 44)

"I was closer to giving up . . ." Bomann-Larsen (2006: 250).

"We saw nothing . . ." Amundsen, diary, in Bomann-Larsen (2006: 273). In *My Life as an Explorer*, Amundsen stated (p. 125) that he and his comrades worked for twenty-four days to flatten the runway, but this appears to conflate several earlier efforts to get the plane into a position to take off with the last attempt, described here (cf. Pool 2002).

"one huge balloon . . ." Bomann-Larsen (2006: 321). Richard Byrd's claim to have reached the North Pole by airplane only two days earlier (May 9) is not widely accepted as genuine.

"salaried airship commander . . ." Amundsen (1927: 137), as paraphrased by Bomann-Larsen (2006: 314).

"more of a suicide bid . . ." Bomann-Larsen (2006: 324).

Royal Norwegian Navy See http://www.searchforamundsen.com/cms; accessed September 10, 2009.

"when his work was done . . ." Nansen, in Bomann-Larsen (2006: 362).

CHAPTER 16

After The End

"[T]here is precious little . . ." Cherry-Garrard (1937: 577).

"'Is it worth it?' . . ." Cherry-Garrard (1937: 575).

"no journey made . . ." Scott (1905, 1: 467).

"[c]ontinually on the panic . . ." C. R. Royds, diary, February 21, 1904, in Huntford (1980: 185).

"Wilson and [Cherry] to prepare . . ." Cherry-Garrard (1937: 160).

"the land that joins . . ." Cherry-Garrard (1937: 159).

References Cited

Amundsen, R. 1912. *The South Pole: An Account of the Norwegian Antarctic Expedition in the "Fram" 1910–1912*. Trans. A. G. Chater. 2 vols. London: Murray.

Amundsen, R. 1927. *My Life as an Explorer*. Garden City, NY: Doubleday.

Bomann-Larsen, T. 2006. *Roald Amundsen*. Trans. I. Christophersen. Stroud, UK: Sutton.

Bull, C. and P. F. Wright. 1993. *Silas: The Antarctic Diaries and Memoir of Charles S. Wright*. Columbus, OH: Ohio State University.

Cherry-Garrard, A. 1937. *The Worst Journey in the World*. London: Chatto & Windus.

Crane, D. 2005. *Scott of the Antarctic*. New York: Knopf.

Decleir, H. 1999. *Roald Amundsen's* Belgica *Diary: The First Scientific Expedition to the Antarctic*. Trans. E. Dupont and C. Le Piez. Bluntisham, UK: Erskine.

Ellis, A. R., ed. 1969. *Under Scott's Command: Lashley's Antartic Danes*. London: Gollancz.

Evans, E. R. G. R. 1952. *South with Scott*. London: Collins.

Fiennes, R. 2003. *Captain Scott*. London: Hodder & Stoughton.

Fisher, M. and J. Fisher. 1957. *Shackleton*. London: Barrie.

Gwynn, S. 1929. *Captain Scott*. London: John Lane.

Hattersley-Smith, G., ed. 1984. *The Norwegian with Scott: Tryggve Gran's Antarctic Diary 1910–1913*. Trans. E.-J. McGhie. Greenwich, UK: National Maritime Museum.

Horwitz, T. 2002. *Blue Latitudes: Boldly Going Where Captain Cook Has Gone Before*. New York: Picador.

Huntford, R. 1980. *Scott & Amundsen: The Race to the South Pole*. New York: Putnam.

Huxley, L., ed. 1914 (4th ed.). *Scott's Last Expedition*. London: Smith, Elder.

Joerg, W. L. G. 1930. *The Work of the Byrd Antarctic Expedition, 1928–1930*. New York: American Geographical Society.

Jones, M., ed. 2006. *Robert Falcon Scott, Journals: Captain Scott's Last Expedition*. Oxford University Press.

Kennet, Lady [Kathleen Bruce Scott Young]. 1949. *Self-Portrait of an Artist*. London: Murray.

King, H. G. R., ed. 1972. *Edward Wilson: Diary of the "Terra Nova" Expedition to the Antarctic 1910–1912*. London: Blandford.

Kløver, G. O. 2009. *Cold Recall: Reflections of a Polar Explorer*. Oslo: Fram Museum.

Lewis-Jones, H., ed. 2009. *Face to Face*. Cambridge: SPRI/Polarworld.

Lowe, P. R. and N. B. Kinnear. 1930. Birds. *Natural History Reports of the British Antarctic ("Terra Nova") Expedition, 1910: Zoology* 4(5): 103–193.

Lyons, H. G., comp. 1924. *Reports of the British Antarctic ("Terra Nova") Expedition 1910–1913: Miscellaneous Data*. London: Harrison.

Mason, T. K. 1979. *The South Pole Ponies*. New York: Dodd, Mead.

Mills, W. J. 2003. *Exploring Polar Frontiers: A Historical Encyclopedia*. 2 vols. Santa Barbara, CA: ABC/Clio.

Parsons, C. W. 1934. Penguin embryos. *Natural History Reports of the British Antarctic ("Terra Nova") Expedition, 1910: Zoology* 4(7): 253–62.

Ponting, H. 1923. *The Great White South, or with Scott in the Antarctic.* London: Duckworth.

Pool, B. H. 2002. *Polar Extremes: The World of Lincoln Ellsworth.* Fairbanks, AK: Universtity of Alaska Press.

Pound, R. 1966. *Scott of the Antarctic.* London: Cassell.

Priestley, R. E. 1914. *Antarctic Adventure: Scott's Northern Party.* London: Unwin.

Roberts, B. 1967. *Edward Wilson's Birds of the Antartic.* London: Blandford.

Rosove, M. H. 2000. *Let Heroes Speak; Antarctic Explorers 1772–1922.* Annapolis, MD: Naval Institute Press.

Ross, J. C. 1847. *A Voyage of Discovery and Research in the Southern and Antarctic Regions, During the Years 1839–1843.* 2 vols. London: Murray.

Scott, R. F. 1905. *The Voyage of the* Discovery. 2 vols. London: Macmillan.

Seaver, G. 1933. *Edward Wilson of the Antarctic: Naturalist and Friend.* London: John Murray.

Smith, M. 2002. *I Am Just Going Outside: Captain Oates—Antarctic Tragedy.* Stroud, UK: Spellmount.

Solomon, S. 2001. *The Coldest March: Scott's Fatal Antarctic Expedition.* New Haven, CT: Yale.

Speak, P. 2008. *Deb: Geographer, Scientist, Antarctic Explorer.* Guildford, UK: Polar Publishing.

Tarver, M. C. 2006. *The S. S.* Terra Nova *(1884–1943), from the Arctic to the Antarctic: Whaler, Sealer and Polar Exploration Ship.* Brixham, UK: Pendragon.

Taylor, T. G. 1916. *With Scott: The Silver Lining.* London: Smith, Elder.

Thomson, D. 1977. *Scott's Men.* Allen Lane/Penguin; London (reissued in 2002 as *Scott, Shackleton, and Amudsen: Ambition and Tragedy in the Antarctic.* Adenaline Classics: New York.)

Williams, E. A. 2008. *With Scott in the Antarctic: Edward Wilson, Explorer, Naturalist, Artist.* Stroud, UK: History Press.

Wilson, D. M., and D. B. Elder. 2000. *Cheltenham in Antarctica: The Life of Edward Wilson.* Cheltenham, UK: Reardon.

Wright, C. S. 1924. Notes on sledging. *Reports of the British Antarctic ("Terra Nova") Expedition 1910–1913: Miscellaneous Data*: 40–44.

www.historicalstatistics.org (concerning historical relative value of currencies; accessed 15 June 2009).

www.measuringworth.com (concerning historical relative value of currencies; accessed 15 June 2009).

www.searchforamundsen.com (concerning Royal Norwegian Navy mission to look for Amundsen's plane; accessed September 10, 2009).

Image Credits

©akg-images/The Image Works: p. 64

Antipodean Books, Maps & Prints, David & Cathy Lilburne, photography by Gilbert King: Cover and pp. 18–19, 214

American Museum of Natural History, Special Collections—Memorabilia Collection 48 (photography by Craig Chesek): pp. 34, 62, 152

©The Art Archive/Culver Pictures: p. 86

©The British Library Board. Add. MS 51035, f.39: p. *183*

©Christie's Images/The Bridgeman Art Library: p. 74 inset

©Mary Evans Picture Library: p. 66

©Mary Evans Picture Library/Everett Collection: pp. 198, 210

©Zenobia Evans: pp. 1 (aerial view of Scott's hut), 52 right, 119 bottom, 149 bottom, 221

©The Fram Museum, Oslo: pp. 36, 203

©Hulton Archive/Getty Images: p. 78

©Ross D.E. MacPhee: p. 40

National Library of Australia: pp. VII (Map NK 10001), 81 (Scott portrait by J. Thomson, nla.pic-an11208027), 156 top (nla.pic-an23814300)

National Library of Norway: drawing by Kristian Prestrud from the book, *The South Pole* by Roald Amundsen, 1912: p. 70

National Library of Norway, Manuscript Collection: pp. 49 (Brevs. 48), 161 (Ms.4° 2730), 187 (Ms.fol. 1924:5:3 (1912)),

National Library of Norway, Newspaper Collection: p. 7 right (AP_08_03_1912)

National Library of Norway, Picture Collection: pp. V & VI (NPRA740, detail), 12 (SURA42), 37 (NPRA3118), 65 (NPRA1105), 69 (NPRA1117), 73 (SURA66), 88 right (NPRA139), 104 (NPRA1479), 107 (NPRA1356) and 107 inset (NPRA111), 108 (NPRA1038), 109 (NPRA1099), 122 (NPRA643), 123 (NPRA1100), 130 (NPRA1436), 142 (NPRA741), 154 (NPRA740), 156 bottom (NPRA132), 170 (NPRA779), 171 (NPRA107), 199 (NPRA3122), 201 (NPRA2969), 205 (NPRA232), 206 (NPRA93), 208 (FMRA246), 211 (NPRA847)

National Portrait Gallery, London: pp. 6 (Scott portrait by C. Percival Small, NPG x22554), 31 (Wilson portrait, by Elliot and Fry, NPG x82251, detail of photograph)

Norsk Folkemuseum, photographs by Anders Beer Wilse: pp. 39 (NF.W 09963), 43 (NF.WA 01855), 45 top left (NF.WA 01829*A), 45 top right (NF.WA 01818), 45 bottom left (NF.WA 02064), 45 bottom right (NF.WA 01811), 88 left (NF.WA 01789)

©Popperfoto/Getty Images: pp. II, 146, 151, 158

©Private Collection/The Stapleton Collection/The Bridgeman Art Library: p. 7 left inset

Courtesy Royal Geographical Society: p. 82

Licensed with permission of the Scott Polar Research Institute, University of Cambridge: pp. 4 (P2005/5/1699), 5 (P2005/5/1290), 23 (P2005/5/1168), 48 (P2005/5/28), 48 inset (P2005/5/916), 50 (P2005/5/379), 53 bottom (P54/16/386b), 56–57 (P2005/5/936), 74 (P2005/5/534), 76 (P2005/5/1287), 77 (P83/6/1/5/60), 84 (P2005/5/798), 89 (P2005/5/1709), 90 (P2005/5/576), 91 inset (P2005/5/540), 97 (P2005/5/381), 116 (P2005/5/399), 118 (P2005/5/360), 132 (P2005/5/964), 134 (P2005/5/553), 136 (P2005/5/960), 157 (P2005/5/1286), 194–195 (P48/14/10)

Licensed with permission of the Scott Polar Research Institute, University of Cambridge (photography by Craig Chesek): pp. 8 (SPRI Archives), 10 (SPRI Archives), 11 (SPRI Archives (*7):91(080)[1910-13]), 14 (Y: 97/13, SPRI Library), 20 (N: 79), 32 (SPRI Archives (*7):91(080)[1910-13], 46 (N: 1044, N: 1045), 55 (66/13/10, Y: 66/21, 2004/3), 93 (N: 7; N: 24a-b; N: 1134), 110 (Y: 66/20b, SPRI Library), 112 (SPRI Library), 113 bottom (SPRI Library), 114 (SPRI Library), 127 (SPRI Newspaper Collection), 128 (N: 616), 135 (N: 77/7/9, SPRI Library), 137 (Y: 61/18/22), 139 (SPRI Library), 140 (Y: 79/17/1, N: 943, N: 744, N: 749, N: 944), 145 (Y: 61/3, N: 1232), 149 (Y: 53/25), 150 (N: 273), 155 (SPRI Archives), 162 (Y: 83/7/6), 163 top (SPRI Library), 163 bottom (N: 1038, SPRI Library), 164 (N: 1039), 165 (N: 1040), 166-167 (top left, P48/281/3; bottom left, P48/281/11; top right, P48/281/15; bottom right, P48/281/14), 168 (Y: 61/18/19), 173 (N: 1195), 174 (N: 800), 176 (SPRI Library), 177 (Y: 73/7/8, Y: 70/2b), 178 (Y: 2007/23, Y: 66/20b), 181 (MS 984), 182 (Z: 120; N: 1037), 184 (SPRI Archives), 188 (SPRI Archives), 190 top (DE46 [Debenham album]), 190 bottom (N: 1231, N: 1238b, Y: 61/3, N: 1192a-b), 191 (N: 857), 192 (MS 1317/1/4), 197 (SPRI Archives), 212 (N: 1394), five foldout panoramas (SPRI Newspaper Collection), foldout of Wilson's annotated hand-drawn map (N: 1036)

Watercolors by Edward Adrian Wilson, licensed with permission of the Scott Polar Research Institute, University of Cambridge: p. 30: *Hut Point, McMurdo Sound, 7 April 1911*, N: 423; pp. 51, 53 top, 54: *Wandering and Black-browed Albatrosses,* Diomedea exulans *and* Thalassarche (=Diomedea) melanophoris. September 1910, N: 1634, details of sketches; p. 61: *Noon, looking South, April 29 1911,* N: 513, detail; p. 98: *Sunset. Apr. 10. 11. 6pm.,* N: 438, detail; p. 143: *Mt. Discovery and Inaccessible Is. Aug. 14. 1911, 1pm.,* N: 485, detail; p. 159: *July 22. 1910. 6.15am. looking W. Moon and afterglow,* Y: 67/1/3, detail; p. 200: *White-headed Petrel,* Pterodroma lessonii, *in flight and afloat,* N: 1681, detail; p. 202: *Royal Society Range. Sept. 14. 1911. 5.30pm.,* N: 482, detail; p. 215: *Aug. 8. 1911. 3pm. Cape Evans. Looking north,* N: 527, detail; pp. 218, 219: *Beaufort Island. Ross Sea. Jan 4. 11. 1 am.,* N: 416, details

©Morten Skallerud 2008 –The Fram Museum, Olso: p. 68

©John Thomson/Hulton Archive/Getty Images: p. 15

Photographs by Herbert George Ponting, from the British Antarctic ("Terra Nova") Expedition 1910–1913 Album, Alexander Turnbull Library, Wellington, New Zealand: pp. 24 (Reference No. PA1-f-067-007-2), 26 (Ref. No. PA1-f-067-008-1), 52 left (Ref. No. PA1-f-067-030-1), 59 (Ref. No. PA1-f-067-087-6), 91 top (Ref. No. PA1-f-067-019-4), 95 (Ref. No. PA1-f-066-05-09), 103 (Ref. No. PA1-f-067-070-1), 113 (Ref. No. PA1-f-067-040-4), 115 (Ref. No. PA1-f-067-050-2), 117 (Ref. No. PA1-f-067-046-2), 121 (Ref. No. PA1-f-067-043-2), 148 [attributed to Robert F. Scott] (Ref. No. PA1-f-066-05-02)

Photograph by Steffano Francis Webb, from the Stefano Webb Collection, Alexander Turnbull Library, Wellington, New Zealand: p. 25 (Ref. No. G-31141-1/2)

Alexander Turnbull Library, Wellington, New Zealand: pp. 29 (Ref. No. F-032270-1/2), 33 (Ref. No. Eph-E-ANTARCTICA-1912-03)

©Patricia Wynne: pp. 13, 17, foldout map *Routes of Amundsen and Scott to the South Pole*

Craig Chesek, additional photography (items from author's collection and AMNH Library): pp. 2, 42, 58, 99, 125, 133, 189 top, 189 bottom, 217

Index

M

N

O

P

Q

R

S

T

U

V

W

Y

About the Author

Ross D. E. MacPhee was born in Edinburgh, Scotland, and grew up in western Canada. He received his Ph.D. at the University of Alberta in 1977. Prior to joining the American Museum of Natural History in 1988 as Curator in the Division of Vertebrate Zoology, he was Associate Professor of Anatomy at Duke University Medical Center. He has also taught at Columbia University, New York University, and several universities in Canada. Dr. MacPhee's research interests span the evolutionary history of mammals, island biogeography, and the biology and causation of extinction. He has led or participated in more than 45 scientific expeditions in 14 countries, including both polar regions. Most recently, he has been at work on islands in the James Ross group in the northern Weddell Sea, looking for fossil evidence of early mammals that crossed into Antarctica 45 million years ago, when southernmost South America and the Antarctic Peninsula were connected by a now-sundered land bridge. He lives in Manhattan with wife Clare Flemming.

Photo by Clare Flemming

About the Natural History Museum

Open to visitors since 1881, the Natural History Museum in London looks after a world-class collection of 70 million specimens. It is also a leading scientific research institution, with groundbreaking projects in 70 or so countries. About 350 scientists work at the Museum, researching the valuable collections to better understand life on Earth, its ecosystems and the threats it faces.

Every year more than 4 million visitors, of all ages and levels of interest, are welcomed through the Museum's doors. They come to enjoy the many galleries and exhibitions, which celebrate the beauty and meaning of the natural world and encourage us to see the environment around us with new eyes.

Panoramas

Folding Maps

The panels on the following foldouts are taken from *The Sphere*'s edition of February 22, 1913, issued at the height of emotional outpouring over the tragic end of Captain Scott and his companions. Although the initial reports of his death had come through almost two weeks previously, there was still uncertainty about what had actually happened. *The Sphere*'s editors tried to allay some of the misinformation while, of course, capitalizing on one of the biggest stories of the year. This sequence reproduces a series of obsessively detailed panoramic panels that was designed to aid readers in following the story of Scott's pole party. Some details (such as showing the tents with large, wigwamlike entrances, or ascribing Oates's decline to "fatigue") are incorrect, but the point should not be lost that the public evidently wanted to know everything about the expedition. Covert jingoistic attitudes are not hard to detect: In panel VI, it is tacitly suggested that Amundsen in fact had not reached the pole because his tent was a half mile off. Scott (naturally) found the error and planted the Union Jack on the proper spot. This completely ignores the efforts Amundsen went to in order to ensure that he crossed 90°S.